The Odyssey of the Western Spirit

An Account of Human Reality

Jack Meyer

CSU Publications
Green Bay, Wisconsin

ISBN: 0-9631727-3-5

CSU Publications
P.O. Box 11701
Green Bay, Wisconsin 54307-1701

Printed by BookMasters
Mansfield, Ohio

Available at:
www.bookmasters.com

Dedication

To the Spirit of Edmund Husserl

1859-1938

TABLE OF CONTENTS

Preface
A World in Crisis

Quite obviously, our world is in fundamental crisis. Difficult conditions and circumstances confront us daily that indicate both short and long term disaster. Somewhat less evident is the fact that any understanding of these problems requires the broadest philosophical and historical perspective. The intent here is to initiate discussion concerning that perspective in the context of three questions. The first is philosophical, the second historical, and the third psychological and political. What is at issue are the conditions for the possibility of fundamental social and political change, or the terms by which we can carry through a positive program of deep and difficult cultural transformation.

At the beginning, the most difficult question can be asked. *What are the general conditions for the possibility of human existence?* In other words, what is the essential reality that must be present for there to be human existence of any kind? What is the essential common denominator that is evident with any and every possible human being? *What* are we at the most general level, before any kind of differentiation, be that of time, place, language, or tradition? This central question suggests nothing of the mysterious or occult, it is simply asking as to *what* a human being is as such.

1

Whether one is alive today as an American, an Oriental, an African, or one has lived in Ancient Greece, Persia, or India, or whether one is to live in any possible future, it is all the same. *What* is the essential and common reality that is universally the same for everyone, anywhere and at anytime?

An obvious and immediate fact is that it is essential that one have a *body*. No one, ever, has existed as a human being without a physical body. Having a body places one within the dimension of material nature. Any human being is a piece with material conditions which are determined by the physical laws of nature. This fact is of a profound importance and, in coming to terms with these conditions, much of human history has been written. Another essential fact lies at the center of the possibility of human existence. As it is necessary to have a body, it is equally necessary to have a mind. Being an object of material conditions, so too, one is subject to the conditions of the mental. As materiality defines one limit, so too, mentality defines another, and, between the two, the real and the ideal, the general conditions for the possibility of human existence are established. Part One will work through the historical and philosophical details of this relationship and lay the foundation for the second question.

Given this twofold general condition of human existence, it is necessary to ask about *specific* conditions. *What are the specific conditions for the possibility of human existence as that has been played out in the history of the Western world?* What are the particular details that distinguish the West from all other historical traditions? How is the West uniquely itself, in contrast, for example, to China or India? Of central importance here will be the traditions of the Biblical Old Testament, Ancient Greece, and the New Testament. As these traditions are woven together there is established the cultural formations that will determine the subsequent development of the West. This of course underlies and is the foundation of the modern and scientific technological culture that shapes most of the world today. It will be necessary to present this historical development in detail as it moves forward from the Romans, to Roman Catholicism, to the Lutheran Reformation, to the Modern Age of science and technology, to the capitalism of the New World, and, finally, to the world today. The critical task will be to show how the general condition of materiality and mentality has been specifically played out in the history of the West. Something unique occurs here that will make all the difference. This concerns the nature of self-consciousness and the power of the person to think for himself. The circumstances of this thinking will provide the impetus for self-responsibility, and this in turn will transform the conditions of social and political life. A dichotomy will be established between cultures of tradition, where the activities of the individual are determined in advance, and the culture of the West, where the possibility arose for the individual to find his[1] way outside of a pre-determined tradition and is able instead to think and *act* on his own behalf. Of course there is never a complete freedom to step beyond the limits of tradition but a decisive exception was made that is essential for the cultural formation of the West. This too can be referred to as a "tradition" but now qualified by an exception. With this account of the history of the West, there will emerge general structures that will appear in various guises. The experiences of religion, capitalism, nationalism, and romanticism will be shown to be various expressions of an underlying theme.

The third and final questions brings us to the present. In light of questions one and two, what could this mean for our world today? With the end of the Cold War, *where do we go from here*? The world is now in the midst of the greatest transition in all of history. How is this to be understood? What role are we to play as active and concerned participants? In a way it is a struggle between the negative and the positive, between the ideologies of the past that no longer apply, and the possibilities of the future, that requires untried methods and unproven initiative. This will concern the "political" as the place where power and policy meet on behalf of the possible well being of the world.

This then is the task of this book, to ask three questions that span the historical horizon from the general to the specific to the political. But the question of method immediately arises and before advancing to the central task it is necessary to address this preliminary concern.

In the most general way the method here could be defined as a matter of *description*, but with a peculiar style and intention. Before one can even begin it is necessary to determine a general attitude of inquiry. Here that is defined by the term *epoche*.[2] This concerns a preliminary resolve *not to judge in advance*, not to bring presuppositions to bear, that would easily convert description into ready explanation. Much is involved here. "...at first we shall put out of action all the convictions we have been accepting up to now, including all our sciences."[3] All opinions and judgment whatsoever are "put out of action." All beliefs of a personal kind, anything at all that could obstruct a clear, direct, and first look "at the things themselves," is put out of play. This is not to deny the possible validity of these opinions and insights, rather it is just to say that *in advance* they cannot be instrumental to our task.

Complimentary to *epoche* there stands another methodological component. When looking at and describing a thing of either a general or specific nature, what is important is its *essential* structure. For example, when drawing triangles in the sand,[4] in the hopes of understanding geometrical figures, it is not the drawing, or the sand, or the imperfections of the lines, that express an essential structure, rather the drawing, sand, and imperfections *exemplify* the perfect figures of geometry, figures that "exist" only in the ideally perfect dimension of geometrical shapes as such. This exemplification is a reference to essential structure. Facilitating this concern with the essential is the ability to "freely vary" the thing in question, to look at it in different ways, to sort through the many ways in which a thing appears as it does, in order to determine more precisely the "invariant structure," its "essence." This essence is not something mysterious or mystifying but rather simply that which is absolutely necessary for there to be the thing itself. It is essential that humans speak, but it is not essential whether that speaking is in one language or another. It is essential that one eat, but not exactly what it is that is eaten. The interplay between the essential and the unessential is evident in all situations and methodologically it is of the greatest importance. Only with the essential is it possible to see *what* a thing is as the unessential naturally falls away.

A third component needs to be aligned with *epoche* and the essential, something of great difficulty and controversy but promising equally great results. When looking at something it is not that thing itself that is the focus but rather *how* that same thing is *meant*, intended, how the viewing subject perceives that thing. It is a matter of "intentionality." When I look at the lamp nearby it is not the lamp itself as lamp that is the primary interest, but rather *how* that lamp appears. It is seen from one side at a time, it can be looked at from differing perspectives, it can be recollected in memory as one's eyes are turned away. It can be seen by someone else *over there.* What is of the greatest importance here is that the *subjective* conditions for the possibility of experiencing the thing itself are the central concern. How is any experience whatsoever built up in the subjective activities of the thinking person himself? The focus, for example, is upon the geometer himself, his mental activities of geometrizing, in relation to the objects of geometry. The task of this type of methodological attitude is to understand the subjective activities of the thinking person that "constitutes" any objects whatsoever. How does geometry first become geometry through the mental activities of the first geometer? The recourse to subjectivity makes all the difference when viewing the development of the West. Without an understanding of subjective intentions there can be no true account. Human affairs will then be seen as an *accomplishment* of that subjectivity. The traditional view of the priority of the objective will be contested here and turned upon its head. The great objective structures of human affairs, such as government, science, art, architecture, etc., will be shown to be what they are only when seen in light of their essential foundation in the subjective activities of the thinking person. The seemingly self-sufficient objective edifice of science is possible only as an accomplishment of subjectivity. Generations of active participants, stretching across millennia, will contribute to the building up, or constitution, of all objective accomplishments. The objective is bounded by absolute necessity to the underlying reality of mentality. It is only through thinking that all else becomes possible. Mentality does not *create* the physical world rather it *constitutes* the reality that is meaningful to us as human beings.

The methodological components of *epoche*, essence, and intentionality can be exemplified in the telling example of the archer and archery. The archer steadily draws his bow, taking aim, and with a momentary pause, lets loose the arrow that arches through the air on its way to the intended target. What are we to make of this? As a matter of contrast it will be useful to sketch a natural scientific account, what could be termed the "physics" of force, projection, trajectory, and impact. The resistance of the bow creates an energy that can be directed through the drawing and releasing of the string, thereby projecting the arrow across a trajectory of space with sufficient force at impact to create penetration of the object struck. A natural scientific account of this phenomenon would have recourse to a mathematical physics that would be able to measure force, trajectory, and impact in a mathematical formula. Using this, an expanded account could be created that would provide a model for all such events of force, trajectory, and impact. General laws of physics

6

would be enumerated that would state the physical principles of archery. While it is obvious that these principles would be of great usefulness it would *exclude* as a matter of scientific principle the subjective reality of the archer himself, as his motives and intentions cannot interfere with physical law. This may appear to be reasonable enough yet an account of archery without the archer is an astounding piece of scientific omission. The natural scientific account of nature in general then is without persons, including the scientist himself. But of course it is the archer who is so decisive for an understanding of archery. His subjective intentions are of an essential importance. It is now necessary to begin again and provide an account based upon the methodology of *epoche,* essence, and intentionality.

Who and *what* is this archer? First of all, we know nothing about scientific theory, we know nothing about the physics of force, trajectory, and impact. All of this is "put out of action." The first and most immediately obvious fact is that the archer lives in a "world." He is a human being among others, participating and sharing the tasks of life, living between a vague past and an indefinite future, that places him in his concerns of the present. He lives in a society, however small or large, among other societies that compete for the fundamental requirements of life. Society, history, culture, and personality then, contribute to his make-up or constitution in the world. The person here, though, is a Persian archer on Xerxes' march to defeat the Greeks. He is part of an army that will subdue the Greeks into submission to Oriental tyranny. But fate would have it otherwise and the decisive battle would be fought at sea and the archer scrambles home without letting go a single shot. But history was being made.

The Greco-Persian War was the most momentous in European history, for it made Europe possible. It won for Western civilization the opportunity to develop its own economic life--unburdened with alien tribute and taxation--and its own political institutions, free from the dictation of Oriental kings. It won for Greece a clear road for the first great experiment in liberty; it preserved the Greek mind for three centuries from the enervating mysticism of the East, and secured for Greek enterprise full freedom of the sea.[5]

To say that the archer lives in a "world" then is to place him somewhere in all of history.

But what of the act of archery itself? In drawing and aiming the bow the archer intends the arrow to a specific target. The factors that comprise this event are his subjective awareness that chooses the target, the flight of the arrow toward the target, and the target itself. Subjective motive provides quite varied intentions and expectations. He could be practicing in order to improve his skill so as to be allowed entry into an elite division of archers. He could be a lone hunter in the field hoping to feed himself and his family with the kill of a deer. He could be William Tell fictionally taking extra careful aim. The range of these possible intentions is as vast as the circumstances of history that have required its effect, the delivering of force at a distance. Secondly, the flight of the arrow exists throughout a range of conditions. Wind, distance, and obstructions along the way dictate. The archer's intention may fall to nothing as the arrow projects itself through a variety of adverse conditions. Only sometimes is the target hit upon as intended. Thirdly, the target itself exists under a variety of changing conditions. It may be stationary and simply there for practice, or it may flee for its life or, most urgently, the target may be another archer with subjective intentions of his own. The event of archery then is comprised of the archer's subjective intentions, the conditions of the flight of the arrow, and the uncertainty of the target, all of which takes place in the world to which all are involved.

Furthermore, though, archery is the act of delivering force, it

8

is essentially a *killing* force. In the primitive struggle for survival its usefulness was exemplary, it was of the highest value. The struggles of living and dying, of winning and losing, of being and not being, were bound up in the possibility offered by the bow and arrow. Summarily then, the natural scientific account of the physics of archery does not touch upon these deeper level human concerns. A pre-eminent example suggests itself here.

The trials of Odysseus in Homer's *Odyssey* culminates in a display of archery, or "the test of the bow." With the end of the battle at Troy, the war hero searches for home but is left scattered about the Mediterranean. Sundry adventures and mis-adventures send him here and there, escaping at times with only his life but always abiding by his firm resolve to arrive home again. His will to persevere becomes tied to the fortunes of chance and finally he finds himself on the shores of his beloved and long lost Greece. But his absence has taken its toll and circumstances have come to an impasse. Without a King, the kingdom requires that the queen Penelope take a new husband but she resists the claims of the hopeful suitors as best that she can, hoping against all hope for the return of her first and only love, Odysseus. As she delays, the suitors nightly consume in drunken feasting the substance of the house. The moment of decision is at hand.

My lords, hear me: suitors indeed, you commandeered this house to feast and drink in, day and night, my husband being long gone, long out of mind. You found no justification for yourselves--none except your lust to marry me. Stand up, then: we now declare a contest for that prize. Here is my lord Odysseus' hunting bow. Bend and string it if you can. Who sends an arrow through iron axe-helve sockets, twelve in line? I join my life with his, and leave this place, my home, my rich and beautiful bridal house, forever to be remembered, though I dream it only.[6]

9

The bedraggled and disguised Odysseus has returned and has quickly assembled a small band of co-avengers. The suitors can now be tested directly. "...the great horn bow...,"[7] was brought forward. Each in turn gripped "...the great bow of Odysseus...,"[8] attempting to set the string in place but achieving only failure. All were thwarted in their desires to string and shoot the great bow and secure the prize of Penelope. The King though has finally returned. Recognized only as a beggar he has the audacity to request a chance for himself. The suitors scoff at this arrogance of one not of their kind but Penelope is intrigued. "Give him the bow and let us have it out!"[9] The vanquished suitors are not pleased but finally begrudge consent. "Eumaios picked up bow and quiver...and there he placed them in Odysseus' hands."[10] They taunted him as he inspected his old and familiar weapon. The bow was *in his hands*, to do with what he will.

But the man skilled in all ways of contending, satisfied by the great bow's look and heft, like a musician, like a harper, when with quiet hand upon his instrument he draws between his thumb and forefinger a sweet new string upon a peg: so effortlessly Odysseus in one motion strung the bow. Then slid his right hand down the cord and plucked it, so the taut gut vibrating hummed and sang a swallow's note.[11] He picked one ready arrow from his table where it lay bare: the rest were waiting still in the quiver for the young men's turn to come. He nocked it, let it rest across the handgrip, and drew the string and grooved butt of the arrow, aiming from where he sat upon the stool. Now flashed arrow from twanging bow clean as a whistle through every socket ring, and grazed not one, to thud with heavy brazen head beyond.[12]

Revelation and retribution were at hand. Comeuppance was due as the truth would stand.

Odysseus faced the crowd and spoke clearly. "So much for that. Your clean-cut game is over. Now watch me hit the target that no man has hit before, if I can make this shot. Help me, Apollo."[13]

The carnage begins. "Odysseus' arrow hit him under the chin and punched up to the feathers through his throat."[14] His co-avengers had closed all exits and the scramble to flee is futile, their destruction will be complete. "And Odysseus looked around him, narrow-eyed, for any others who had lain hidden while death's black fury passed. In blood and dust he saw that crowd all fallen, many and many slain."[15] The deadly deed had been done, the suitors were no more. Penelope only slowly allows herself to recognize her long lost husband, but finally sees.

Now from his breast into his eyes the ache of longing mounted, and he wept at last, his dear wife, clear and faithful, in his arms, longed for as the sunwarmed earth is longed for by a swimmer spent in rough water where his ship went down under Poseidon's blows, gale winds and tons of sea.[16]

He has arrived home.

Who is this Odysseus? The purpose of this book is to recount the story of the odyssey of the Western spirit, at the beginning of which stands this Odysseus. Something entirely unique occurs here that occurs nowhere else, something absolutely essential for our world today. Outside of the West societies and culture have long since established a "traditional" structure. The rules and procedures, the laws, of life, based upon religious principles, have been set in place from which there can be no dissent. For the person this means that his life has been determined *in advance*. He will be whatever tradition has already determined him to be. With Odysseus a first glimmer, an inkling, appears on the world horizon of something entirely different, something that will take millennia to come to full recognition. The issue is the matter of self-consciousness. It is the possibility of the individual coming to think for himself such that he is able to act on his own behalf. Rather than *passively* existing in the tradition of his birth, the person establishes his own center of validity and takes the opportunity to *actively* participate in a world of his partial making. Thinking for himself, he is equally able to act for himself. No greater contrast with tradition is possible. But the career of this thoughtful action, willful intent, is long and arduous and finally will lay the foundation for the Western world. All the great "players" in history will have been touched by the audacious spirit of Odysseus. The Greeks and their philosophers, Jesus and his followers, Michelangelo and the great Renaissance creators, the superb mathematicians of the Modern era, and anyone who takes upon himself the labor and responsibility of thinking and doing for himself, are all part of this single "tradition." Of course, this will always occur in a greater society, a "tradition" of its own, but it is the *inspiration* of the person that is decisive and that will make all the difference. This making is responsible for the formation of the unique institutional structures that make our world what it is. It also gives us the courage to think that the deeds that have been done can be re-done anew, that we have the power and ability, if we only have the courage, to change our world for the better. Where do we go from here, or what are we to make of the 21st century? This final question now comes into clearer focus.

Amazingly, in simply trying to describe the essential conditions for the possibility of archery one is led back to the subjective intentions of the archer, then back further to his world, which includes the larger historical world, where we find Odysseus in search of home. Arriving there, it is then possible to *turn forward* and re-live and re-think the ensuing historical and philosophical development of the West, at the end of which we find ourselves. An amazing thing indeed.

Introduction
A Note to the Reader

The Odyssey of the Western Spirit falls into the category of philosophical idealism. It will show that the primary condition of human reality is a matter of mentality, a labor of the spirit. The western tradition is supported by three philosophical idealists. They are Plato of the 5th century BC, Descartes of the 17th century AD, and Husserl of the 20th century. All great thoughts of the West are indebted to one or the other or all of these original thinkers. The central prejudice of our time is that of material realism, or the theory that there is no such thing as mentality at all, but only a material network of neurological events. The task here is to marshal the evidence required for a convincing description of the realm of the spirit, and to show that any theory of realism is a contradiction in terms, as it cannot account for the theorizing itself. Thinking in terms of theory is an activity strictly of mentality and spirit and must be understood as such. Realism seemingly accounts for much indeed but finally fails in any completed theory. Only idealism includes all of existence, both the material and the mental, the real and the ideal.

While this is a work of idealism it is decidedly not a work of scholarship. It does not organize the authoritative thoughts of others, but tries instead to think for itself. It defers to authority in terms of example and illustration but not regarding theory. This is both a virtue and a vice. It is able to range freely without tethered constraint to existing opinion, yet perhaps at times ranges too freely. The reader will need to judge one way or the other. But there is an "authority" to which one must necessarily defer and that is the descriptive record of western history itself. Any interpretative account naturally emerges from this record, having allowed "the things to speak for themselves." But interpretation, philosophical theorizing, is a difficult thing and the author must finally rest with the theory presented. Scholars may not be convinced but nonetheless they may find it to be worthy of their attention.

Of immense help has been the giant work of Will Durant entitled *The Story of Civilization*. Its 11 volumes and 7,000 pages provides an historical vista and scope that sets matters into proper perspective, *in one place*. He has worked through the historical "story" and provides moments of perfect insight and balanced clarity. At times he is allowed to speak at length when that is simply the best that can be done.

The philosophy of Edmund Husserl provided the original inspiration for this work. His *Crisis of European Sciences and Transcendental Phenomenology* is an idealistic masterpiece that established a philosophical methodology that needed to be applied to all of history. Accepting his challenge, this work surely falls short but is nonetheless a serious and dedicated attempt to think through the issues of the Western spirit. The attempt itself is necessarily an idealistic success even though there may be a shortcoming of details. Most importantly, here is found an asking of *big* questions. The limitation to the *small* question has so severely limited intellectual life that breaking free of this "academic" imposition is a welcome departure. But, finally, it is one thing to ask a big question and another entirely to put forth a reasonable *answer*. No apologies here. The answer hopes to tie together the historical, philosophical,

14

economic, social, and scientific into a final insight into the political. Idle theorizing needs to defer to political action, and that is done here.

Hopefully, at the start, the reader will be a little disturbed by all this. The goal is to de-construct all of historical, philosophical, religious, and personal belief, only to re-construct that belief on the far side of the account of the odyssey of the western spirit. Believing what we will, a journey back through the historical sources can only add insight, if not revelation. But the reader must be willing. Without relinquishing all of one's beliefs, at least experimentally, for the time being, there will be little achieved except perhaps a bit a rage. Duly warned, the reader may need to read and then re-read, certainly a pretentious request by any author, but do with it what you will.

In sorting through a theory of idealism, it has been essential to cross paths with the religious traditions of the world in general and of the West in particular. In so doing it is necessary to distinguish "institutional" religion from the experience of the individual that is a personal revelation of the larger universe. The one deals with social, political, and economic ideology, where men contest for worldly power, whereas the other deals with the matters of the personal spirit where the individual seeks to achieve a heightened awareness of the greater grandeur of existence itself. In hoping to clear the way for the latter, it has been necessary to take issue with the former. The one is a theism that imposes its will in the world, whereas the other is a *pantheism* which recognizes the greater good in the wonder of the universe pure and simple.

Part One

Materiality and Mentality:

The General Condition of Human

Existence

Chapter One

Materiality and the Experience of Scarcity

Obviously, human existence is not possible without the body. The laws of physical nature determine the conditions of this body. Any and all human beings, anywhere, are subject to these laws with respect to the necessities of food, water, and shelter. It is always and everywhere necessary to find enough to eat and drink, and to secure adequate shelter from the elements of wind, rain, sun, and cold. In primitive existence the struggle to possess these necessities and avoid these elements was the defining reality of life. All effort was directed to this end. The general *lack* of these goods led to an uncertain and difficult existence. Life was fundamentally an experience of general scarcity and physical privation. Alongside of this experience there was the occasional experience of *plenty.* There would have been times when the hunt was successful, the weather mild, and one's shelter well secured. Within the general experience of privation then there would have occurred brief times of plenty. But there exists another level of privation, as it is both physical and *psychological.* The physical privation of hunger, thirst, and cold is amplified by the psychological privation of uncertainty, fear, and anxiety in the face of the unknown. Physical and psychological privation then together circumscribe the conditions of life. This would be equally true of both primitive and advanced levels of existence. No one ever has been able to step outside of the fact of this privation. Interestingly, whereas the experience of physical privation would cause pain, the experience of psychological privation would cause *anxiety*. Early accounts of this anxiety are to be found in the Biblical Old Testament.

And your dead body shall be food for all birds of the air; and for the beasts of the earth; and there shall be no one to frighten them away. The Lord will smite you with the boils of Egypt, and with the ulcers and scurvy and the itch, of which you cannot be healed. The Lord will smite you with madness and confusion of the mind; and you shall grope at noonday...Your sons and your daughters shall be given to another people, while your eyes look on and fail with longing for them all the day; and it shall not be in the power of your hand to prevent it. A nation which you have not known shall eat up the fruit of your ground and of all your labors; and you shall be only oppressed and crushed continually; so that you shall be driven mad by the sight which your eyes shall eye.[1] You have sown much, and harvested little; you eat, but you never have enough; you drink, but you never have your fill; you clothe yourselves, but no one is warm...[2]

The experience of this privation then stands at the center of life anywhere. The need for some sort of emotional resolution to this anxiety will power subsequent religious experience.

The essential feature of this experience is that it pertains only to human beings, as animals appear to be oblivious to any anxiety. The distinguishing fact is *awareness*. It is only human beings who are aware of their own privation. It is precisely the heightened awareness of their condition that aggravates the emotional anxiety of privation. It is memory and expectation, abilities of mentality, that determines this anxiety. But, while mentality enhances anxiety, it equally allows for the possibility of reaching beyond the strict limits of material existence. With the abilities of memory and expectation it is possible to *act* in a way that would reduce the conditions of privation. It is possible to hunt more effectively, for example, with forethought and planning, so that a more plentiful and stable food supply is secured. It is possible to more effectively protect a water supply, And, it is possible to fashion a dwelling that is more secure from both the elements and unwelcome intruders, both human and animal. Simply, through the mental abilities that comprise thinking, it is possible to do better, to more effectively secure oneself from the generally overriding experience of privation. The possibility of thinking allows one to *distance* oneself from the experience of anxiety, but a contradiction is put into place. Ironically, thinking is the awareness that both creates anxiety and is the tool for overcoming it. At the center of the human experience this contradiction will never be displaced.

Without entering into the labyrinthine philosophies of thinking, it is possible to sketch a preliminary definition. Naturally, all thinking requires the brain as a material cause but here the concern is not with a scientific account of the material conditions but rather simply with a descriptive account of the mental functions involved. What is essential is thinking as thinking as such, and not as possibly conditioned by materiality. The general domain of thinking can be termed consciousness or, more precisely, self-consciousness. A comparison of animal existence to human thinking can illustrate the special circumstances of this thinking. A human being is able to *see,* while an animal merely looks on, a human is able to *remember* a variety of things already seen, while the animal has already forgotten and, as a consequence, a human is able to *compare* that which was once seen and now remembered with that which is now being seen. The animal *learns* nothing from its "experience," whereas the human being can accumulate insight into *what* he sees, and then *how* that is. The primitive man sees the fire of a lightning strike, and sees it burning the underbrush, seeing it consume the fuels that lay about. He feels the warmth of the fire and remembers the chill of the night.

Comparing the two he sees the value of fire. Recognizing the conditions for the possibility of fire he sees how *to build a fire.* Using the mental abilities of thinking he is able to *intervene* in his world on his own behalf. What is essential here is that these abilities allow him to see *what* a thing is apart from the many circumstances of that thing's natural occurrence. He may see the fire of lightning, or the fire of the molten lava spilling from the mountain, or the nurtured fire of his camp, and yet he recognizes in all these instances the essential reality of fire. In seeing this essential *what,* he is in possession of a mental skill that will serve him well in the never ending struggle for survival and well being.

Thinking then is a mental ability that involves the process of seeing, remembering, seeing, comparing, and seeing again. This process is evident in any number of conditions and circumstances. The essential *what* provides the basis for a greater understanding of the network of other interconnected essential *whats.* The tools and technologies for survival are now enhanced in the search for food, water, and shelter. An additional mental ability facilitates this thinking. With the use of the *imagination* one can be lifted out of the strict limits of actual experience into the realm of possible experience. To the ability of thinking is added the ability to picture, to imagine, possible differences of reality. It is the imagination that will set human beings upon a trajectory of technical, cultural, and economic development that will carry through to our world today. At issue is an "economy" of thought. One could remember actual experiences as well as *imagine possible experiences.* One could take a single example and *vary* in one's mind one or another of its features, with an eye to the distinction between the essential and the unessential. One could create an example that has not been experienced in reality, a fiction. In other words, one need not go through the entire series of actual examples in order to distinguish the better from the worse. In comparing and imagining, it is possible to *more quickly* understand.

An example is in order.

The hunter sits by his fire considering his *broken* spear. He sees that a better wood is needed for his purposes. In the heat of the hunt the spear handle shattered with the force of the dying animal's final struggle. Pondering, he sees his need and remembers the various types of trees that could possibly possess the qualities that would be better. Of all that could be remembered only a few are possible. He compares in his imagination three and then two and finally decides upon a test. At dawn he will search out and find the material that he thinks will be the best. Without having the actual wood in hand his hunch is worth the effort. This example of course is a piece of the imagination too, as it would hardly have been so simple and straightforward, yet the *essentials* are in place. With the mental ability of thinking, it is possible to do better and improve one's chances.

On the basis then of seeing, remembering, seeing, comparing, and imagining, and seeing again, an improvement is made in the effectiveness of his spear, thus insuring a more adequate food supply. This process of improvement could develop in all directions, encompassing a wide range of activities as a body of *knowledge* is developed. Of course this process is never confined to a single individual but rather is a collective effort that extends over an expanse of time and place. Every seeing, in continuity with a remembering of results, whether successful or not, allows for a new seeing. One begins to *learn* and learns to build upon that learning. A tradition emerges that is carried forth from generation to generation. But all is good only *until further notice,* as learning and knowledge ever expands. Everything must remain open to re-consideration. Of course in reality it is perhaps not this clear, as that tradition itself will serve to restrict the new, but in principle the power of thinking is to seek out beyond itself and create something new.

If thinking can be about real things, it can equally be about something distinctly different. Thinking about *ideas* is of a unique order all its own. An important example here concerns counting. One initially counts by counting things, particular things, such as the fingers of one's hand or the newborn cows in one's herd. But quickly it becomes evident that such a counting of things has a natural limit and that this limit can be overcome when one learns to count things that are no longer "real." Rather than counting fingers one can count about *ideal* matters, numbers that are numbers alone, pure and simple. With this thinking and counting in terms of ideas, ideal states of affairs, a far wider range of possibilities is laid open. A relative simplicity, the counting on one's fingers, gives way to a relative complexity, the counting of numbers that can become arithmetic.

This expansion of the domain of thinking provides results in many ways. Obviously, the first great level of advancement is with the tools of life, now of an ever expanding variety, that enables human groups to be more successful, both in the procuring of food, water, and shelter, but also in the effective organization of the social group itself. The requirements of settled agriculture provides an important example. With each new season of planting, growing, and harvesting organization and planning is required that allows for a consistent and plentiful result. A far more secure food supply than possible with hunting was achieved through the agency of seeing, remembering, seeing, comparing, and then seeing again. Of course the crop may still fail from the uncontrollable forces of drought and pestilence but, *for the most part,* life is better as the food supply is brought under the jurisdiction of the thinking possible to agriculture. Simply, it is the abilities of mentality that have allowed for these material gains.

Once begun, the momentum of the force of mentality is brought to bear in a variety of ways. It is now that the great ancient civilizations become possible. The wheel, animal domestication, methods of agriculture, and patterns of social organization were developed which took human reality from the tribe and its tools of the hunt to the complex social relations of "civilization" with its machines of building and mass production. The material base was greatly expanded and a "freedom" was accorded to a few to live a life of luxury, a life that could be devoted to the leisure of thinking. But the central tension of human existence remained. While the material base had begun to expand, the forces of scarcity would continue to dominate, but something new was possible. The hand to mouth existence of traditional tribal life could be replaced by the rational methods of agriculture and building. Much more was now seen to be possible. The great civilizations of Egypt, Mesopotamia, India, and China now appear upon the ancient horizon.

Chapter Two

Mentality and the Experience

of Ideality

The greatest contrast distinguishes the experience of material scarcity and privation from the experience of ideality. If the one concerns disease, destruction, and death, then the other concerns the very opposite, eternal health, well-being, and immortality. The distinction is between particular material facts and *universal* truth. Number can again provide a perfect example. The number 1 is 1 for everyone, at all times, the very same. It can suffer no material limitation and is eternally perfectly itself. It is simply a universal truth, something that necessarily lies outside the domain of materiality. It is true once and for all, pure and simple. The quality of this universality intrigued and fascinated early thinkers, as they turned their attention to the reality of God. The global definition of God as omniscient, omnipresent, and omnipotent consummated Him as the highest universality. The great ancient religions took root at this juncture where a leisured few were able to think about a world that was created and governed by the most perfect universality. The mental distance that separated the primitive cave dwellers, caught in the grip of hunger and cold, to the religious clerics of Ancient Egypt, was immense. The power of this religious experience is attested to by the monumental architectural structures that were built in worship to

God.

The religious experience though contains a psychological motive. As human beings existing in the material world, religious thinkers formulated a belief that worshiped God in Himself, but this worship also provided for some emotional alleviation in the hard world of daily life. Simply, the central psychological theme of religious thinking concerns the attempt to overcome and alleviate the circumstances of material scarcity and physical privation. In thinking and worshiping the God in Heaven it is hoped that one will feel less the pain of the world here and now. The anxiety of the want of everyday life is hoped to be overcome by the idea and belief in a life somewhere else that is *without* that anxiety, a life apart, a "heavenly" reality. The emotional belief in this separate realm, a realm that exists in some future dimension, proves to be of sufficient power so that one is able to ignore emotionally any existing privation. The recognition of the awesome divinity of God elevates one out of the domain of the material.

Religious thinking, then, serves to find alleviation from the anxieties surrounding the circumstances of scarcity and privation and throughout the world provides an account of the nature of divinity and of God as the absolute power. Equally, an account is provided of creation, Heaven, or a place without material scarcity, of morality, and of personal immortality. Whether given expression in India, China, Egypt, or Ancient Palestine, these themes are always the central tenets of belief.

In the literature of the Indian Hindu tradition is to be found these recurrent religious themes.

Brilliant is It, the light of lights--That which knowers of the soul do know! The sun shines not there, nor the moon and stars; These lightnings shine not, much less this (earthly) fire! After Him, as He shines, doth everything shine. This whole world is illumined with His light...before...behind, to right and left, Stretched forth below and above.[1]

As in other traditions, the Hindu begins with the deity as the pure Absolute, as the cause of creation. "Of all creations I am the beginning and the end..."[2] There is also the concern with leaving behind the material world and the finding of "heaven."

Simply by being attached to hearing and chanting Your transcendental glories, one can attain the highest perfectional stage and enter into Your kingdom. If a person, therefore, always keeps in touch with You by hearing and chanting Your glories and offers the results of his work into Your supreme abode. You are realizable by persons who have cleansed their hearts of all contamination. This cleansing of the heart is made possible by chanting and hearing the glories of Your Lordship.[3]

Explicitly formulated also is the matter of social relations. The differentiation of the caste system into the rulers, the administrators and warriors, the farmers and businessmen and, finally, the laborers and craftsmen, is a rigid social order based upon religious tenets. The fact of immortality finds direct expression in Hindu literature.

One should know perfectly the Personality of Godhead and His transcendental name, as well as the temporary material creation with its temporary demigods, men and animals. When one knows these, he surpasses death and the ephemeral cosmic manifestation with it, and in the eternal kingdom of God he enjoys his eternal life of bliss and knowledge.[4] Those with the vision of eternity can see that the soul is transcendental, eternal, and beyond the modes of nature.[5]

In the Taoist tradition of China there is an equal concern with matters of God, creation, Heaven, morality, and immortality. Across differences of language, culture, climate, and the particular circumstances of separate traditions, there spans this common interest in these matter of an ideal nature. The ancient Chinese text *The Lao Tzu* speaks of the greatest power.

We look at it and do not see it; Its name is The Invisible. We listen to it and do not hear it: Its name is the Inaudible. We touch it and do not find it; Its name is The Subtle (formless). These three cannot be further inquired into, And hence merge into one. Going up high, it is not bright, and coming down low, it is not dark. Infinite and boundless, it cannot be given any name; It reverts to nothingness. This is called shape without shape, Form without object. It is The Vague and Elusive, Meet it and you will not see its head. Follow it and you will not see it. Hold on to the Tao of old in order to master the things of the present. From this one may know the primeval beginning (of the universe). This is called the bond of Tao.[6]

Matters of creation are of central concern.

The Tao (Way) that can be told of is not the eternal Tao; The name that can be named is not the eternal name. The Nameless is the origin of Heaven and Earth; The named is the Mother of things.[7]

Instruction is also given of Heaven.

Heaven is eternal and Earth everlasting. They can be eternal and everlasting because they do not exist for themselves, And for this reason can exist forever.[8]

Without speaking in specific detail, the general nature of social relations is stated.

When one desires to take over the empire and act on it (interfere with it), I see that he will not succeed. The empire is a spiritual thing, and should not be acted on. He who acts on it harms him. He who holds on to it loses it. Among creatures some lead and some follow. Some blow hot and some blow cold. Some are strong and some are weak. Some may break and some may fall. Therefore the sage discards the extremes, the extravagant, and the excessive. He who assists the ruler with Tao does not dominate the world with force. The use of force usually brings requital. Wherever armies are stationed, briers and thorns grow. Great wars are always followed by famines...Whatever is contrary to Tao will perish.[9]

The issue of immortality is addressed.

Attain complete vacuity, Maintain steadfast quietude. All things come into being, And I see thereby their return. All things flourish, But each one returns to its root. This return to its root means tranquillity. It is called returning to its destiny. To return to destiny is called the eternal (Tao). To know the eternal is called enlightenment. Not to know the eternal is to act blindly to result in disaster. He who knows the eternal is all-embracing. Being all-embracing, he is impartial. Being impartial, he is kingly (universal). Being kingly, he is one with Nature. Being one with Nature, he is in accord with Tao. Being in accord with Tao, he is everlasting, And is free from danger throughout his lifetime.[10]

Egyptian religious thinking goes on in a familiar way, again being concerned with God, creation, Heaven, morality, and immortality. Quoting in detail gives a glimpse of the continuity of intention within varying traditions.

This is the sacred god, the lord of all gods, Amen-Ra, the lord of the throne of the world...the sacred soul who came into being in the beginning, the great god who liveth by right and truth...the being in whom every god existeth, the One of One, the creator of the things which came into being when the earth took form in the beginning, whose births are hidden, whose forms are manifold, and whose growth cannot be known...He shone upon the earth from primeval time (in the form of) the Disk, the prince of light and radiance. He giveth light unto all peoples...He masterth the bounds of eternity, he

31

goeth round about heaven... He is the prince of princes, the mightiest of the mighty...He is the firstborn god, the god who existed from the beginning, the governor of the world by reason of his strength...He is the primeval water which floweth forth in its season to make live all that cometh forth upon the potter's wheel...He is the Lord of time and he traverseth eternity; he is the aged one who reneweth his youth;...He is the young bull that destroyeth the wicked, and his strong arm fighteth against his foes. Through him did the earth come into being in the beginning...He is the Being who cannot be known, and he is more hidden than all the gods...His decrees are gracious and well doing...He giveth long life and multiplieth the years of those favored by him, he is the gracious protector of him who he setteth in his heart, and he is the fashioner of eternity and everlastingness.[11]

All flows out of the principle of the divine and the holy. "...the sacred god...the lord of all gods...the creator...(who) came into being in the beginning...he mastereth the bounds of eternity...the heavens and the earth were made by his conception..." The divine God is the creator of the universe and responsible for affairs upon the earth. He is "...the mightiest of the mighty...governor of the world..." who concerns himself with the affairs of men. He is responsible for good harvest and prosperity. "He is the primeval water which floweth forth in its season...the lord of life..."

May the gods grant that I go into and come forth from my tomb, may the Majesty refresh its shade, may I drink water from the cistern every day, may all my limbs grow, may Hapi give unto me bread and flowers of all kinds in their season, may I pass over my estate every day without ceasing, may my soul alight upon the branches of the groves which I have planted, may I make myself cool beneath my sycamores, may I eat the bread which they provide...let not my soul be imprisoned, but may I be among the venerable and favoured ones, may I plough my lands in the Field of Aaru, may I arrive at the Field of Peace, may one come out to me with vessels of ale and cakes and bread of the lords of eternity, may I receive meat from the altars of the great...[12]

While providing this account of material plenty, morality and social relations among men are seen to be gifts of the deity. God is the force which is concerned with acts of justice and injustice. "...he destroyeth the wicked...he directeth the world in his course...(with) an aweful terror...his decrees are gracious and well doing...human affairs prosper or decline according to his mandate...he is the gracious protector of him who he setteth in his heart... He is an absolute force who cares for the people of the world." "Live life, not shall thou die."[13] "Thou shall exist for millions of millions of years..." "...my soul is eternity..." "Thy essence is in heaven, thy body to earth." As everywhere throughout the world, Ancient Egyptian religious thinking expresses the same universal ideas about God, creation, Heaven, morality, and immortality.

One of the two root sources of the Western world is the Biblical Old Testament and there too is found a religious thinking that gives similar expression to the universal themes of religion. *Genesis* provides an account of divinity as the absolute power of creation. "In the beginning God created the heavens and the earth."[14] He goes on to create all that inhabits the earth, and Adam and Eve commence human existence. The third day witnesses this divine power.

And God said, "Let there be lights in the firmament of the heavens to separate the day from the night; and let them be for signs and for seasons and for days and years, and let them be lights in the firmament of the heavens to give light upon the earth." And it was so. And God made the two great lights, the greater to rule the day, and the lesser light to rule the night; he made the stars also.[15]

God is necessarily the cause of material abundance.

In the day that the Lord God made the earth and the heavens, when no plant of the field was yet in the earth and no herb of the field had yet sprung up--for the Lord God had not caused it to rain upon the earth, and there was no man yet to till the ground; but a mist went up from the earth and watered the whole face of the ground--then the Lord God formed man of dust from the ground, and breathed into his nostrils the breath of life; and man became a living being. And the Lord God planted a garden in Eden, in the east; and there he put the man whom he had formed. And out of the ground the Lord God made to grow every tree that is pleasant to the sight and good for food, the tree of life also in the midst of the garden, and the tree of knowledge of good and evil.[16]

But, as God is responsible for abundance, He is also there as man chooses scarcity.

The Lord God said to the serpent, "Because you have done this, cursed are you above all cattle, and above all wild animals; upon your belly you shall go, and dust you shall eat all the days of your life. I will put enmity between you and the woman, and between your seed and her seed; he shall bruise your head, and you shall bruise his heel." To the woman he said, "I will greatly multiply your pain in childbearing; in pain you shall bring forth children, yet your desire shall be for your husband, and he shall rule over you." And to Adam he said, "Because you have listened to the voice of your wife, and have eaten from the tree which I commanded you, 'You shall not eat of it,' cursed is the ground because of you; in toil you shall eat of it all the days of your life; thorns and thistles it shall bring forth to you; and you shall eat the plants of the field. In the sweat of your face you shall eat bread till you return to the ground, for out of it you were taken; you are dust, and to dust you shall return."[17]

As a man feels his want, in the here and now, he will know the cause of his condition as a just God demands his due. But the fact of scarcity is bound up with matters of immorality. A plentiful life is a life according to the laws of God. The statues and ordinances, the

Law, is the basis of social relations. Each will deserve his own just reward, be that eternal bliss or eternal damnation. With the Old Testament all aspects of life come under the divine law, every detail being set within the religious judgment. Accordingly, the anxiety of material scarcity and physical privation is alleviated in a comprehensive way. Simply, remain within the statutes and ordinances and all has already been made better.

If you walk in my statutes and observe my commandments and do them, then I will give you rains in season, and the land shall yield its increase, and the trees of the field shall yield their fruit...And I will give you peace in the land, and you shall lie down, and none shall make you afraid; and I will remove evil beasts from the land, and the sword shall not go through your land. And you shall chase your enemies, and they shall fall before you by the sword...And I will walk among you, and will be your God, and you shall be my people. I am the Lord your God, who brought you forth out of the land of Egypt, that you shall not be their slaves; and I have broken the bars of your yoke and made you walk erect.[18]

Not to respect the Law will command disaster.

...I will appoint over you sudden terror, consumption, and fever that waste the eyes and cause life to pine away. And you shall sow your seed in vain, for your enemies shall eat it; I will set my face against you...I will break the pride of your power, and I will make your heavens like iron and your earth like brass; and your strength shall be spent in vain, for your land shall not yield its increase, and the trees of the land shall not yield their fruit.[19]

Although the idea of personal immortality was not clearly developed in the Old Testament, there are passages that lay the basis for its full statement in the New Testament. "For I lift up my hand to heaven, and swear, As I live forever..."[20] "We have wrought no deliverance in the earth, and the inhabitants of the world have not fallen. Thy dead shall live, their bodies shall rise." [21] In one of the dominant expressions of religious thinking, the Bible too is concerned with the universal themes of God, creation, Heaven (scarcity and plenty), morality, and immortality. As in India, China, and Egypt, the theme is the same with each expression differing but little.

A closer look needs to be taken at the Old Testament as it moves toward idealities, as it moves from particularity and difference to generality and sameness, as it moves from the many to the One. The most profound advance of the Jewish Testament is the fact of a single God. Rather than a multitude of deities swarming the heavens to the distraction of human beings there is now conceived a single Deity that reigns over all. "And God said to Moses, 'I am the Lord.'"[22] The special trauma of the Old Testament is precisely this overcoming of the belief in many gods, as the mass of people were yet to believe in the singularity of the Lord. "Hear, O Israel: The Lord our God is one Lord..."[23]

And the people of Israel again did what was evil in the sight of the Lord, and served the Baals and the Ashtaroth, the gods of Syria, and the gods of Sidon, the gods of Moab, the gods of the Ammonites, and the gods of the Philistines; and they forsook the Lord, and did not serve him. And the anger of the Lord was kindled against Israel...[24]

Of a truth, O Lord, the kings of Assyria have laid waste all the nations and their lands, and have cast their gods into the fire; for they were no gods, but the work of men's hands, wood and stone; therefore they were destroyed. So now, O Lord our God, save us from his hand, that all the kingdoms of the earth may know that thou art the Lord.[25]

The many gods can be only of destructible stuff, material beings, while the single and true Lord is necessarily everlasting and indestructible. Simply, the Old Testament accomplishes the transition

36

from the thinking of the many gods of the world to the single idea of the God of the Universe, the unification of the many into One, the transformation of the material into the ideal.

This unification also occurs at the level of Law. The Ten Commandments constitute this Law. Rather than living according to one convention or another, one habit or another, there is established the *one* Law. There will be but one way of doing things. The multiplicity of random convention is to be replaced by a singular statement of Law. The Ten Commandments represent a movement away from conventional practice to a single idea, as that practice becomes "idealized" into the formal code of Law. All ambiguity and confusion of convention is removed, as the Law is the final standard.

I am the Lord your God, who brought you out of the land of Egypt, out of the house of bondage. You shall have no other gods before me. You shall not make for yourself a graven image, or any likeness of anything that is in heaven above, or that is in the earth beneath, or that is in the water under the earth; you shall not bow down to them or serve them; for I the Lord your God am a jealous God, visiting the iniquity of the fathers upon the children to the third and fourth generation of those who hate me, but showing steadfast love to thousands of those who love me and keep my commandments. You shall not take the name of the Lord your God in vain; for the Lord will not hold him guiltless who takes his name in vain. Remember the sabbath day, to keep it holy. Six days you shall labor, and do all your work; but the seventh day is a sabbath to the Lord your God; in it you shall not do any work, you, or your son, or your daughter, your manservant, or your maidservant, or your cattle, or the sojourner who is within your gates; for in six days the Lord made heaven and earth, the sea, and all that is in them, and rested the seventh day; therefore the Lord blessed the sabbath day and hallowed it. Honor your father and mother, that your days may be long in the land which the Lord your God gives you. You shall not kill. You shall not commit adultery. You shall not steal. You shall not bear false witness against your neighbor. You shall not covet your neighbor's house; you shall

37

not covet your neighbor's wife, or his manservant, or his maidservant, or his ox, or his ass, or anything that is your neighbor's.[26]

Everyday life is brought under the single rule of Law, which serves as the principle of *comparison* and then judgment. Instances of behavior will be judged according to the universality of the Law. The habits of conventions are replaced by the rule of Law. The transition to Law is an accomplishment of thinking that recognizes ideality in its own right. This creates the possibility of thinking *only* in terms of ideality, *only* in terms of the One. This is of course a significant cultural advance as the many give way to the One, as the many gods of antiquity give way to the God of Israel, as the many evils of the world give way to the single evil of Satan, as the many just acts of the person give way to the single idea of Justice. The particulars of life are now to be judged with respect to an ideality of Law.

The Chosen People of the one God are brought under a single Law for the ordering of the affairs of the community.

You shall appoint judges and officers in all your towns which the Lord your God gives you, according to your tribes; and they shall judge the people with righteous judgment. You shall not pervert justice; you shall not show partiality; and you shall not take a bribe, for a bribe blinds the eyes of the wise and subverts the cause of the righteous. Justice, and only justice, you shall follow, that you may live and inherit the land which the Lord your God gives you.[27]

Only the *idea* of what is in accordance with the Law is to serve as the basis of justice.

There, hear me, you men of understanding, far be it from God that he should do wickedness, and from the Almighty that he should do wrong. For according to the work of man he will requite himself, and according to his ways he will make it befall him. Of truth, God will not do wickedly, and the Almighty will not pervert justice.[28]

38

The idea of a single God has absolute consequences for the particular affairs of the social community.

As the Old Testament represents a movement from particularity to generality, from the many to the One, from the real to the ideal, so too is this movement found in Ancient Greek thinking, the second root of the Western spirit. In Plato's *Republic* is found the same movement to generality. It presents the movement from the many deeds of the just and the unjust to the singular idea of justice itself. Stated otherwise, it is an attempt to determine the single essential characteristic, the common feature, of justice which must necessarily participate in the example of it that would be given in fact. Initially justice is said to be a "giving to each what is owed," [29] as well as "doing good to friends and harm to enemies," [30] and "the advantage of the stronger." [31] After much discussion, justice is defined as a "...mean...between what is best--doing injustice without paying the penalty--and the worst--suffering injustice without being able to avenge oneself."[32] It is also a matter of the "minding of one's own business," [33] as well as "...the power by which all these (moderation, courage, and prudence) come into being..." [34] Justice is something "...not with respect to a man's minding his external business, but with respect to what is within, with respect to what truly concerns him and his own." [35] He "...sets his own house in good order..." [36] All of this one must see for oneself. But justice refers beyond itself to something called the Idea of the Good.

...in the knowable the last thing to be seen, and that with considerable effort, is the *idea* of the Good; but once seen, it must be concluded that this is in fact the cause of all that is right and fair in everything...[37]

Justice is a matter of the Idea of the Good which is not a thing of the physical world, rather it can be understood only by the mind. This

Idea exists separate and distinct from all things of the world. By *analogy* these things of the world may serve as a means to see the Idea of the Good. The geometer uses figures that have been drawn in the sand, figures which can be only rough approximations of the perfect figures of geometry itself. The drawn imperfections of lines and circle in the sand can lead the mind to understand lines and circles as such. By analogy, in considering the many imperfect approximations of "good" things, it is possible to recognize in each that which is essential to its being called good at all and that which is merely an attending circumstance. The essential is distinguished from the unessential. It is unessential that the cup is made of glass or clay, as what is essential is that the circumstance of "cup-ness" be fulfilled, that liquid be contained until one's thirst has been quenched. With this mental movement from the unessential to the essential, from the many to the One, from the real to the ideal, there is seen a central "what-ness." In Plato's view there is a greatest of all things in the realm of the essential that is the *Idea of the Good.* From this all else is made possible. Justice comes about as the child of the Good. Understanding this was a difficult task and it was "the greatest study."[38] What distinguished the study of the *Idea of the Good* from all other studies, such as that of geometry, was that geometry could be learned from someone else, but the *Idea of the Good* was something that one needed to learn for oneself. A teacher could perhaps assist in the early going of such a study but any final insight could be achieved only when one was able to see for oneself. These special requirements for the thinking person had great consequences for all subsequent cultural development in the Western world.

Plato provides another telling example of the process of thinking that proceeds from the many to the One. In the *Symposium* the essential what-ness concerns the question of *love.* The occasion for the discussion is rather amusing. Suffering hangovers from the prior night's bout of alcoholic intoxication, a gathering of men have decided upon a more restrained evening. The customary dancing girls have been sent away and, "merely by way of refreshment," a modest amount of wine has been made available. Emerging from the mental fog of a drunken stupor, the men decide upon a discussion concerning the nature of love. Each is to provide a speech on love's behalf, with the anticipation of a final definition, a statement as to love's essence. There will be six speeches with Socrates bringing up the rear. It is claimed, first of all, that "...Love is the oldest and most glorious of the gods, the great giver of all goodness and happiness to men, alike to the living and the dead." [39] The next speaker asserts that the Love of Aphrodite is "...heavenly in himself and precious alike to cities and to men, for he constrains both lover and beloved to pay the most earnest heed to their moral welfare."[40] With excesses naturally accompanying matters of love, this higher love of Aphrodite guides one to the more noble course. One's "moral welfare" ought to hold sway over the darker business that often becomes involved. Another speaker provides a medical account. As the body is comprised of many conflicting forces, it is the function of Love to find a harmony and balance. The physician is he who "...must be able to reconcile the jarring elements of the body, and force them, as it were, to fall in love with one another," [41] and "...medicine is under the sole direction of the god of Love." [42] Aristophanes then provides some comic relief that goes to the heart of the matter. Love is "...a desperate yearning for the other..." [43] He recounts a tale. In the long past, the male and the female were a single being.

...each of these beings was globular in shape, with rounded back and sides, four arms and four legs, and two faces, both the same, on a cylindrical neck, and one head, with one face one side and one the other, and four ears, and two lots of privates, and all the other parts to match. They walked erect, as we do ourselves, backward or forward, whichever they pleased, but when they broke into a run they simply stuck their legs straight out and went whirling round and

41

round like a clown turning cartwheels. And since they had eight legs, if you count their arms as well, you can imagine that they went bowling along at a pretty good speed.[44]

This rather innocent play came to an end when they set upon the gods "trying to scale the heights of heaven..." [45] Their disrespect towards the gods was rectified by their being "cut in half."

...when the work of bisection was complete it left each half with the desperate yearning for the other, and they ran together and flung their arms around each other's necks, and asked for nothing better than to be rolled into one. [46]

Our "primeval wholeness" had been lost and the desire of the lover is to be merged "into an utter oneness with the beloved." [47] Or, simply,

...the happiness of the whole human race, women no less than men, is to be found in the consummation of our love, and in the healing of our disserved nature by finding each his proper mate. [48]

Before Socrates can speak there is a final speech that enthralls the imagination. It asserts that Love is simply a god and it is our main responsibility to extoll and praise Love as Love.

...Love was born to be the enemy of old age, and shuns the very sight of senility, clinging always to his like in the company of youth...[49]

As a preserve against the ravages of time, the ravages of physical privation, love is an affirmation of youth and a freedom from the results of old age. But it is more too.

And so I say...that Love, besides being in himself the loveliest and the best, is the author of those very virtues in all around him. And now I am stirred to speak in numbers, and to tell how it is he that brings: Peace upon the earth, the breathless calm that lulls the long-tormented deep, rest to the winds, and that sweet balm and solace of our nature, sleep. And it is he that banishes estrangement and ushers friendship in; it is he that unites us in such friendly gatherings as this--presiding at the table, at the dance, and at the altar, cultivating courtesy and weeding out brutality, lavish of kindness and sparing of malevolence, affable and gracious, the wonder of the wise, the admiration of the gods, the despair of him that lacks, and the happiness of him that has, the father of delicacy, daintiness, elegance, and grace, of longing and desire, heedful of the good and heedless of the bad, in toil and terror, in drink or dialectic, our helmsman and helper, our pilot and preserver, the richest ornament of heaven and earth alike, and, to conclude, the noblest and the loveliest of leaders, whom every one of us must follow, raising our voices in harmony with the heavenly song of Love that charms both mortal and immortal hearts. [50]

Echoing the Biblical 23rd Psalm, this speech in praise of love gives rise to the higher emotions of gratitude and worship that rightfully serve this greatest power for the good.

A summation is needed on the verge of the speech of Socrates. Each speech has focused upon a single aspect of Love and then praised it as if that aspect were the whole. (This mistaking of a part for the whole will create continuing grief throughout the world.) But, for the time being, love is surely a giver of happiness, a moral constraint, a harmony and balance, medically good for the body, a passionate yearning for one's soulmate, and the cause of all that is good in world. Each of these definitions do its part but a re-consideration is necessary in order to see all of the parts as parts of a single whole. While each speaker has said his piece, it is necessary to say more. The speech of Socrates enters a new dimension and will point the way for the continuing odyssey of the Western spirit.

Socrates begins. Love must a love *of something.* "...Love is always the love of something, and...that something is what he lacks."[51] It must be in *relation* to something else, as it cannot stand alone, isolated unto itself, as if it were a "god," something only to worship. Socrates here admits his ignorance and acknowledges that he knows nothing about love himself and anything that he would say he learned from an aged woman named Diotima. She had agreed to instruct him in his ignorance, as she was "...deeply versed in this and many other fields of knowledge...,"[52] and taught him all that he knows about "the philosophy of love." Not being a god at all, love is instead an intermediary, being "...halfway between mortal and immortal...halfway between god and man."[53] Love is *in-between*.

They are the envoys and interpreters that ply between heaven and earth, flying upward with our worship and our prayers, and descending with the heavenly answers and commandments, and since they are between the two estates they weld both sides together and merge them into one great whole. They form the medium of the prophetic arts, of the priestly rites of sacrifice, initiation, and incantation, of divination and of sorcery, for the divine will not mingle directly with the human, and it is only through the mediation of the spirit world that man can have any intercourse, whether waking or sleeping, with the gods. And the man who is versed in such matters is said to have spiritual powers, as opposed to the mechanical powers of the man who is expert in the more mundane arts. There are many spirits, and many kinds of spirits, too, and Love is one of them.[54]

As an intermediary love is "...neither mortal nor immortal...and is never altogether in or out of need, and stands, moreover, midway between ignorance and wisdom."[55] But a final purpose is involved.

I know it has been suggested, she continued, that lovers are people who are looking for their other halves, but as I see it, Socrates, Love never longs for either the half or the whole of anything except the good. For men will even have their hands and feet cut off if they are once convinced that those members are bad for them. Indeed I think we only prize our own belongings in so far as we say that the good belongs to us, and the bad to someone else, for what we love is the good and nothing but the good. Or do you disagree? [56]

Summarily, "...Love longs for the good to be his own forever." [57] The *activity* of love is to bring forth the beautiful, to bring forth into the world the power of the good.

Conception, we know, takes place when man and woman come together, but there's a divinity in human propagation, an immortal something in the midst of man's mortality which is incompatible with any kind of discord. [58]

The longing for this "immortal something" is the greatest power on earth. It is the yearning to step outside and beyond the limits of mortality, the limits of material necessity and physical privation, and it is to become almost "like a god." But human choice is also involved as there are two ways in which to embrace this immortality.

Well then, she went on, those whose procreancy is of the body turn to woman as the object of their love, and raise a family, in the blessed hope that by doing so they will keep their memory green, "through time and through eternity." But those whose procreancy is of the spirit rather than the flesh--and they are not unknown, Socrates,--conceive and bear the things of the spirit. [59]

Some turn to the body and find an immortality in the life of their children, while others turn to the things of the spirit and find an immortality in the wisdom of the spiritual domain. This wisdom "...is that which governs the ordering of society, and which goes by the name of justice and moderation." [60] The proper ordering of society is possible only with an understanding of the reality of the Highest Good. Only when one has set aside all partial and limited aspects and has come to see and appreciate the most general good, only then is it possible to order society properly. The reality of Love culminates in the common welfare of society as a whole. The parts fit perfectly into the greater vista of the whole. Political philosophy and the philosophy of Love embrace the same reality. Diotima continues. Love is...

...an everlasting loveliness which neither comes nor goes, which neither flowers nor fades, for such beauty is the very same on every hand, the same then as now, here as there, this way as that way, the same to every worshiper as it is to every other. Nor will his vision of the beautiful take the form of a face, or of hands, or of anything that is of the flesh. It will be neither words, nor knowledge, nor anything that exists in something else, such as a living creature, or the earth, or the heaven, or anything that is--but subsisting of itself and by itself in an eternal oneness, while every lovely thing partakes of it in such sort that, however much the parts wax and wane, it will be neither more nor less, but still the same inviolable whole. [61]

Having borne witness to the "eternal oneness," the cause of all that is good, one equally sees the proper way in which society is to be ordered, the best way in which people can live and prosper in harmony. In having seen the truth of the Highest Good one can see the reality of the best social organization. Without this vision of the Good, this illumination, there can only be a stumbling blindness and confusion, a perpetual struggle and antagonism among viciously competing special interests who recognize only their own advantage. Each special interest elevates its partial "philosophy" to the position of universal truth, as the part masquerades as the whole and the common interest will be crushed against the jagged reefs of special interest. But Diotima concludes her speech in praise of the Highest Good and its relationship to Love. "...if, my dear Socrates...man's life is ever worth the living, it is when he has attained this vision of the very soul of beauty." [62] Love is a much more profound reality than any of the previous speeches could ever have suspected. It is a matter of coming to comprehend the Highest Good, seeing this as the true cause of all that is good in the world, and then caring to return to the world of partial half-truths, and finally attempting to set a balance in place that serves the greatest good. There is simply no arguing with this. The Teaching of Diotima, this vision of Love, is of the highest order of truth and establishes the principle upon which we could live in peace and harmony. Of course none of this happened in fact, few read the great *Symposium* and fewer still cared at all. The world would continue upon its career of death and destruction, an experience still fresh after 2,500 years, *yet* a difference was made, as the *idea* of a *possible* harmony was born into the world. We are the beneficiaries of this birth.

The Old Testament and the Teaching of Plato then stand together as initiating a common tradition that serves as the foundation of the Western world. The essential fact is that with each there is a movement from the particular to the general, from the many to the One, from convention to Law, from partial acts of justice and love to the total insight into Justice itself and Love itself, from the real to the ideal. It allows human beings for the very first time to "stand upon their own feet" and think for themselves. Again, few were so inclined, but those few would make all the difference. Plato in particular created the mental tools for thinking in terms of ideality, simply said, conceptualization.

Our modern world of complex scientific, technological, economic, and social relations would not have been possible without this spectacular transformation of thinking. The Teaching of Plato then presents for the first time in world history a *self-conscious* thinking in terms of idealities. The Old Testament moves upon this same road but only as an intimation, as it lacks this self-conscious intent. But together these two traditions created something new. The advantages are breathtaking. There occurs a tremendous economy and efficiency of thinking, something that in due time will power the

47

cultural expansion of our own time. a single example will do. Rather than counting real things there appears the possibility of mathematics. Rather than counting upon one's fingers, one will be able to calculate "in one's head." Mathematics will be divested of its moorings in "reality," in concrete numbers and real relations, and instead there will be established the principles of thinking in terms of the idealities of number and relation. Thinking "leaps," as it were, from the world and is able for the first time to "conceptualize" as it pleases. The full impact of this will be realized only in the Modern Era, beginning in the 17th century. Much difficulty and confusion lay between Plato and then but the fact nonetheless remains that a mental breakthrough has been made and that only time and good fortune will be needed for its fruition in the transformation of the world.

As the Old Testament and the Teaching of Plato together comprise the movement towards ideality, it is important to consider what this will mean as an *experience*. What does the possibility of ideality and conceptualization mean for the person? Set alongside of the experience of material scarcity and physical privation there could be no greater difference. This difference itself is a revelation in its own right. On the one hand, there is the experienced fact of hunger, thirst, the cold, pain, disease, and death. On the other hand, there is none of this, but rather the mental possibility of plenty, perfection, and immortality. All the anxiety that attaches to living in the world of material scarcity is *alleviated* with the *idea* of a world that is without that scarcity, as reality is alleviated by an ideality. As the Old Testament becomes transformed by the New these concerns will become central but in order to see the experience of ideality as it becomes the "religious experience" it is necessary to return to the trail of Odysseus. The Odyssey of the Western spirit begins with his struggles and we are indebted to the Ancient Greeks for having acted upon his beginning. Before going forward it is necessary to briefly return to that beginning.

A full appreciation of the mental breakthrough of the Greeks is possible only when contrasted with the Oriental despotism with which it struggled.

The ancient world, in so far as we can reconstruct it, bears everywhere the same stamp. In Egypt, in Crete, in Mesopotamia, wherever we can read bits of the story, we find the same conditions: a despot enthroned, whose whims and passions are the determining factor in the state; a wretched, subjugated populace; a great priestly organization to which is handed over the domain of the intellect.[63]

The Greeks present a possible break with this tyranny, meaning simply that the conditions are being established for the individual to *think for himself.*

High spirit and the energy of great vital powers had worked in them to assert themselves against despotic rule and to refuse to submit to priestly rule. They would have no man to dictate to them and being free from masters they used their freedom to think. [64] The Greek mind was free to think about the world as it pleased, to reject all traditional explanations, to disregard all the priests taught, to search unhampered by any outside authority for the truth. The Greeks had free scope for their scientific genius and they laid the foundations of our science to-day. [65]

We are reminded of Odysseus. In his journey towards home he needed to rely upon himself alone, his own wits and guile. He needed to think for himself, in order to act upon circumstances for his own behalf. Rather than passively praying homage to the gods, yet without forsaking them, he chooses instead to act for himself and to take his chances and to live or die by the results. This choice places him on the threshold of the self-conscious thinking self, and the experience of ideality will be its greatest accomplishment. This is the divide between consciousness and self-consciousness, between strict tradition and the possible initiative of individual thinking and action, between tyranny and freedom. This is best exemplified in the long struggle between Greece and Persia. The vastly superior army of Persians descended upon the Greeks with a host of five million and came to grief at their hands. Much was at stake.

The Greco-Persian War was the most momentous conflict in European history, for it made Europe possible. It won for Western civilization the opportunity to develop its own economic life-- unburdened with alien tribute and taxation--and its own political institutions, free from the dictation of Oriental kings. It won for Greece a clear road for the first great experiment in liberty; it preserved the Greek mind for three centuries from the enervating mysticism of the East, and secured for Greek enterprise full freedom of the sea.[66]

The hard lesson of war was that enthusiasm for battle cannot be commanded from above and that only the individual can call upon himself to do the duty that he sees as his own. It is no coincidence then that the experience of an emerging self-consciousness is the very condition for the possibility of the experience of ideality. The way has been cleared to *Know Thyself.*

Chapter Three
The Religious Experience

The mental ability for *written* language is central to the possibility of ideality. It provided a means for remembering and comparing, for taking the thinking process into more complex formations. As written, language became *objective* and therefore transferrable in time. One generation passes on to the next the accumulation of its own efforts. With the passage of centuries the written word achieved the status of the sacred and became part of the religious experience itself. But before the word could become sacred it needed to be *named*. This involves the formation of concepts and the process of idealization.

In everyday life any person would have had experience with the color *red*. In would have been experienced in its many shades and textures, such as that of the evening sky, or the blood of the sacrificed lamb, or the fruits of the field, and so on. The color would always have been presented as the color *of something*. But the realization would have finally emerged that while red must appear with the thing that it colored, there was such a "thing" as *red itself*. This conceptual red is nowhere to be found among things, but rather it is an *idea*, an ideality that exists separate from reality. It exists only through the agency of thinking. Just as the number *one* is nowhere yet

51

"somewhere," so too with the color *red*. The *naming* of this special red forms the generic concept, the red that is absolutely itself without the limitations of reality. It is the conceptual red that gives meaning to all experiences of red things. All reds are relative to this *red*. Each experienced red is a matter of identity and difference, of sharing in the generic ideality yet being distinguished from it in fact. This possibility of moving between ideality and reality gives to human life its depth and richness. It is only here that *meaning* becomes possible.

The achievement of language in the written word then creates a separation, a freeing, from the circumstances of particular experiences. This freeing allows human beings to think in the terms of conceptual idealities. This is an accomplishment of the greatest importance and can be better appreciated by an example from Ancient Arabic culture. The camel there was the central fact of life, the standard of wealth and prosperity. This importance was evident in language. There were over 6000 words that dealt with the camel. There was a distinct term for every conceivable variation and difference that was possible *yet,* there was *not* a word for the generic term *camel* itself. A word for the inclusive concept was lacking. [1] The linguistic equivalent for the generic *red* was not there. Being accustomed to the highly conceptual languages of today, it is difficult to imagine such an omission. Apparently there was no *need* for the term as daily life was conducted with the 6000 specific terms. Certainly Arabic language used the process of idealization, as any language must, but that process had simply not been completed so as to include the end generic term. The point here is that this conceptualization and idealization, this possibility of thinking and ideality, is not to be taken for granted, and that it is an *active accomplishment* and not a passive given. Once formulated though, the concept was understood in terms of religious feeling. To have come upon a term that would include such a wide range of experiences and yet essentially existed *apart* was a "revelation" that inspired wonder and awe. To recognize the reality of *red* among other reds, to recognize *One* among many things, and to have found *God* among the many gods, was to have witnessed a religious revelation. "In the beginning was the *Word,* and the *Word* was with *God,* and the *Word* was *God.*" [2]

The achievement to conceptual thinking was put to a specific use. The leisured few gave themselves to religious considerations. What was it that they saw and pondered? Obviously, the overwhelming reality of life was the fact of material scarcity and physical privation. Life was hard, painful, and brief. With this realization there came an emotional anxiety and terror which was heightened by an enhanced awareness. To know that one knew was to make the experience worse. A great contrast is now formulated. These earliest religious thinkers saw the ideality of the number One, the unity and power of a single God, and the majesty of the ideas of Justice, Love, Eternity, Immortality, and of Heaven. Conceived here was the idea of a *place,* a possible world, that was *without* the fact of scarcity and privation. A greater difference of reality could not have been imagined. Two distinct experiences lay side by side, two realities, one suffered through every day in anxiety and terror, and the other imagined to be somewhere else that was perfectly free of all such terror. The one produced anxiety and the other ecstasy. An emotional feeling of joy was possible simply with the *idea* of a perfect abundance. An absolute *schism* was evident, a division that defined human experience. Thinking then is both the cause and the condition for the fact that there are *two* realities and this contradiction and antagonism lies at the center of human experience. A re-statement is necessary.

The anxiety of privation continues unabated. While it was possible to have experienced glimpses of a world without privation, glimpses that were essentially the idealities of conceptual thinking, in absolute fact, privation was the reality of the experienced world. A divergence appears. The idealities of thinking came to be *re-interpreted*, they came to be understood more as "reality" itself, more real, than the actual reality of everyday experience. But before this re-interpretation could be carried through in fact, an emotional re-alignment was necessary. The mere thought of a world *without* the experience of scarcity and privation was found to be enough to create a feeling that was so powerful that it was felt to be a *greater* reality than the experienced reality itself. A feeling proved to be more powerful than actual experience, and consequently it was possible to *deny* that actual experience of its value and deplete it of its significance. A de-valuation and then denial of the actualities of everyday experience was carried through in the wake of an idealized emotion. The Good, the Beautiful, and visions of God were accorded the highest value, as anything to do with the world was de-valued to the level, of dirt, evil, disease, sin, rot, and death. There was a rush to exaggeration with this re-structuring of reality.

There is no soundness in my flesh because of thy indignation; there is no health in my bones because of my sin. For my iniquities have gone over my head; they weigh like a burden too heavy for me. My wounds grow foul and fester because of my foolishness, I am utterly bowed down and prostrate; all the day I go about mourning. My loins are filled with burning, and there is no soundness in my flesh. I am utterly spent and crushed; I groan because of the tumult of my heart.[3]

The idealities of conceptual thinking are now thought to make up reality as such, as everyday experience was re-interpreted as the domain of "evil." Reality is now thought to be concerned only with God, Heaven and Immortality, whereas all of the world, the earth, is a domain of darkness and terror that is to be shunned.

Dominion and fear are with God; he makes peace in his high heaven. Is there any number to his armies? Upon whom does his light not arise? How then can man be righteous before God? How can he who is born of woman be clean? Behold, even the moon is not bright and the stars are not clean in his sight; how much less man, who is a maggot, and the son of man, who is a worm! [4]

The degradation of man and the world comes to be a consistent theme in religious thinking. But one step more is necessary in order to complete the inversion of reality. The men who used conceptual thinking to find God and Heaven must necessarily *continue* to live in the world that is now so thoroughly degraded and deprived of value. One final assault on the world is at hand. To rid one's experience of the taint of the world, there is invoked a *substitution.* The newly re-valued reality of ideality, of Heaven, that is a world without the material factor, the pure domain of God, is now felt to be the *whole* of reality itself and is substituted in the place of the already de-valued and denied reality of living experience. *Denial and Substitution.* Reality is no longer what it is experienced to be but rather what it is felt to be subsequent to the force of denial and substitution. The emotional relief and advantage is absolutely tremendous. If the reality of the anxiety concerning scarcity and privation was no longer felt to be of any value, and if instead the ideas of ideality could be taken as being the only value, and if denial and substitution could be carried out convincingly, then, simply put, the anxiety and terror of the world here and now would no longer be felt, it would have been comprehensively alleviated. One could emotionally proceed *as if* there were no world at all except the one remaining after denial and substitution had been completed. The everlasting pain of scarcity and privation, of disease, and death would have been silenced, even though that pain and disease would continue to exist as before, it was simply *not felt*, as the emotional feeling of abundance, comfort, and everlasting life extinguished the experience of that pain. One had become oblivious, sealed off, from the anxieties of privation. The machinery of denial and substitution was complete and the degree of emotional alleviation immense.

The Psalms express the feeling of this alleviation in great detail.

The Lord is my shepherd, I shall not want; He makes me lie down in green pastures. He leads me beside still waters; he restores my soul. He leads me in paths of righteousness for his name's sake. Even though I walk through the valley of the shadow of death, I fear no evil; for thou art with me; thy rod and thy staff, they comfort me. Thou preparest a table before me in the presence of my enemies; thou anointest my head with oil, my cup overflows. Surely goodness and mercy shall follow me all the days of my life; and I shall dwell in the house of the Lord for ever. [5]

The process of denial and substitution can be traced through each line of this most famous Psalm. "The Lord is my shepherd..." The "Lord" is an idealization and conceptualization of all that is *Good*, all that is powerful in one's experience, as He is all-knowing, all-loving, and all-powerful. He is the greatest reality and the final force in the Universe. He is the Universe. To have the Lord then as one's "shepherd," as one's personal guardian from all possible harm, as one's ever-present and ever-loving protector, is to have a *personal* relationship with the absolute power of all being. "I shall not want..." As the greatest power, He is the shepherd that can turn back the laws of nature, those laws and forces that had given one over to such a wrenching privation, those very circumstances that had provoked such a bitter anxiety. All of this will be no more, as one is fully protected. "He makes me lie down in green pastures..." He allows one to rest when there has been no resting, when the demands of survival require a frenetic chase day after day. Rest is inconceivable in the terms of real life. And that rest will take place "in green pastures." The desert landscape of heat, sand, rock, bandits, and wild animals was the actual experience that would contrast to the "green pastures" of one's restful repose. "He leads me beside still waters..." There may be no greater horror than that of drowning, of being engulfed by the raging waters of the Sea of Galilee, and to be lost into the great cold depth. Many fisherman have left widows and orphans when the calm morning breeze gave way to the quickly forming storm that left a shattered empty craft bobbing on the still churning sea. Seemingly calm waters can beguile into a final disaster. One is never safe. When the Lord "leads" and "protects" from these treacherous seas a lasting fear has been alleviated. "He restores my soul." Having lived in fear and trembling, one's soul having been scattered about in the tribulations of survival, it is no small consolation to come under divine protection. "He leads me in paths of righteousness for his name's sake." The way of the world is not of righteousness, but rather of greed, malice, envy, sin, violence, and brutality or, simply, the pursuit of selfishness at the expense of someone else. One may *prefer* righteousness but it would be nothing more than an innocence which would be immediately taken advantage of by the more powerful. Nothing could be better than marching in the grand army of the righteous, in the name of the Lord, against satanic evil. "Even though I walk through the valley of the shadow of death, I fear no evil." In the midst of tribal bloodshed, the shadow of death casts its pall everywhere, but the Lord protects. Throughout all of these feelings of this great Psalm there is a de-valuation and then denial of the world which is followed by the substitution in its place of an idealized reality that has been purified through the emotions of alleviation, a reality that is finally purged of all elements of actual experience. This denial and substitution and degradation of the world provides the greatest feeling of emotional alleviation. One simply believes that all of this is true as God becomes personal. "...for thou art with me, thy rod and thy staff, they comfort me..." One assures oneself that this is one's rightful entitlement and it is to this assumption that many will return again and again over the generations in order to advance individual interests at the expense and death of others. Consolidation of this assumption continues. "Thou preparest a table for me in the presence of my enemies, thou anointest my head with oil, my cup overflows." One's good fortune will be delivered only at the *exclusion* of others, as one's enemies must be seen to suffer the fact of wretchedness. One must be allowed to gloat in order to consummate one's personal relationship with God, or so it is assumed. Life is divided in half, between one's own special tribe, and all others, one's natural enemies. A summary statement follows. "Surely goodness and mercy shall follow me all the days of my life." God has personally bestowed His grace upon thee and a final repose is achieved. The everlasting terror is now denied. "...and I shall dwell in the house of the Lord for ever." Death itself, the ultimate privation, is set aside. One will *live* in the House of the Lord, *forever.* Death will not be allowed to reap its grim harvest on one's behalf.

Elsewhere in *The Psalms* is found this same denial of reality as is and the substitution in its place of an altered reality based upon the desire for emotional alleviation.

I will bless the Lord at all times; his praise shall continually be in my mouth. My soul makes its boast in the Lord; let the afflicted hear and be glad. O magnify the Lord with me, and let us exalt his name together! I sought the Lord, and he answered me, and delivered me from all my fears. Look to him, and be radiant; so your faces shall never be ashamed...The Lord redeems the life of his servants; none of those who take refuge in him will be condemned. [6]

He who dwells in the shelter of the Most High, who abides in the shadow of the Almighty, will say to the Lord, "My refuge and my fortress; my God in whom I trust." For he will deliver you from the snare of the fowler and from the deadly pestilence...Because you have made the Lord your refuge, the Most High your habitation, no evil shall befall you, no scourge come near your tent. [7]

I love the Lord, because he has heard my voice and my supplications. Because he inclined his ear to me, therefore I will call on him as long as I live. The snares of death encompassed me; the pangs of Sheol laid hold on me; I suffered distress and anguish. Then I called on the name of the Lord: "O Lord, I beseech thee, save me life!" [8]

When one's anxiety is so extreme, when life is but an affliction, these Biblical passages offer a vision of abundance, repose, and personal immortality that achieves an emotional alleviation *as if* there were no suffering at all. The fact of this alleviation here will be termed the Theology of Faith.

The Theology of Faith involves *prayer* as its special *work*. The belief and faith in the vision of the world that is without the material factor is sustained by the emotional force of just believing that it is so. This takes the explicit form of prayer and chanting. With the perpetual repetition of the *words* of one's belief, the prayers, one comes to further believe. The meaninglessness of repetition creates an emotional force where it is impossible to believe otherwise. One's reality becomes enshrined in the rote repetition of empty words. The special meaning of the prayer is given over to meaningless sound. Ironically, prayer then takes on the quality of work. One's "labor" is of the spirit and is accorded the highest value as the work of the world has already been de-valued and deeded over to the forces of evil. Dissent is no longer possible, as the reiterated belief that the world is such and such creates that very world. One is able to while away one's time in the prayers of the spirit and an exquisite alleviation from the anxiety of the world has already been achieved.

Even though denial and substitution was able to provide a comprehensive personal feeling of alleviation, more was required. There was a *political* dimension to this Theology of Faith. The feeling of alleviation did not diminish in the least the fact that there was still not enough to go around, some would still need to go without and a principle of *exclusion* was necessary. A religious sanction was required in order to justify this exclusion. *The Psalms* speak clearly.

The Lord is in his holy temple, the Lord's throne is in heaven; his eyes behold, his eyelids test, the children of men. The Lord tests the righteous and the wicked, and his soul hates him that loves violence. On the wicked he will rain coals of fire and brimstone; a scorching wind shall be the portion of their cup. For the Lord is righteous, he loves righteous deeds; the upright shall behold his face. [9]

Divine sanction justifies exclusion. Any sort of violence may be put upon those who are left out. The belief of the *Chosen People* carries this into the world of struggle and violence. When justified by God, any deed is possible.

While the Old Testament provides this sanction for exclusion, it is the New Testament and then Christianity which will carry this *Ideology of Exclusion* to the level of political doctrine. This will establish a legacy of violence that is with us today.

Not every one who say to me, "Lord, Lord," shall enter the kingdom of heaven, but he who does the will of my Father who is in heaven. On that day many will say to me, "Lord, Lord did we not prophesy in your name, and cast out demons in your name, and do mighty works in your name?" And then will I declare to them, "I never knew you; depart from me, you evildoers." [10]

Do not think that I have come to bring peace on earth; I have not come to bring peace, but a sword. For I have come to set a man against his father, and a daughter against her mother, and a daughter-in-law against her mother-in-law; and a man's foes will be those of his own household. He who loves father or mother more than me is not worthy of me; and he who does not take his cross and follow me is not worthy of me. He who finds his life will lose it, and he who loses his life for my sake will find it. [11] For many are called, but few

60

are chosen. [12]

The Ideology of Exclusion was to be maintained. Tolerance was not a virtue, as this type of social partition would be used again and again in the continued struggles of one group against another.

The harsh economic realities in Palestine provided the stage for the Teaching of Jesus. The poor and powerless flocked to his call, those excluded from both Hebrew and Roman privilege. The vigor of the Chosen People had settled into a system of priestly power that took to the few the labors of the many. Roman power was a foreign imposition that allowed no compromise. The New Teaching came at a time when nothing of this world encouraged hope and there was not the slightest inkling of something better. The extreme squalor and desperation enhanced a Teaching that preached of "another world."

Therefore I tell you, do not be anxious about your life, what you shall eat or what you shall drink, nor about your body, what you shall put on. Is not life more than food, and the body more than clothing? Look at the birds of the air: they neither sow nor reap nor gather into barns, and yet your Heavenly Father feeds them. Are you not of more value than they? And which of you by being anxious can add one cubit to his span of life? And why are you anxious about clothing? Consider the lilies of the field, how they grow; they neither toil nor spin; yet I tell you, even Solomon in all his glory was not arrayed like one of these. But if God so clothes the grass of the field, which today is alive and tomorrow is thrown into the oven, will he not much more clothe you, O men of little faith? Therefore do not be anxious, saying, "What shall we eat?" or "What shall we drink?" or "What shall we wear?" For the Gentiles seek all these things; and your heavenly Father knows that you need them all. But seek first his kingdom and his righteousness, and all these things shall be yours as well. [13]

There was no need to worry as "the kingdom of heaven is at hand."[14] Heaven is but a world without the material factor, a world above and beyond, a world without need, that has been transformed through the labor of denial and substitution.

Jesus said to them, 'I am the bread of life; he who comes to me shall not hunger, and he who believes in me shall never thirst...' [15] Jesus said to her, 'Every one who drinks of this water will thirst again, but whoever drinks of the water that I shall give him will never thirst; the water that I shall give him will become in him a spring of water welling up to eternal life...' [16]

There would be no disease.

When he came down from the mountain, great crowds followed him; and behold, a leper came to him and knelt before him, saying, 'Lord, if you will, you can make me clean.' And he stretched out his hand and touched him, saying, 'I will; be clean.' And immediately his leprosy was cleansed. [17]

There would be no hard labor.

Come to me, all who labor and are heavy laden, and I will give you rest. Take my yoke upon you, and learn from me; for I am gentle and lowly in heart, and you will find rest for your souls. For my yoke is easy, and my burden is light. [18]

There would be no death.

While he was speaking to them, a ruler came in and knelt before him, saying, 'My daughter has just died; but come and lay your hand on her, and she will live.' And Jesus rose and followed him, with his disciples...And when Jesus came to the ruler's house, and saw the flute players, and the crowd making a tumult, he said, 'Depart; for the girl is not dead but sleeping.' And they laughed at him. But when the crowd had been put outside, he went in and took her by the hand, and the girl rose. And the report of this went through all that district. [19] ...on this rock I will build my church, and the powers of death shall not prevail against it...[20]

The Teaching of Jesus then is of another world, not of the Jews or the Romans, but "elsewhere," without hunger, thirst, pain, disease, and death. To those caught in the clutches of extreme want this is a powerful message. The emotional force of this will prove to be the greatest force on earth. But this Teaching needs the final sanction of the Word of God.

When Jesus had spoken these words, he lifted up his eyes to heaven and said, "Father, the hour has come; glorify thy Son that the Son may glorify thee, since thou hast given him power over all flesh, to give eternal life to all whom thou hast given him. And this is eternal life, that they know thee the only true God, and Jesus Christ whom thou hast sent. I glorified thee on earth, having accomplished the work which thou gavest me to do; and now, Father, glorify thou me in thy own presence with the glory which I had with thee before the world was made...I am praying for them; I am not praying for the world but for those who thou hast given me, for they are thine; all mine are thine, and thine are mine, and I am glorified in them. And now I am no more in the world, but they are in the world, and I am coming to thee...I have given them thy word; and the world has hated them because they are not of the world, even as I am not of the world...Sanctify them in the truth; thy word is truth...I made known to them thy name, and I will make it known, that the love with which thou hast loved me may be in them, and I in them. [21]

Convinced in their belief in this *love*, this global feeling of alleviation and assurance, the Teaching of Jesus became a power to conquer the world.

Before this Teaching could become a force in the political affairs of the world, it was already a new force in the life of the individual. It was the individual *person* to whom the Teaching was addressed, as a new understanding of the self proved to be a personal revelation. One was now to stand accountable *directly* before the Son and the Father, there was to be no mediation by the "authorities." Personal life and the possibility of individual choice enter human affairs for the first time. The statutes and ordinances of the Jewish Law had been amplified and codified into a system of social relations whose interpretation and implementation required an entire class of practioners. Every conceivable nuance of dispute and controversy had already been judged upon by the Hebraic Code. Accordingly, there was nothing left to the "individual," the person, as the Law stood absolutely. One could only passively accept this final judgment. The Teaching of Jesus was so attractive exactly upon this point, as rather than being nothing but a passive "object" before the Code, one was instead an active "subject" to oneself in the immediate presence of God. There was to be no intermediaries, save Jesus himself, between oneself and one's God. But this new relationship was no longer defined by the fear of tradition but rather was to be based upon *love,* a personal feeling of goodness and caring and assurance. The difference was between *who* one was before the majesty of God and his Son on earth and *what* one was already determined to be by the tradition of Hebraic Law. A *personal* and loving relationship with God was the revelation of the new Teaching.

But I say to you that hear, Love your enemies, do good to those who hate you, bless those who curse you. To him who strikes you on the cheek, offer the other also; and from him who takes away your coat do not withhold your shirt. Give to every one who begs from you; and of him who takes away your goods do not ask them again. And as you wish that men would do to you, do so to them. If you love those who love you, what credit is that to you? For even sinners love those who love them. And if you do good to those who do good to you, what credit is that to you? For even sinners do the same. And if you lend to those from whom you hope to receive, what credit is that to you? Even sinners lend to sinners, to receive as much again. But love your enemies, and do good, and lend, expecting nothing in return; and your reward will be great, and you will be sons of the Most High; for he is kind to the ungrateful and the selfish. Be merciful, even as your Father is merciful. [22]

The astonishing insight was that love was one's own possession to either give or not, that it could not be *commanded* but rather must be freely given. Only from *within*, only as a matter of one's personal resolve, only through one's heart, was it possible to love one's enemies, to turn the other cheek, to take upon oneself the entirely unexpected attitude of love and care. Each person would need to be responsible for himself in his own choice of either the old hate or the new love. Love could no more be commanded than a Persian tyrant could command his troops to defeat the Greeks. This new responsibility, this new experience of inner life, was the revolutionary advance of the Teaching of Jesus. Little of this would be fully appreciated at the time, but the intimation of this responsibility announced a different kind of world entirely. "...You shall love the Lord your God with all your heart, and with all your mind; and your neighbor as yourself." [23] The force of one's whole being, of one's heart, soul, and mind, delivered an experience the likes of which had never been seen. Only on the basis of oneself, *as oneself,* was this new truth to be possible. Nothing lese would make a difference. The personal *choice* to love was one's very own, pure and simple. But this transformation of the spirit could not have taken place all at once. While the Teaching of Jesus introduced the *possibility,* the idea, of enhancing the dimensions of inner life, of personality, it would be another seventeen centuries before this possibility would come to much. The Teaching of Jesus was soon to become the Church of Paul, or Christianity, and the process towards personality would be undermined. A new group of intermediaries were interjected between the person and God. The new clergy would be quick to convince the

65

first adherents of Jesus that all this talk of personal love would need to be converted into something else. The structure of the Church would need to be upon rock. People need not worry themselves with matters of choice and responsibility, as that would best be left to others. But, regardless of the fact that the process would not go too far, the breakthrough had been made and the world was a different place.

The emergence of idealization and its embodiment in conceptual language allowed for a deepening cultural advancement. This is the process of *building,* of construction, through the agency of ideality, as that is brought to bear upon the physical fact of nature. Ideality produces a result in two intimately related ways. Ideality proper is the strictly mental aspect of thinking in conceptual terms. Mathematics is the best example. But it is the second aspect of ideality which actually *builds.* Thinking is put to work in the conception and architectural organization of stone in the formation of a building. Thought and physical work labor together in the planning, construction, utilization, and maintenance of permanent structure. The continual renewal and expansion of this process of building finds its genesis in the force of ideality and is to be termed *constitution.* Everything that includes thinking and its results in the world is a matter of *constitution.* Only when the great cultural and physical formations of the world today are understood in the greater historical context of these beginnings in ideality is it possible to fully appreciate the power and force of constitution. It is necessary to understand human reality as a comprehensive historical process that has been forged through the labor of thinking, something then that has been collectively achieved throughout the world.

With the fact of constitution and building comes the possibility of the *expansion* of the economic base. Something once built provides value for many years and then serves as a basis for the creation of additional value. A compounding effect becomes evident.

66

Once an aqueduct has been built, for example, bringing valued water to a place, it is possible to create economic expansion as the compounding effect, such as greater agricultural returns. One structure allows for the possibility of heightened return elsewhere. The peoples of the great civilizations of the ancient world were great precisely because they were *builders*. The many local cultural tribes throughout the world have remained local because they were not builders. Of course, this process of constitution and building was never allowed to advance unobstructed. War and destruction, greed and covetousness, has always intervened to consume both the compounded return as well as the original principle. Much comes to nothing. In the context of scarcity and privation, anything whatsoever would be subject to the threat of immediate consumption. This would involve hierarchies of force and principles of extortion. Having considered the "religious experience," it is now necessary to turn to Constitution and Power.

Part Two

Constitution and Power:

The Specific Conditions of
Human Reality

Chapter Four
Denial and Substitution and Power

The Teaching of Jesus offered to the common man, who was beaten by the combined forces of Hebraic Law and Roman power, a new sense of himself, a feeling of self-respect, that came as a profound sense of personal awakening. His choice to "turn the other cheek" was his own personal decision that gave to him a great pride. But, regardless of this new feeling, the harsh conditions of scarcity and privation continues as before. Hunger, disease, pain, and death were just as dreadful. But the *idea* of something else had come forth and it would be through *faith* that this idea would be nurtured and sustained. In the face of an overwhelming privation, it was necessary to *believe* that things could be otherwise. It was a vision of reality that stood on the far side of life, a vision though that stood at the center of the New Teaching. Faith is the willingness to believe in something that is without evidence in experience. "Now faith is the assurance of things hoped for, the conviction of things not seen." [1] This passage continues with an elaboration of Old Testament faith but there occurs an important difference with the New. Old Testament faith is a matter of tribal commandment while with the New it is a matter of personal decision. While proclaiming the possibility of love rather than retribution, compassion rather than vengeance, it is necessary that one just *believe* that this is the case when all proof and evidence is lacking. *Nothing had changed except one's attitude.* This faith allows one to live *as if* one's belief is true as well. Faith allows one to endure

71

and await a promised future.

If we are afflicted, it is for your comfort and salvation; and if we are comforted, it is for your comfort, which you experience when you patiently endure the same sufferings that we suffer. [2]

This patient endurance of the woes of the world will be the cornerstone of the Christian experience, with the immense reward being personal salvation.

And he said to all, "If any man would come after me, let him deny himself and take up his cross daily and follow me. For whoever would save his life will lose it; and whoever loses his life for my sake, he will save it...But I tell you truly, there are some standing here who will not taste death before they see the kingdom of God." [3]

Everlasting life and immortality, the Kingdom of God, is the reward for a faith in the Lord and for having endured the indignities of worldly experience. This Kingdom is at hand. "...the time is near..."[4] "I am coming soon." [5] The faith that this is so is the added assurance that it is, as the power of emotion simply reinforces and sustains itself. It is here that Christianity breaks into two entirely distinct experiences, two ways in which alleviation is to be found.

The first experience is that of faith or, as has been termed, the *Theology of Faith.* This is the experience of "patient endurance," of whiling away one's time until a life after death relieves one once and for all from the anxiety of scarcity and privation. "Life is a long awaiting of God's peace." [6] One simply needs to wait it out and keep oneself busy with the common work of daily existence. "Do things without grumbling or questioning, that you may be blameless and innocent, children of God..." [7] This *idea* of relief from the world is enough for the great mass to live in resigned peace and quiet expectation. Simple faith is sufficient. But for some few this is not enough.

An entirely different sort of experience involves those who would lead and shepherd the great mass. There are the many and then there are the few. This involves those who would hope to rule.

Then said Jesus to the crowds and to his disciples, "The scribes and the Pharisees sit on Moses' seat; so practice and observe whatever they tell you, but not what they do; for they preach, but do not practice. They bind heavy burdens, hard to bear, and lay them on men's shoulders; but they themselves will not move them with their finger. They do all their deeds to be seen by men; for they make their phylacteries broad and their fringes long, and they love the place of honor at feasts and the best seats in the synagogues, and salutations in the market places, and being called rabbi by men. But you are not to be called rabbi, for you have one teacher, and you are all brethren. And call no man your father on earth, for you have one Father, who is in heaven. Neither be called masters, for you have one master, the Christ. He who is greatest among you shall be your servant; whoever exalts himself will be humbled, and whoever humbles himself will be exalted." [8]

Even though Jesus preached against the strict rule of Law of the Jewish Authorities, especially their attitude of condescension, when the Teaching of Jesus became the Christianity of Paul, a similar rule was put into place, as again an authority would be necessary. A special divine dispensation was forthcoming. "...I think that I have the Spirit of God." [9] This personal belief in this warrant from God and Christ assured Paul of his place at the head of the new Church, as a new Authority was ready, willing, and able to take power. Paul broadened his claim.

"Am I not free? Am I not an apostle? Have I not seen Jesus our Lord? Are not you my workmanship in the Lord? If to others I am not an apostle, at least I am to you; for you are the seal of my apostleship in the Lord." [10]

With his belief and faith in this divine sanction, Paul appointed himself as the shepherd of the new flock and all power and authority was to be vested in him. The mandate of God was to be carried forth through the agency of Paul.

We know that in everything God works for good with those who love him, who are called according to his purpose. For those whom he foreknew he also predestined to be conformed to the image of the Son, in order that he might be the first-born among many brethren. And those whom he predestined he also called; and those whom he called he also justified; and those whom he justified he also glorified. [11] We who are strong ought to bear with the failings of the weak...[12]

The invigorating experience of self-awareness and personal responsibility that had been announced by the Teaching of Jesus, the possibility of love and compassion, was now to be taken over by the new clergy of the Church, at the front of which stood Paul. Even though Paul never stood as pope in Rome, he was the central conceptualizing force that established the institutional basis for the subsequent development of the Papacy. The experience of personal power and self-awareness that had been such a revelation for the followers of Jesus would *not* be allowed in the Church. Power and control would be maintained and dispensed by the Few from above. The "democracy" of the first days would be supplanted by the "aristocracy" of the newly constituted Church. In contrast to the *Theology of Faith,* that was denial and substitution for the many, there is now established the *Theology of Power*, that is denial and substitution for the Few. A precise psychological description of the personal exercise of power is now possible.

The reality of power involves two dimensions. There is the manner of its acquisition and the quality of the experience itself. In the *Acts* is described the manner of its acquisition. An imposition of guilt is necessary.

Now the company of those who believed were of one heart and soul, and no one said that any of the things which he possessed was his own, but they had everything in common. And with great power the apostles gave their testimony to the resurrection of the Lord Jesus, and great grace was upon them all. There was not a needy person among them, for as many as were possessors of lands and houses sold them, and brought the proceeds of what was sold and laid it at the apostles' feet; and distribution was made to each as any had need. Thus Joseph who was surnamed Barnabas (which means, son of encouragement), a Levite, a native of Cyprus, sold a field which belonged to him, and brought the money and laid it at the apostles' feet. [13]

Sharing a consensus of the spirit, it was only natural and proper that all private possessions be turned over to the common welfare, as within the context of the greatest good private needs would be sacrificed. But some individual reluctance remained, as not *all* was relinquished to the common pot. But the ever increasing demands of the Church would allow no truck with such personal *greed.* The great mission on earth would have no tolerance here. The passage continues.

But a man named Ananias with his wife Sapphira sold a piece of property, and with his wife's knowledge he kept back some of the proceeds, and brought only a part and laid it at the apostle's feet. But Peter said, "Ananias, why has Satan filled your heart to lie to the Holy Spirit and to keep back part of the proceeds of the land? While it remained unsold, did it not remain your own? And after it was sold, was it not at your disposal? How is it that you have contrived this deed in your heart? You have not lied to men but to God." When Ananias heard these words, he fell down and died. And great fear came upon all who heard of it. The young men rose and wrapped him up and carried him out and buried him. After an interval of about three hours his wife came in, not knowing what had happened. And Peter said to her, "Tell me whether you sold the land for so much." And she said, "Yes, for so much." But Peter said to her, "How is it that you have agreed together to tempt the spirit of the Lord? Hark, the feet of those that have buried your husband are at the door, and they will carry you out." Immediately she fell down at his feet and died. When the young men came in they found her dead, and they carried her out and buried her beside her husband. And great fear came upon the whole church, and upon all who heard of these things.[14]

The Apostle Peter had made an effective example of this simple couple, as they both lay dead. The many followers quickly came to feel the guilt of their reluctance, of their natural desire to keep but a bit of their material goods for themselves, as the Apostle rained down upon their heads accusation, incrimination, and death. There would be no love here. Any reluctance to come forth clean was deemed the work of Satan. The highest crime is charged of the simple person in need. Death to him who refuses, he who chooses to protect himself and his family. Peter wanted it all, as the idea and faith in a life after death was to be enough for all the rest. *Everything was to be turned over to the Church.* The many were commanded to deed over to the Few all the fruits of their hard labor. An additional lifetime tax, over and above that of the Caesar, would be extracted. The Financing of the Church was secured.

At present, however, I am going to Jerusalem with aid for the saints. For Macedonia and Achaia have been pleased to make some contribution for the poor among saints at Jerusalem; they were pleased to do it, and indeed they are in debt to them, for if the Gentiles have come to share in their spiritual blessings, they ought also to be service to them in material blessings. When therefore I have completed this, and have delivered to them what has been raised, I shall go on by way of you to Spain, and I know that when I come to you I shall come in the fulness of the blessing of Christ. [15]

As the first spokesman of Christ, the Apostle must be funded for his work.

If we have sown spiritual good among you, is it too much if we reap your material benefits? If others share their rightful claim upon you, do not we still more? [16]

In leading the way to salvation, Paul entitles himself to "reap your material benefits." An irony intrudes. He who claims so forcefully that there is nothing good in the material aspects of the world, nothing that can be meaningful for everlasting life, *demands* that those who would produce such goods hand them over to the leaders of the Church. The condemnation of material goods is made by those who are set to take possession of those very same goods.

Whatever your task, work heartily, as serving the Lord and not men, knowing that from the Lord you will receive the inheritance as your reward; you are serving the Lord Christ. [17]

To "work heartily," with patient good cheer, is the mandated task of the many. They are to work the fields so that the Few may be supported in the Lord's Work. The fruit of the sweat of one's brow goes to the possession of others. Keeping the many poorer than they otherwise would have been creates a dependency which provides an opportunity for the further exercise of power by those Few, an opportunity which quickly and continually will come to be abused. The psychological experience of this exercise of power is central for the subsequent development of both Church and Empire.

It is important to consider in detail the content of Paul's "vision." How was it that Paul was the initial conceptualizing force which came to constitute the Church? Paul is an example of the psychological experience that has been described as denial and substitution but, in a fundamental way, he is *the* example. His exemplification of denial and substitution has had the greatest impact upon the world that followed. Furthermore, his understanding encompassed *both* the Theology of Faith and the Theology of Power. While the common man knew only about faith and the Few knew about power, Paul conceived of both as but differing aspects of the same problem and solution. Scarcity and privation was the problem. The solution was infinitely more complex.

So if there is any encouragement in Christ, any incentive of love, any participation in the Spirit, any affection and sympathy, complete my joy by being the same of mind, having the same love, being in full accord and of one mind. Do nothing from selfishness or conceit, but in humility count others better than yourselves. Let each of you look not only to his own interests, but also to the interests of others. Have this mind among yourselves, which is yours in Christ Jesus, who, though he was in the form of God, did not count equality with God a thing to be grasped, but emptied himself, taking the form of a servant, being born in the likeness of man. And being formed in human form he humbled himself and became obedient unto death on the cross. Therefore God has highly exalted him and bestowed on him the name which is above every name, that at the name of Jesus every knee should bow, in heaven and on earth and under the earth, and every tongue confess that Jesus Christ is Lord, to the glory of God the Father. [18]

This account was simply inconceivable except on the basis of faith. One must simply believe. It was a speech of just words, language without meaning. The explanation was incomprehensible. So with faith Paul must proceed. One could only presume to understand the conception of Jesus and his relationship to God and how that would involve one's own personal salvation from the anxiety of the physical world. How *Three* (Father, Son, and Holy Ghost) in *One* made *Three* or *One* was impossible to discern. Faith was the only possibility.

The question of the precise relationship between God and Christ was still current in A.D. 451 at the Council of Chalcedon when confusion was once and for all resolved.

Following, then, the holy Fathers, we all with one voice teach that it should be confessed that our Lord Jesus Christ is one and the same Son, the Same perfect in Godhead, the Same perfect in manhood, truly God and truly man, the Same [consisting] of a rational soul and a body; *homoousious* with the Father as to his Godhead, and the Same *homoousious* with us as to his manhood; in all things like unto us, sin only excepted; begotten of the Father before all ages as to his Godhead, and in the last days, the Same, for us and for our salvation, of Mary the Virgin *theotokos* as to his manhood; One and the same Christ, Son, Lord, Only begotten, made known in two natures [which exist] without confusion, without change, without division, without separation; the difference of the natures having been in no wise taken away by reason of the union, but rather the properties of each being preserved, and [both] concurring in one Person and one *hypostasis*-- not parted or divided into two persons, but one and the same Son and Only begotten, the divine Logos, the Lord Jesus Christ; even as the prophets from the old [have spoken] concerning him, and as the Lord Jesus Christ himself has taught us, and as the Symbol of the Fathers has delivered to us. [19]

Only faith could deliver one to the promised land of understanding, as rational thinking could hardly "crack such a nut" as this. The common man found himself to be in theological arrears and he was left simply believing what he was told. The special vision of Paul was that he thought *himself* to be the specially appointed *medium* for the delivering of salvation to the worthy of the world. It was he, Paul, who would tell all the rest what to believe. He thought of himself as chosen to do the work of God on earth. Even though he would not live to see the church, its structure and agenda could be easily imagined. A hierarchy of power would marshal the forces of the world in the name of the Lord and to the strict exclusion of all else. Political reality would be constituted in order to consolidate these forces so as to insure a *single,* universal, and catholic Church. But with such a concentration of power there would be hell to pay and much grief lay ahead. Persons of a quite human dimension would participate to their own advantage. "Ambition is a weed of quick and early vegetation in the vineyard of Christ." [20]

A hierarchy of power was essential because so many would need to be *excluded* from the Grace of God. The inclusive love that had been preached by Jesus would need to be replaced by an exclusive retribution. Extraordinary powers were required for this selection process. Only a few would be allowed to achieve the reward of personal salvation as obviously so many would be undeserving, worthy only of eternal damnation. The first difficulty though was establishing the criterion for salvation. It would be a full 200 years before the final text of the New Testament would be settled upon. Competing "authorities" fought in open battle for the right to determine who was to be saved. The rest were all *heretics*, natural troublemakers, who would need to be dealt with quickly and decisively if the power of the new church was to be maintained. Only through a severe discipline could Paul's work achieve global importance.

With the Theology of Faith there is denial and substitution for the many, as they were led to peacefully toil in the fields, working with the expectation of a divine reward. With the Theology of Power there is denial and substitution for the Few, those who would profit personally from the labor of others. Their experience of the exercise of power would have a "divine" quality about it that was nothing short of 'intoxicating" *here and now.* Preaching of another world, they would gather to themselves the fruits of *this* world. The matter concerns the special experience of ideality and divinity.

God's thinking is absolute in that there is no distinction between thought and deed. To think is to have already done. Human thinking is relative in that there *is* a distinction between thought and deed. It is a question of ends and means, as on the one hand they are the same and on the other they are different. Human thinking always involves a sequence that is qualified by space and time whereas divine thinking is simultaneous onto itself. Thought and power are the same. The divine thought of the universe is already that universe's creation. A beginning and an end are simultaneously contained in the same thought. Regardless of this essential difference between the divine and the human there is an essential *sameness* that will "intoxicate" humans for millennia to come. There occurs an *approximation* to the divine experience that will ensnare the Few as they think as if they were thinking the thoughts of God.

Power is a matter of command and control over either things or people. The Few achieved a power over things when the many were convinced to hand over the productivity of their labor. But, in so doing, the many handed over to the Few a power over themselves. This dominion created a special psychological experience. If divine thinking is the simultaneous fact of thought and deed, then the exercise of power of one person over another is the closest thing on earth to divinity. While the experiences are not exactly the same, one could proceed *as if* they were. The king says, "Let there be a great temple to myself!" With this command there is no temple, no simultaneous creation, but a chain of events is set into motion and the result will be a temple to the king. Thousands are set to quarrying the stones, moving them to the site, and then setting them one atop another so that the king may have his house of death. As greater numbers are commanded to this task, with nothing expended in their welfare, everyone is sacrificed to the temple. As the construction years pass by, nearing completion, the king will have his wish. He has done nothing but *command* and yet here stands a temple. Just as God could have commanded, so too now the king has commanded with the only difference being simultaneity. God's command is accomplished fact, the king's command must be executed over time and distance. *Nonetheless* the king's experience enthralls him as if divine.

The king though has other ways to fancy his presumed divinity. "Off with your head!" Immediately, nearly simultaneously, someone's head loses its footing in the shoulders. "Off comes this beautiful head whenever I give the word." [21] Caligula so addresses one of his lovers. The long and tortured history of the singular exercise of power by king and lord is but the desire to feel the simultaneity of divinity, the identification of thought and deed, *at the expense of someone else.* There is no greater feeling on earth, albeit negative.

David also defeated Hadadezer the son of Rehob, king of Zobah, as he went to restore his power at the river Euphrates. And David took from him a thousand and seven hundred horsemen, and twenty thousand foot soldiers; and David hamstrung all the chariot horses. And when the Syrians of Damascus came to help Hadadezer king of Zobah, David slew twenty-two thousand men of the Syrians. Then David put garrisons in Aram of Damascus; and the Syrians became servants to David and brought tribute. And the Lord gave victory to David wherever he went. [22]

Being the king of the Chosen People, being convinced of divine sanction, David is free to impose his special form of terror on whomever he pleases. The feeling of this command is simply divine. "Go, do all that is in your heart; for the Lord is with you." [23] With this injunction to violence, transformed in an infinite variety over centuries, millions will be consigned to grief. To command others to do whatever it is that one wants is to have the experience which approximates that of God, *even if for but a moment.* This is an *otherworldly* experience that constitutes denial and substitution for the Few. This feeling of divinity alleviates if but momentarily the anxiety regarding material existence. To act *as if* one were God is no longer to feel oneself to be subject to the conditions of being human. An overriding arrogance drives this feeling deeper.

And David returned to bless his household. But Michal the daughter of Saul came out to meet David, and said, "How the king of Israel honored himself today, uncovering himself today before the eyes of his servant's maids, as one of the vulgar fellows shamelessly uncovers himself!" And David said to Michal, "It was before the Lord, who chose me above your father, and above all his house, to appoint me as prince over Israel, the people of the Lord--and I will make merry before the Lord. I will make myself yet more contemptible than this, and I will be abased in your eyes; but by the maids of whom you have spoken, by them I shall be held in honor." And Michal the daughter of Saul had no child to the day of her death.[24]

As the one chosen of God, David assumes to himself every prerogative and privilege, respecting only himself. He does whatever he pleases as if that were the command of God. In so doing he is no longer of this world, but has become like a god, divine, sharing in the power of the Lord. He feels himself to be rightfully the king of the world. Others *will* obey his command. But one need not be a king to clutch after this experience. In all human relationships there is the opportunity for one or another to impose his will, to achieve that "*moment of divinity.*"

All the lieutenants and henchmen throughout history have yearned for this possibility of violence to others in the name of the king, pope, fuhrer, or generalissimo. There will be a *post mortem* denial of responsibility but the lieutenant will exercise his deed of

83

violence *on his own*. There may be a sanction from above but the individual below will share in a full responsibility. Group sanctioned violence comes so easily precisely because the individual is provided *cover* for his crime. But in the end he desires that same feeling of divinity as his tyrant and is equally responsible.

The psychological experience of power then is twofold. The Few bring to themselves the productivity of others, having convinced them that laboring without a fuss is in the proper order and arrangement of God's plan. With this material resource under their dominion, the Few then find a more refined experience in the ruthless imposition of power on those very same people who have given up the profits of their labor. Excess accumulation by the Few heightened the scarcity for the many. A social and political structure of dominion and power has been put into place that will serve well the demands of both Church and Empire. This "totalitarian" view is thought to be nothing but the requisite of God and rightfully mandated for his flock here on earth. Society will be ordered top to bottom in a hierarchical structure of power and production. Everyday life will be regimented according to the instructions of the Few who have called upon themselves to interpret the word of God. But none of this had reached to the world yet, it being only a glimmer in the emerging structure of the Church. A great distance remained in order to bring this view into reality.

From the time of Paul to that of Augustine, in the 5th century, the Teaching of Jesus would be transformed from a heretic sect of Judaism to the state religion of the Empire. Christianity would be transformed from a private belief to an established political reality. As the early Christians became more numerous, having recruited from the mass of downtrodden and hopeless, they came to represent an alternative to the tired and worn polytheism of Rome. This was nothing more than a pretense, a convention of ritual, that left the emotions untouched. Educated and prosperous Roman citizens began

84

to convert until the Emperor Constantine did so on his deathbed in A.D. 337. Thereafter the consolidation of Church and Empire would rest upon theological doctrine. Uniformity of belief would insure a uniformity of power, and hierarchy was the first priority. A central issue here was the remission of sin. Certain so-called heretics had claimed that any true believer had an immediate and direct relationship with Jesus and God and therefore was in full possession of the various rights of the Church. According to this interpretation each individual was self-sufficient in his religious life. The Teaching of Jesus had preached just such a view. With this there would be no need for the intermediaries, clergy, as the Church would be thoroughly democratic, without centralized authority. Of course the Church could not tolerate such an assault upon its position and this type of interpretation would be labeled heresy and subject to physical extermination. The Church view was that there would be no such democracy and that all authority must flow through a bishop who stood in lineage with St. Peter and St. Paul. In other words, a priesthood was essential, the laity to be distinguished from the clergy, and the common man would be disqualified from finding God on his own. Only the Church could remit sins and not anyone who took it into his head to declare himself a spokesman of God. The Few further consolidated their power, as the many could only hope to be shepherded to salvation. This issue of the necessity of the intercession of the clergy would erupt over and over again until it finally split the Church entirely with the Lutheran revolt. The point here is simply that as the Church established itself as a state religion, it needed to consolidate its power through theological doctrine. This meant the elimination of all possible dissent and the hunt for the heretic became a centuries long anguish to the people of Europe. Scripture was clear.

See to it that no one makes a prey of you by philosophy and empty conceit, according to human tradition, according to elemental spirits of the universe, and not according to Christ. [25]

Under this specific injunction, prosecution of contrary opinion became more and more vicious as the Church more comfortably fit into the mantle of Empire.

But the Christians formed a numerous and disciplined society; and the jurisdiction of their laws and magistrates was strictly exercised over the minds of the faithful. The loose wanderings of the imagination were gradually confined by creeds and confession; the freedom of private judgment submitted to the public wisdom of synods... [26]

With Augustine (354-430) there is a Christian authority equal to the task of imposing Catholic uniformity and power. Under his guidance, there is established a new level of terror over and above the original terror of scarcity and privation. The notion of "love," as preached by the Teaching of Jesus, was to be exterminated and replaced by Church accusation and incrimination. Confessions of sin and heresy were to be extracted by torture. The rack and the whip were now tools for social control and could be used freely by the Few. Augustine had only contempt for anything but his totalitarian vision of absolute Catholic domination. All of the world was purely evil and needed to be purged and purified through his authority and that of the Church. He was the Church Father most responsible for the wholly negative attitude of the Church towards sexuality which exists to this day. Sexuality of course represented an experience of *personal* life and *that* could not be tolerated if Catholic uniformity was to be maintained. But his experience was rather mixed, as his "closet" was not bare.

Clouds arose from the slimy desires of the flesh and from youth's seething spring. They clouded over and darkened my soul, so that I could not distinguish the calm light of chaste love from the fog of lust. Both kinds of affection burned confusedly within me and swept my feeble youth over the crags of desire and plunged me into a whirlpool of shameful deeds. [27]

While confident to accuse and condemn others for "sins" of the flesh he himself is a first practioner. This First Inquisitor then consummates another theme that will cling to Church tradition and that is hypocrisy. In the name of Jesus his Lord any sort of double dealing will be possible in support of Catholic power.

Augustine had lived out of wedlock with a woman who had given birth to his son, Adeodatus. She was not a Christian being a "pagan" from Augustine's homeland of North Africa. Monica, Augustine's mother, was intent upon his marrying within the Church, so that his salvation would be more easily secured. Arrangements were made, the son's mother sent packing, and a new and more acceptable Christian bride was brought forth by Monica. Unfortunately, though, for Augustine, his marriage would have to wait two years as the future bride had yet to reach the age of consent. The *eight year old* would need to wait until she was 10, the then rightful age of consent, before becoming the Church sanctioned wife of this future Church Father. In the meantime further arrangements were made and a concubine engaged for the servicing of his immediate desires. This occurs before his famous Conversion when all is changed, presumably. Augustine becomes a changed man and any taint of his past will not be a hindrance to his establishment of Church policy that would root out all behavior, albeit sexual or otherwise, that would compromise total control. His own past was no deterrence to the condemnation of the very same deeds. Christian "love" would not obstruct the imposition of force. Wedded to Catholic power then is arrogance, intolerance, and hypocrisy. Augustine himself did not see the realization of this religious power but when in due course it was achieved his principles would be executed to perfection and many "sinners" would be more quickly shown the way to hell. Ironically, Augustine witnessed the fall of Rome with the Germanic invasion from the North, not the last time that Rome would collide with the forces beyond the Rhine, but he conveniently interpreted this as being but the prelude to the return of Christ. Of course it was not and he died quietly confident in his terror that was about to be.

The collapse of Rome signaled a significant shift in worldly power. This so-called "fall" was a matter of both change and continuity. The "barbarians" were not necessarily bent upon destruction. They had heard of Rome as a place of plenty, a sort of mystical place of abundance. Their own privations naturally drove them to seek relief. After achieving military victory they were quick to establish a working relationship with the many elements of the Old Empire. Christianity was in a privileged position to prosper from this new situation. The obvious superiority of Roman culture, witnessed by its physical edifice, led the many tribes to convert willingly to Christian belief, hoping to come under the protection of a more powerful deity.

A period of "Dark Ages" was entered upon where economic activity reached low levels and rural life was the rule. Work upon the land though witnessed improved production. Benedictine monasticism preached a simple life, and busying oneself with the toil of the land was the proper way to personal salvation. Great tracts of land in Europe came under cultivation for the first time. Swamps were drained, forests cleared, and there was a general improvement in agricultural production. In the eleventh century a Benedictine order called the Cistercians improved matters more. Shunning urban life they sought isolation in the rural countryside. They brought into production marginal lands and working for no wage they were able to re-invest their surpluses into further improvements. This would lay the foundation for subsequent economic expansion. Schools were also maintained by Christians during this period, nurturing the sacred texts. While little of originality was done, the tradition of letters was preserved. It would be upon this base in agriculture and learning that any further European advancement would be made.

The social and economic structure of this period was feudalism. At the local level, the lord provided daily protection from bandits, robbers, and the like to an agricultural community in exchange for part of the proceeds of its labor. Military protection was traded for work and food. Advantage easily went to the lord. The list of laborer obligations was long.

(1) He paid annually three taxes in money: (a) a small head tax...; (b) a small rent; (c) an arbitrary charge levied by the owner yearly or oftener. (2) He annually gave the lord a share--usually a *dime* or tenth--of his crops and livestock. (3) He owed his lord many days of unpaid labor... (4) The serf was obligated to grind his corn, bake his bread, brew his beer, press his grapes, at the lord's mill, oven, vat, or press, and pay a small fee for each such use. (5) He paid a fee for the right to fish, hunt, or pasture his animals, on the lord's domain. (6) His actions at law had to be brought before the baronial court, and cost him a fee varying with the gravity of the case. (7) He had to serve at call in the baron's regiment in war. (8) If the baron was captured, the serf was expected to contribute to the ransom. (9) He contributed also to the substantial gift due to the lord's son on being made a knight. (10) He paid the baron a tax on all products that he took for sale to market or fair. (11) He could not sell his beer or wine until the lord had two weeks' prior time to sell the lord's beer or wine. (12) In many cases he was obliged to buy a prescribed quantity of wine yearly from the lord... (13) He paid a fine if he sent a son to higher education or gave him to the Church, for thereby the manor lost a hand. (14) He paid a tax, and required the lord's consent, in case he or his children married a person not belonging to the manor... (15) In scattered instances we hear of the *ius primae noctis*...whereby the lord might claim the "right of the first night" with the serf's bride; but in almost all cases the serf was allowed to "redeem" his bride by paying

a fee to the lord... (16) If the peasant died without issue residing with him, the house and land reverted to the lord by escheat... (17) On some--especially on ecclesiastical--manors he paid an annual and an inheritance tax to the *vogt* who provided military defense of the estate. To the Church the peasant paid an annual tithe or tenth of his produce. [28]

While his taxes were certainly high, the peasant could hopefully live in peace, under the lord's protection. Life was structured by repetition and work, with little opportunity for change. Given the requirement of agriculture, feudalism was a comfortable arrangement that demanded the recurrence of the same. Nothing could change.

Overarching the rural life of the lord and his domain was the presence of the Church which itself became the greatest cause of violence and strife. The Church's attitude had become arrogant and condescending as it penetrated into more and more areas of life. In 1300 the pope was inspired, *ex cathedra,* to declare of the spiritual and the temporal that...

...both are in the power of the church, the spiritual sword and the material. But the latter is to be used for the church, the former by her; the former by the priest, the latter by kings and captains but at the will and by the permission of the priest. The one sword, therefore, should be under the other, the temporal authority subject to the spiritual...If, therefore, the earthly power err, it shall be judged by the spiritual power...But if the spiritual power err, it can only be judged by God, not by man...For this authority, though given to a man and exercised by a man, is not human, but rather divine...Furthermore, we declare, state, define and pronounce that it is altogether necessary to salvation for every human creature to be subject to the Roman pontiff. [29]

The pope and the Church were above the law, they were the law, beyond reproach. Nothing was to be left outside of this dominion. This is denial and substitution and the Theology of Power taken to its refined perfection. Assured of their priority, the Church and its clergy took for itself the *lion's share* and accumulated to themselves all the riches of the land, living in a pomp that left the peasant smoldering in rage. One figure has it that while the clergy made up only one percent of the population, they consumed a full twenty five percent of the wealth. The clergy extracted a horrendous charge for its services. But this was not without a cost to the Church itself. A gulf was created between it and the people that at times flared into open hostility. A system of *purchased* salvation, mechanical Christianity, was fostered where anything at all involved a charge payable to the Church. Death taxes were required, alms were paid to remit sins, and crusaders who did not return had their property confiscated. Papal and Church credibility was sacrificed as more and more people refused to believe in its mission. Alternatives were tried but the Church would tolerate no such breaches of its position. All deviations would be dealt with severely.

Two developments sought to reverse the corrosion of Christian belief and the authority of the papacy, the Crusades and the Inquisition. Both were born and breed in the violence of fanatical belief. In 1070 the Turks took final control of Jerusalem. Christians were denied access to the holy places and were subject to Muslim violence. Reports reached back to Europe of the "atrocities" and there went out the call to arms, the call to holy war. The Holy Land must be re-conquered for the true faith. Popular support was garnered and the Church orchestrated the move to the east.

O race of Franks! race beloved and chosen by God!...From the confines of Jerusalem and from Constantinople a grievous report has gone forth that an accursed race, wholly alienated from God, has violently invaded the lands of these Christians, and has depopulated them by pillage and fire. They have led away a part of the captives into their own country, and a part they have killed by cruel tortures. They destroy the altars, after having defiled them with their uncleanliness. The kingdom of the Greeks is now dismembered by them, and has been deprived of territory so vast in extent that it could not be traversed in two month's time...Let none of your possessions keep you back, nor anxiety for your family affairs...Let hatred, therefore, depart from you; let your quarrels end. Enter upon the road to the Holy Sepulcher; wrest that land from a wicked race, and subject it to yourselves. Jerusalem is a land fruitful above all others, a paradise of delights. That royal city, situated at the center of the earth, implores you to come to her aid. Undertake this journey eagerly for the remissions of your sins, and be assured of the reward of imperishable glory in the Kingdom of Heaven. [30]

Domestic difficulties were to be set aside and the spirit of international conquest affirmed. Masses of men, women, and children were marshaled and moved east to the devastation of everyone and everything that was encountered. Christian slaughtered Christian in order to have the right to slaughter the infidel.

Of the first crusaders, three hundred thousand had already perished, before a single city was rescued from the infidels, before their graver and more noble brethren had completed the preparation of their enterprise. [31]

The lucky few that made it to Jerusalem achieved the fruition of their dreams, Holy Slaughter.

...wonderful things were to be seen. Numbers of the Saracens were beheaded...others were shot with arrows, or forced to jump from the towers; others were tortured for several days and then burned in flames. In the streets were seen piles of heads and hands and feet. One rode about everywhere amid the corpses of men and horses. [32]

This eyewitness account was given by the priest Raymond of Agiles. And then further.

...women were stabbed to death, suckling babes were snatched by the leg from their mothers' breasts and flung over the wall, or had their necks broken by being dashed against posts; and 70,000 Moslems remaining in the city were slaughtered. The surviving Jews were herded into a synagogue and burned alive. The victors flocked to the church of the Holy Sepulcher...they wept with joy and release, and thanked the God of Mercies for their victory. [33]

This victory confirmed the righteous crusader of his belief in his personal salvation. But, finally, it was all a failure, as crusade followed crusade until there was the particularly gruesome failure called the Children's Crusade. It was a massive butchery with the few survivors being sold as slaves to Christian masters.

The principle of the crusaders was a savage fanaticism; and the most important effects were analogous to the cause. Each pilgrim was ambitious to return with his sacred spoils, the relics of Greece and Palestine; and each relic was preceded and followed by a train of miracles and visions. The belief of the Catholics was corrupted by new legends, their practice by new superstitions; and the establishment of the inquisition, the mendicant orders of monks and friars, the last abuse of indulgences, and the final progress of idolatry, flowed from the baleful foundation of the holy war. The active spirit of the Latins preyed on the vitals of reason and religion; and, if the ninth and tenth centuries were the times of darkness, the thirteenth and fourteenth were the age of absurdity and fable. [34]

From 1095 to 1291 Europe and Asia became acquainted with each other through the arts of mutual slaughter. Both Catholic and Saracen reached to new heights of barbarity as they each fought to the death to defend their respective God. Each could tolerate nothing in the other's faith to their One True God. But, as attacks upon the east proved to be without success, the popes turned the perfected idea of "crusade" inward. Dissent *within* Europe was now to be met with the call to arms, the call to Crusade. Any dispute with Vatican power was liable to attack by crusaders. The social, political, and economic disruption that naturally followed in the wake of the crusades in the east brought to life many sects of belief that sought to find a different way. This heresy and dissension threatened to weaken an already exhausted Church. Trouble was breaking out all over and the discredited Church needed to institute drastic measures. The failure to convince men's minds gave way to the success in breaking their bodies. In the lasting spirit of Augustine, the Inquisition was reincarnated.

"If a man does not abide in me, he is cast forth as a branch and withers; and the branches are gathered, thrown into the fire and burned." [35] In the absolute struggle with evil and the Great Satan there was sufficient Biblical justification for extreme measures. A papal decree in 1280 clarified policy.

We hereby excommunicate and anathematize all heretics--Cathari, Patarines, Poor Men of Lyon...and all others, by whatever name they may be called. When condemned by the Church they shall be given over to the secular judge to be punished...If any, after being seized, repent and wish to do penance, they shall be imprisoned for life...All who receive, defend, or aid heretics shall be excommunicated. If anyone remains under excommunication a year and a day, he shall be proscribed...If those who are suspected of heresy cannot prove their innocence, they shall be excommunicated. If they remain under the ban a year, they shall be condemned as heretics. They shall have no right of appeal...Whoever grants them Christian burial shall be excommunicated until he makes proper satisfaction. He shall not be absolved until he has with his own hands dug up the bodies and cast them forth--We prohibit all laymen to discuss matters of Catholic faith; if anyone does so he shall be excommunicated. Whoever knows of heretics, or of those who hold secret meetings, or of those who do not conform in all respects to the orthodox faith, shall make it known to his confessor, or to someone else who will bring it to the knowledge of the bishop or the inquisitor. If he does not do so he shall be excommunicated. Heretics and all who receive, support, or aid them, all their children to the second generation, shall not be admitted to an ecclesiastical office...We now deprive all such of their benefices forever. [36]

All dissent was lumped together and given over to the harshest punishment. Suspicion was sufficient to conviction. To be charged was already to be doomed. Oddly, to even speak of the Lord, one's savior, was a punishable offense. Nothing was to be said. A special case was the heresy of the Albigensians, the Cathari.

(The Cathari) denied that the Church was the Church of Christ; St. Peter had never come from Rome, had never founded the papacy; the popes were successors to the emperors, not to the apostles. Christ had no place to lay His head, but the pope lived in a palace; Christ was propertyless and penniless, but Christian prelates were rich...the Roman Church... was the Whore of Babylon... [37]

This was a devoutly Christian belief but without deference to Rome. What it sought was a simpler belief but, most importantly, a higher moral standard for its clergy. It leader, or "perfects,"

...were those who had renounced the world in a solemn public ceremony. They gave up their property; they promised never to eat meat, eggs, or any other product of animal intercourse; they were never to lie, to take an oath, or to renounce their faith. [38]

Providing this example of a higher moral standard, they wandered the countryside in pairs sharing their belief and message. Little more was involved. "The essential acts of Cathar ritual were repeated recitals of the Lord's Prayer, the laying on of hands, and the exchange of the kiss of peace." [39] It was a belief that left much to the feeling of the person in direct rapport with the higher being of Jesus Christ. The Church in Rome would have none of this. Its power and influence would be lost, as would its ability to collect taxes. When its discredited voice of persuasion was exhausted, the Church orchestrated a military intervention that would force belief at the cost of wholesale destruction. Many were in for extermination. The Albigensian Crusade was on and Innocent III would extract his due and the dues of the Church. The slaughter that lay ahead is simply beyond present day comprehension.

An army was organized in the north of France, with papal promises of spoils and easy pickings from those who were to be chastised. Its first target was the fortified city of Bezier. Mistakes by the defenders led to a quick entry.

There followed one of the most pitiless massacres of the Middle Ages. No one was spared, Catholics and heretics, men and women, clerics and children were all put to the sword...In reporting the victory to the pope, the legate Arnaud Amaury said cheerfully that neither age nor sex was spared and that about twenty thousand people were killed...the legate expressed no regret about the massacre, not even a word of condolence for the clergy of the cathedral who were killed in front of their own altar. A southern, but Catholic chronicler of the Crusade believed that the massacre was a deliberate act of policy. He says that the leaders had agreed 'that in any fortified place that would not surrender, all the inhabitants were to be killed when the place was taken. Then they would find no one to resist them... This is why Bezier was ruined and destroyed, why the inhabitants were slain. All were killed, even those who took refuge in the church. Nothing could save them, neither crucifix nor altar. Women and children were killed, the clergy were killed by those crazy, damnable foot-soldiers. No one escaped; may God, if He will, receive their souls in Paradise. I do not believe that such an enormous and savage massacre ever took place before, even in the time of the Saracens.' [40]

What is beyond comprehension is that "no one was spared." Thousands were systematically put to the sword, hacked to death, as the butchers of Rome roamed the city flushing out of hiding every last victim. What is this? People without any real cause, simply led on by the encouragement of the Vicar of Rome, murder everyone in sight. Of course the easy reply is that they did it *in the name* of their God, whom they were led to believe was threatened by the presumed heresy of these people, a heresy that was but a slightly different belief in the same God. But, psychologically, it is not in the name of God but *as "God"* themselves that they murdered and pillaged so enthusiastically. In the very act of indiscriminate murder they feel for themselves the power of life and death that is normally the sole preserve of God. This experience "transubstantiates" them from the worldly experience of themselves to the divine experience of God. Just as God is this power absolutely, the foot soldiers of Innocent III feel the relative power of something godlike. Their future Nazi brethren will experience the same. In the end of course they find that they are not God as the relative merits of their duty give rise to the stench of slaughter, but *for the moment* the experience was divine and for that it was worth it, or so they would like to believe once the full machinery of justification is put into play. This is a "religious experience" to which the world will return again and again, as one holocaust follows another. All innocence is lost.

The Inquisition turned society into a police state that could destroy anyone, anywhere, anytime.

The Inquisition had a long arm, a sleepless memory, and we can well understand the mysterious terror inspired by the secrecy of its operations and its almost supernatural vigilance. [41]

The Inquisitor was convinced of his mission and mandate especially as he could personally profit from confiscated goods. His enthusiasm was as deep as his greed was long.

One third was given to local authorities, one third to the officials of the Inquisition, and one third to the bishop and inquisitor, to be expended in the assault on heresy... [42]

But advantage went to the stronger and the three-part division of the spoils was quickly subverted.

The papal division into thirds was generally disregarded; the inquisitors monopolized the whole and spent it on themselves or enriched their kindred at their pleasure. [43]

The Inquisitor was accorded absolute power.

The inquisitor, with endless iteration, was empowered and instructed to proceed summarily, to disregard forms, to permit no impediments arising from judicial rules or the wrangling of advocates, to shorten the proceedings as much as possible by depriving the accused of the ordinary facilities of defence, and by rejecting all appeals and dilatory exceptions. [44]

The damage done to society was immense, all acts of goodwill could not be risked. Total fear shrouded the Catholic universe in a mist of misery. The legacy of this tradition of accusation, torture, confiscation, and death tainted everyday life for centuries to come.

Of all the curses which the Inquisition brought in its train this, perhaps, was the greatest--that, until the closing years of the eighteenth century, throughout the greater part of Europe, the inquisitorial process, as developed for the destruction of heresy, became the customary method of dealing with all who were under accusation; that the accused was treated as one having no rights, whose guilt was assumed in advance, and from whom confession was to be extorted by guile or force. [45]

It would be impossible to compute the amount of misery and wrong, inflicted on the defenceless up to the present century, which may be directly traced to the arbitrary and unrestricted methods introduced by the Inquisition and adopted by the jurists who fashioned the criminal jurisprudence of the Continent. [46]

It was a system which might well seem the invention of demons, and was...the Road to Hell. [47]

Denial and Substitution and the Theology of Power had reached into new heights of perversion and misery. The Crusades and the Inquisition had heaped bodies high in the name of the Father, Son, and Holy Ghost.

Matters only worsened. By the beginning of the 16th century new lows had been reached. Recently as many as three popes had simultaneously declared themselves to be the single head of the Church. Rome itself had been abandoned, as for 68 years the popes resided in Avignon as the political and military wars of worldly power continued with divine fury. Not surprisingly, the question was one of *money*. The Church needed vast sums in order to fund its far flung operations. As it got entangled in the political wranglings among rulers, the Church collided with secular power over the right to extract revenue from the peasants. England and Germany would deny papal demands for money when the Church would side with France. There could be no end to these struggles. Many had witnessed the cause of the vicious circularity in the play of human disaster. "...peace brings livelihood, livelihood wealth, wealth pride, pride strife, strife war, war poverty, poverty humility, humility peace." [48] In this battle for survival the Church indulged in any sort of dealing in order to raise cash. It was the issue of indulgences that would bring the continent to full war and serve to divide the Church in two, and then three, and then shatter it entirely. A person needed to have a remission of their sins in order to enter into the promised land of personal salvation, Heaven.

Through the powers apparently delegated by Christ to Peter (Matt. 16:19), by Peter to bishops, and by bishops to priests, the clergy were authorized to absolve a confessing penitent from the guilt of his sins and from their punishment in hell, but not from doing penance for them on earth. Now only a few men, however thoroughly shriven, could rely on dying with all due penances performed; the balance would have to be paid for by years of suffering in purgatory, which a merciful God had established as a temporary hell. On the other hand, many saints, by their devotion and martyrdom, had earned merits probably in excess of the penances due to their sins; Christ by his death had added an infinity of merits; these merits, said the theory of the Church, could be conceived as a treasury on which the pope might draw to cancel part or all of the temporal penalties incurred and unperformed by absolve penitents. Usually the penances prescribed by the Church had taken the form of repeating prayers, giving alms, making a pilgrimage to some sacred shrine, joining a crusade against the Turks or other infidels, or donating money or labor to social projects like draining a swamp, building a road, bridge, hospital, or church. The substitution of a money fine for punishment was a long established custom in secular courts; hence no furore was caused by the early application of the idea to indulgences. A shriven penitent, by paying such a fine, i.e., making a money contribution, to the expenses of the Church, would receive a partial or plenary indulgence... [49]

Having nothing to do with virtue of any sort, this "mechanical Christianity" laid the gates of Heaven open to a *cash purchase*. A new low had been achieved. Abuses quickly accumulated and compounded, as pope, bishop, and priest found an even greater need for worldly money. Confident of a divine sanction, it was only the extent of one's greed that limited the take. The common man expected to find virtue, humility, and compassion in his Church but instead encountered avarice, arrogance, and license. One important commentator waxed eloquently.

If Rome thus believes and teaches with the knowledge of popes and cardinals (which I hope is not the case), then in these writings I freely declare that the true Antichrist is sitting in the temple of God and is reigning in Rome--that empurpled Babylon--and that the Roman Curia is the Synagogue of Satan...If the fury of the Romanists thus goes on, there will be no remedy left except that the emperors, kings, and princes, girt about with force and arms, should attack these pests of the world, and settle the matter no longer by words but by the sword...If we strike thieves with the gallows, robbers with the sword, heretics with fire, why do we not much more attack in arms these masters of perdition, these cardinals, these popes, and all this sink of the Roman Sodom which has without end corrupted the Church of God, and wash our hands in their blood? [50]

Furthermore.

Some have estimated that every year more than 300,000 gulden find their way from Germany to Italy...*We have come to the heart of the matter*...How comes it that we Germans must put up with such robbery and such extortion of our property at the hands of the pope?...If we justly hang thieves and behead robbers, why should we let Roman avarice go free? For he is the greatest thief and robber that has come or can come into the world, and all in the holy name of Christ and St. Peter. Who can endure it or keep silence? [51]

On their way to Heaven, these men of great belief had found instead the Road to Hell.

The final insult was sexual. As the highest levels of the Church indulged in a behavior unbecoming of the tenets of the Teaching of Jesus, so the lower levels followed this example. The village priest got whatever he could. Reports of pervasive sexual predation resounded upon the land. In a position of power, the "celibate" preacher indulged his physical appetites. Speaking of entry into Heaven, he finally sought entry elsewhere. Preaching one thing, indulging in another, the hypocrisy was witnessed by all. Wives and daughters, and young sons, were never safe from violation. Time was nearly up. Clergy lived by one set of rules, privilege, while the rest of society labored by another, work. The Church was due a comeuppance.

On October 31, 1517 delivery was made. An Augustinian monk by the name of Martin Luther cited ninety five objections to the practice of indulgence and nailed them to the door of the Church. While not seeking or expecting revolution, but only reform, there was nonetheless set into motion a legacy of violence that claims victims to this day. A full fledged confrontation with the Church quickly ensued and just as quickly there was established German support for their outspoken monk. Virtually overnight, Luther became a force in the world and the war was on. But, while his complaints against indulgences and Church excesses were important, his greatest contribution came in presenting a new understanding of one's relationship with God and Christ. Salvation was not a matter of indulgences, clerical intervention, or social standing, rather simply of *faith*. It alone mattered. All the ceremonies, rituals, and pious wishful thinking of the Church, clergy, and laity was perfectly useless to a man's attainment of salvation. Faith and faith alone would do.

For not by the doing of works, but by believing, do we glorify God and acknowledge that He is trustful. Therefore, faith alone is the righteousness of a Christian man and the fulfilling of all the commandments. For he who fulfills the First, has no difficulty in fulfilling all the rest. But works, being insensate things, cannot glorify God, although they can, if faith be present, be done to the glory of God. [52]

Luther sought to free the individual from the clutches of the priest, or so it first appeared. The person was to have a direct relationship to God, an experience that would be made possible by faith alone. Without the trappings of Church, faith could assure for oneself a divine reward. Essentially, it was a matter of allowing the person to *think for himself*. But political demands and the requirements of power quickly intervened to squash any such freedom. In going to war with the Vatican it was not free thinkers but rather foot soldiers that would be needed. So while this possibility of the individual was suggested it was not allowed the light of day. Perhaps it would have a future, but for the time being it did not. The freedom to think one's own thoughts would again become a heresy and punishable by death but the *idea* of that possibility was alive in the world and not to be returned to its religious dungeon.

Luther himself had his own personal problems. His was perhaps a personal resentment that it was the pope in Rome who had a single authority with God. This was something that he craved for himself. "I was the first who God entrusted with this matter; I was the one to whom He first revealed how His Word should be preached to you." [53] As with all of the megalomaniacs to enter world affairs Luther was convinced of the Lord speaking exclusively through himself. All worldly matters must defer to him. Luther was to be the new Moses and the one leader of the world to salvation. He was not to bring love but rather vengeance.

And let whosoever can, throw brimstone and pitch upon them; if one could hurl hell-fire at them, so much the better...And this must be done for the honor of Our Lord and of Christianity, so that God may see that we are indeed Christians. Let their houses also be shattered and destroyed...Let their prayer books and Talmuds be taken from them, and their whole Bible too; let their rabbis be forbidden, upon pain of death, to teach henceforth any more. Let the streets and highways be closed against them. Let them be forbidden to practice usury, and let all their money, and all their treasures of silver and gold be taken from them and put away in safety. And if all this be not enough, let them be driven like mad dogs out of the land. [54]

His attack upon the Jews was matched only by his attacks upon everyone else. "I do not admit that my doctrine can be judged by anyone, even by angels. He who does not receive my doctrine cannot be saved." [55] "The hand that wields the secular sword is not a human hand but the hand of God. It is God, not man, Who hangs, and breaks on the wheel, and decapitates, and flogs; it is God who wages war." [56] He had appointed himself to be the hand of God and there would be devastation upon the land.

The Lutheran revolution carried on, and the Catholic/Lutheran war was taken to the people. But finally, perhaps it had nothing to do with religion and everything to do with worldly political power. A new force was taking shape, something that would organize war for centuries to come, *nationalism.* The great linguistic and ethnic groups were taking political and geographical shape, as the French, Germans, English, Spanish, and Italians began a tradition of war on social, economic, and political grounds. And of course there was now the mad rush for gold in the New World. Continental devastation would be financed by the destruction of innocent peoples elsewhere. Times were good, or so was the feeling of those bent upon their own gain at the expense of others.

The Lutheran belief quickly splintered into competing sects, with each demanding total submission. Where before there had been one, now there were many, tearing at the body and spirit of people who hoped only to be left alone.

It (Presbyterian authority) took the right to ordain the religious worship and moral conduct of every inhabitant; it sent a minister and an elder to visit every house and family annually; it could summon any person before it for examination; it could publicly reprove or excommunicate offenders, and could rely on the Council to banish from the city those whom the Consistory banned from the Church. ...no one was to be excused from Protestant services on the plea of having a different or private religious creed; Calvin was as thorough as any pope in rejecting individualism of belief; this greatest legislator of Protestantism completely repudiated that principle of private judgment with which the new religion had begun. [57]

The Catholic Church fought back.

No one shall print, write, copy, conceal, sell, buy, or give, in churches, streets, or other public place, any book or writing made by Martin Luther, John Oecolampadias, Ulrich Zwingli, Martin Bucer, John Calvin, or other heretics reprobasted by the Holy church...We forbid all lay persons to converse or dispute concerning the Holy Scriptures, unless they have duly studied theology, or have been approved by some renown university... [58]

The Jesuits were established at this time as a military arm of the Vatican in order to win back the lands lost to Lutheran heresy. Their mission and principle was clear. "We ought always to be ready to believe that what seems to us white is black if the hierarchical Church so defines it." [59] Absolute obedience would be the cornerstone of yet another attempt to impose upon others one's own belief. A profound commentator perhaps said it best.

In one sense the drama of religious, political, and martial conflict that filled the front of the sixteenth century was superficial, for it proceeded only by permission of a deeper drama played behind the historic scenes or beneath the pompous stage--man's daily and perpetual battle with the soil, the elements, poverty, and death. What, after all, were the bulls and blasts of popes and Protestants, the rival absurdities of murderous mythologies, the strut and succession, gout and syphilis, of emperors and kings, compared with the inexorable struggle for food, shelter, clothing, health, mates, children, life? [60]

The Lutheran revolution then brought little that was new as the old methods of power and domination were to be maintained. The Catholic hierarchy of power is not to be replaced by a de-centralized democracy but rather a new hierarchy would remain in place at the top of which would sit Luther instead of the pope. Even though Luther seemed to suggest that the common man could interpret Scripture according to his own lights, in the end this would not do, not every hare-brained idea could be tolerated. As there was heresy with the Catholic Church so too now there would be heresy with the Lutheran. A *second* system of Inquisition was established. To have escaped the Catholics was often to be grabbed by the Lutherans.

An incredible irony lies at the center of the Reformation. Luther's appeal to the individual's own judgment with respect to God, the principle that clears the way for individual conscience and the right to think for oneself, is completely undercut by the Protestant dogma of predestination, that everything has been decided in advance. One breakthrough is broken against a higher ideology. On the other hand, Catholicism is based upon the principle that there is but one "opinion," that being the pope's, and that the flock must heed accordingly. There was no need to think for oneself, yet Catholicism maintained the principle of free will, that a person indeed was in possession of the right to think. In summary, then, the war between Catholic and Protestant shared in ideologies that masked and confused any final result. The Catholics affirmed and denied the right of the individual to think for himself, starting with faith and then reason, while the Protestants affirmed and denied the individual the right to think for himself, starting from reason and then faith. Yet each failed in that this suppression could not be enforced. The experience of ideality was inherent to human consciousness and it would prove to be a greater force than either combined. Finally, some men would have had enough of the tyranny, hypocrisy, and violence and would chart a new course. Arrogant belief would give way to the possibility of reasoned insight. Death and destruction would give way to a renewal of life and the desire to build a better world for all. But, of course, the road was not straight.

Chapter Five
The Individual and Capital

Certain people in society wanted to have nothing to do with the wars and violence of church against church and church against state. The Lutheran Reformation had shattered the totalitarian view and new churches were being established everywhere. Thoughtful men yearned for a new criterion of truth, a new standard upon which to judge truth from falsity. Any church view was based upon a faith that required no justification from evidence in the world. The "truth" of the Church was a matter of Authority and papal tradition, something codified into a body of belief that had become simply *unbelievable*. Submission to this Church Authority had brought only everlasting violence causing some to decide to *think for themselves.* Evidence would no longer be a matter of Church doctrine but rather a thinking for oneself, a seeing, remembering, seeing, comparing, and seeing again. Developments in the astronomy and mathematics and a re-thinking in philosophy would together establish the basis for a New Science.

Improved technological methods had led to the invention of the telescope. Scripture had claimed that the earth was the at the center of the universe, and that the sun and the planets revolved around this stationary position. New astronomical observations were now possible and indicated the opposite. It was not the earth but rather the sun that stood at the center and the earth was but one of many planets that revolved around it. To suggest such a view was heresy and punishable by death. The infallibility of the Church view could tolerate no such reversal, contrary opinion was inconceivable. The tradition of the Church Authorities would be maintained.

The view that the sun stands motionless at the center of the universe is foolish, philosophically false, and utterly heretical, because contrary to Holy Scripture. The view that the earth is not the center of the universe and even has a daily rotation is philosophically false, and at least an erroneous belief. [1]

To ever once have been proven to be in error would undercut the principle of Church infallibility and open the floodgates to any number of additional claims to contrary truth. The Church would stand firm, committed to its tradition. The New Science was not to emerge uncontested, but the "evidence" that it provided substantiated the fact that truth lay elsewhere.

Although a host of astronomers, mathematicians, and philosophers, such as Copernicus, Kepler, and Galileo, would contribute to the advancement of the New Science, it would be the French thinker Descartes (1596-1650) who would give the most concise and explicit philosophical expression to the new theory of evidence and science in general. He considers the proper manner of beginning and sees that a prior personal resolve is necessary in order to enter into the domain of "science."

It is now some years since I detected how many false beliefs that I had from my earliest youth admitted as true, and how doubtful was everything I had since constructed on this basis; and from that time I was convinced that I must once for all seriously undertake to rid myself of all the opinions which I had formerly accepted, and

108

commence to build anew from the foundation, if I wanted to establish any firm and permanent structure in the sciences. [2]

Having been educated in Jesuit schools, it was clear of what he intended to rid himself. He was looking for a way around Authority so that he could investigate on his own. But it was not just Church doctrine that needed to be purged, as the accumulated beliefs of everyday life too needed to be set aside. This of course would cause a "general upheaval" as life required some sort of belief in order to be possible at all. He would try a methodological experiment that would elevate *doubt* to an odd position of priority. In order to clear away the accumulated "underbrush" of common sense belief, he needed to make a clean sweep.

I feel constrained to confess that there is nothing in all that I formerly believed to be true, of which I cannot in some measure doubt, and that not merely through want of thought or levity, but for reasons which are very powerful and maturely considered... [3]

Everything that comes by the senses, tradition, common sense, and Authority is possible of doubt. The senses can easily deceive, tradition can have forgotten, common sense could be mistaken, and Authority could manifestly be wrong. What can be left when all of this is doubted? There is one thing and one thing alone. "I find here that thought is an attribute that belongs to me; it alone cannot be separated from me. I am, I exist, that is certain." [4] Stated in a more famous formulation.

I noticed that whilst I thus wished to think all things false, it was absolutely essential that the 'I' who thought this should be somewhat, and remarking that this truth '*I think, therefore I am*' was so certain and so assured that all the most extravagant suppositions brought forward by the sceptics were incapable of shaking it, I came to the conclusion that I could receive it without scruple as the first principle of the Philosophy for which I was seeking. [5]

The possibility of individuality, the reward of thinking for oneself, that was a matter of the tribe in the Old Testament, a matter of deference to the gods in Plato, a matter of love and compassion in the Teaching of Jesus, a matter of heresy in the Catholic Church, and an embarrassment for Luther, receives from Descartes its most profound and positive expression. "I think therefore I am" is a principle of personal integrity and responsibility that will serve as the foundation for the emerging edifice of Modern Science. A more decisive break with the past is not imaginable. The thinking individual is to stand at the center of his world, judging for himself, with all else "revolving" around him, following the planetary reversal. The only "authority" could be but himself, as reason, as thinking thing. But this is not an imaginary world of the isolated self, it must reach out to an "objective" reality, there must be a principle of evidence that the thinking person will recognize as distinguishing the true from the false. Having established a foothold from which to begin, it would be necessary to determine *how* one would proceed. What would determine the difference between truth and falsity? "...it seems to me that already I can establish as a general rule that all things which I perceive very clearly and very distinctly are true." [6]

I term that clear which is present and apparent to an attentive mind, in the same way as we assert that we see objects clearly when, being present to the regarding eye, they operate upon it with sufficient strength. But the distinct is that which is so precise and different from all other objects that it contains within itself nothing but what is clear. [7]

Few things would reach to the level of this clarity and distinctness, but the truths of mathematics would. The fact that 1+1=2 is true in a clear and distinct way. It simply cannot be otherwise. To understand

1 and then 1 and then the sum of the two as being 2 is a piece of evidential truth that satisfies Descartes' newly sought after principle of philosophy. On the other hand, the idea, for example, of the infallibility of popes, when speaking *ex cathedra,* is not a clear and distinct idea, as it does not satisfy the new criterion. Such an idea must remain but a mere idea without sufficient evidence. Descartes here has established the foundation for the New Science in mathematics and, by extension, in physics. Mathematical physics will serve as the criterion of truth and the 17th century would witness a tremendous advance of scientific and technological innovation. It is here that the basis was laid for the modern scientific, technological, and industrial world in which we live. Our world is possible only as a result of Cartesian doubt. Descartes' theory though, while serving as a superb beginning, nonetheless would contain deep flaws, as again the road is never straight, but a hard nut had been cracked. The domain of possible investigation had dramatically expanded from the finite and limited world of Church Authority to the infinite and unlimited world of mathematical and scientific thinking. This may not have been fully appreciated to this day.

It is necessary to step back and take an overview of the distance traveled from the time of hunting and gathering to the philosophical breakthrough of "I think therefore I am." All innovation and initiative is based upon this principle of thinking for oneself. While this must always occur in an existing *tradition*, it is possible to *break* with that tradition for the time being. This break has made all of the difference and is the essential quality of the mentality that is the Western spirit. Outside of the West there has not occurred a similar breakthrough. Outside of the West there is to be found only totalitarian traditions where there can be no innovation whatsoever. Only in the West has there developed a "tradition" that has allowed itself to be re-interpreted, where the individual thinking thing can think his own thoughts. There is simply no greater force on earth than this solitary thinker. The mathematical principles that are essential to the constitution of the modern world are accomplishments of this thinker. The musician, artist, philosopher, and legislator of the West are persons who first of all needed to think for themselves. But, while in the West there arose the possibility of this break with tradition, there is nonetheless an overwhelming tendency to *return* to tradition. A break is made, when thinking for oneself achieves some sort of advance, but this in turn is reabsorbed into the tradition as the forces of conservatism reach out to return to the past. But "Pandora's Box" has been opened and although conservatism will attempt to extend its reach there is now a equally powerful "tradition" of innovation. Only in the West is this true, only here did the miraculous thing called thinking achieve cultural legitimacy. The issue here is between a totalitarian tradition, that will tolerate no breach of convention, and a tradition that allows the individual some leeway in which to think his own thoughts. To be sure, the West is a rigid tradition too but not *as* rigid. The world today has been "Westernized" precisely because the success of the achievements of individual freedom and initiative have spread to the rest of the world. No traditional culture would be able to resist this "spirit."

Returning to Descartes' breakthrough, his standard of truth could be met with only in mathematics. The world of actual experience, of real colors and textures, real sights and sounds, does not lend itself to this standard. It is here that the New Science hit upon an error that befuddles to this day, as it prejudiced itself in favor of a single type of experience, to which it reduced all others. A key distinction was made between *primary* and *secondary* qualities. Only primary qualities could be of interest to science. New thinkers entered the debate.

These I call *original* or *primary qualities* of body, which I think we may observe to produce simple ideas in us, viz. solidity, extension,

112

figure, motion or rest, and number. *Secondly,* such qualities which in truth are nothing in the objects themselves but powers to produce various sensations in us by their primary qualities, i.e., by the bulk, figure, texture, and motion of their insensible parts, as colours, sounds, tastes, etc. These I call *secondary qualities.* [8]

The red which is the color that is actually seen, the red of the sunset, is a secondary quality, and is a mere sensation without objective validity, whereas the "red" that is a primary quality is that which has been measured as a mathematical wavelength. As primary the experience is of a measurement and not a real thing. Mathematics can measure wavelengths but it can do nothing with the experience of red itself. The warmth of the fire that is a direct experience is a secondary quality with no scientific merit, as only if converted into a measurable temperature through the use of a thermometer can this "experience" of warmth be useful to mathematical science. The fateful consequence is that measured numbers are accorded a greater reality than the "secondary" reality of lived experience. Only once all secondary qualities have been converted into primary qualities, through a process of indirect mathematization,[9] only once instruments of measurement have been duly consulted, would it be possible to interpret reality as it *really* is. Descartes' goal of clear and distinct ideas achieves fulfillment with this mathematization of nature.

Certainly, without question, the mathematical interpretation has its appropriate place. It is the only possible method for measurements of physical things, of objects in real space and time, but there are places where it does not belong. The fateful error is that a methodology appropriate to one area is misapplied in another. In matters of the "psychological and mental" such a methodology of measurement is fraught with misunderstanding. Mathematical measurement is appropriate for physics but not so for psychology. This will be a bone of contention. Much of modern psychology is exactly patterned after mathematical science. The sciences of the spirit are thought to be equivalent to the sciences of physical existence. The measurement of galactic distances would be the same as measuring the mind as reduced to meurological activity. Achievements of the spirit are rendered into the movement of "stuff" in the brain. Psychology would finally become neurobiology. The final goal of this science is a "material theory of consciousness," which of course is a contradiction in terms. Significant difficulties lay ahead as the psychologist thinks himself to be a physical scientist.

This question of the interpretation of reality as a matter of primary qualities can be expressed in terms of denial and substitution. The real experience of the world, of actual colors and sounds, tastes and odors, is de-valued of significance and relegated to the level of "mere" experience, as only what is mathematical is to be received as true. This mere experience is given a "secondary" status, *denied* its central importance, and *substituted* in its place is a "reality" of purified mathematical relations. Just as the religious experience denied the world as is and substituted in its place a world of purified religious relations, so too, now, the New Science invokes an *identical* ideology and denies the world as is, the world of secondary qualities, in favor of a world of mathematically generated relations. The net effect is essentially the same, as the world of our actual experience is devalued and divested of its real content. With the attainment of the ideas of both "Heaven" and "primary qualities," the reality of lived experience is lost. With both, the common man needs a "clergy" to interpret his world for him, in the one case the priest and in the other the scientist. Each of these castes will claim for themselves an undue reward, as the cleric and the new scientist have much more in common than their separate agendas would seem to suggest. But advancement was made. Descartes' great service was to have philosophically freed the individual to think for himself, but this could not go too far when the method of advancement was prejudiced

114

from the start by mathematical relations, towards a reality that has been run through the machinery of denial and substitution. Historically, though, no one would have been able to see the problem as the early successes and achievements of the New Science simply dazzled the imagination. Compared with the old Authority this new way delivered tangible results. Advances in mathematics, astronomy, and physics led to great technological innovation in navigation, commerce, industry, and war. Navigational instruments were drastically improved with the conquest of the New World as a result, industrial production was improved laying the basis for further prosperity, and trade and commerce expanded delivering more goods and services to more and more people. Only with the recourse to the "primary qualities" of mathematical physics was any of this possible. Material well being was on the rise. Notwithstanding these great and lasting achievements, the New Science was flawed in the aftermath of denial and substitution.

While philosophical and scientific innovation broke new ground, man's inhumanity to man continued apace. Possible prosperity was no block to continued destruction.

There were not two armies but six--German, Danish, Swedish, Bohemian, Spanish, French; armies manned largely by mercenaries or foreigners having no attachment to the German people or soil or history, and led by military adventurers fighting for any faith for a fee; armies fed by appropriating the grains and fruits and cattle of the fields, quartered and wintering in the homes of the people, and recompensed with the right to plunder and the ecstasy of killing and rape. To massacre any garrison that had refused to surrender, after surrender had become inevitable, was a principle accepted by all combatants. Soldiers felt that civilians were legitimate prey; they shot at their feet in the streets, conscripted them as servants, kidnaped their children for ransom, fired their haystacks and burned their churches for fun. They cut off the hands of a Protestant pastor who resisted the wrecking of his church; they tied priests under wagons, forcing them to crawl on all fours till they fainted of exhaustion. The right of a soldier to rape was taken for granted; when a father asked for justice against a soldier who had raped and killed his daughter, he was informed by the commanding officer that if the girl had not been so stingy with her virginity she would still be alive...Moderate estimates reckon a fall, in Germany and Austria, from 21,000,000 to 13,500,000. Count von Lutzow calculated a reduction of population in Bohemia from 3,000,000 to 800,000. Of 35,000 villages existing in Bohemia in 1618, some 29,000 were deserted during the conflict. Throughout the Empire hundreds of villages were left without a single inhabitant. In some regions one might travel sixty miles without seeing a village or a house. Of 1,717 houses standing in nineteen Thuringian villages in 1618 only 627 stood in 1649, and many of these were untenanted. [10]

Participants in this Thirty Years' War could not have cared to take heed of philosophical subtlety but with the Treaty of Westphalia in 1648 religious tyranny was on the wane and the advancement of science and technology set to bound forward.

The knowledge that came with the new mathematical science was directly equated with worldly *power*. The traditional Theology of Power involved the emotional identification of the individual and his exercise of power *as if* that were the same as the power of God. With this new "Mathematics of Power" there is a similar identification, a similar emotional experience that approximates divinity. The natural assumption became that divine thinking must be a mathematical thinking, that in the act of doing algebra or differential calculus, for instance, one must be thinking *exactly* as would God. This would create that "moment of divinity" that would elevate one beyond the normal conditions of human existence, of scarcity and privation, for just the time being, and the emotional experience was simply exquisite. This would power the New Science into technological development and create unprecedented advances. To be able to

116

circumnavigate the globe, proving it was a globe, to transport goods across thousands of miles of land and ocean, to construct large machines of production and commerce, created a heightened sense of personal power. All of this would funnel into a new economic system to replace feudalism, promising a greater wealth of goods than anyone could imagine, that would serve the needs of all to the profit of some. *Capitalism* was born and the Western spirit embraced the idea of *abundance*.

With the feudalism of the Middle Ages the priest and baron controlled all financial matters. Barter was the primary vehicle of exchange and few goods were traded beyond an immediate locality. At the same time, there continued the Church sanction against the making of money on money, or usury, as it was thought to involve the dark forces of Satan. Interest was not to be charged, as this great sin was reserved for the Jews. The mass of common humanity toiled in the fields and need not be bothered by such matters. The Lutheran shattering of the Church lead to the gradual acceptance of interest as a legitimate means for doing business. Without it there would be no way to efficiently *invest*. Money would lay dormant and nothing would come of prior effects. There could be nothing upon which to build. This changed when, at the same time, the discovery and exploitation of America added extensive supplies of gold and silver to economic circulation. Prior to this, the shortage of a circulating currency constricted trade. While the approval of interest and the inflows of precious metals were important in the rise of capitalism, undoubtably the most important element was the individual himself. Many factors contributed. Trade with the East, an expanded awareness of other peoples and places in the wake of all the crusading, the discovery of the world as a globe, the new riches and products of the Americas, the greater familiarity of the peoples within Europe, the emerging scientific and technological advances, and especially the Lutheran revolution that gave sanction to the individual to be his own person, all led to an enhancement of human *desire*.

The great expansion of goods, of technical innovations, of luxuries, and novelties, led to the desire to have them. It was here that the individual was personally motivated to explore the opportunities that the newly expanded economic base offered. Improved methods of interaction, of banking, credit, markets, insurance, and of consensus were put into place. The possibility of "business" was becoming real. Rather than being organized according to religious division, groups of men were organizing an "international" system of rational commerce. Trade was transformed from a dangerous and risky adventure to a standardized system of business. Of course setbacks were many as the world is *only today* for the first time reaching to a global system of consensual commerce, but fundamental progress was being made. Divisions were deep but a different sort of man was emerging from the religious wars, a man who wanted to live his life for himself as best as he saw fit. His domain would be business. His life would no longer be dominated by the Church but rather the market. Great profits were to be made and the "capitalist spirit" energized Europe.

...capitalism...was replacing the old medieval ways of looking at things with new ideas more in accord with the new times. The businessman came slowly to look upon his enterprise as merely a means for making profits. In fact, his search for profits pushed into the background all thoughts of his duty to society, to God, and to his neighbors. There was a growing tendency to value all things in terms of money, to believe that success meant the heaping up of wealth, to think that riches were the chief end of life and the most certain basis of power. In the middle ages, the rich man had been suspected because he was rich. In the sixteenth and seventeenth centuries, the rich man came to be respected because he was rich. [11]

Concern for profits alone, though, does not account for the full experience of capitalism.

The essential quality of capitalistic activity is the production and distribution of *material goods*. The aggregate of goods per capita had remained essentially the same from the time of Christ through the Middle Ages and up to the Modern Era. Any increase had been immediately consumed by continued war, famine, and pestilence. Europe had remained shrouded in scarcity and privation. The emergence of capitalism was the first attempt *ever* to address scarcity at its root. Through the technological innovations of the New Science a rationalized system of business was established that in fact began the process of dramatically increasing aggregate wealth. Only in this way would it be possible to produce more and the capitalist understood his opportunity. The only way in which to reap profits was to have already produced and delivered more and more goods to more and more people. Profits were made *subsequent* to the meeting of other's needs. The majority would nonetheless still go without, but the critical fact in the history of the West, and later the world, was that better methods of production and distribution had appeared. Nowhere else in the world would this innovation occur. Only in the West is production driven upward. But the process is tortured, as the capitalist spirit entrenched itself in the amassing of wealth at any cost to others. In the end the capitalist would take too much. A familiar story will be told.

The amassing of wealth for the capitalist alleviated the fact of his own possible material scarcity. His wealth assured him that he would never go without, that all of his physical needs would always be met. The "man of substance" was a man cushioned from want. This was a distinction not lost on either that man himself or all those others who were so cushioned. The workers and the owner lived separate realities.

The wages of the worker are limited to his subsistence by competition

119

among the workmen...The mere worker, who has only his arms and his industry, has nothing except in so far as he succeed in selling his toil to others...The employer pays him as little as he can; and as he has a choice among a great number of workers, he prefers the one who works for the least wage. The workers are therefore obliged to lower their price in competition with one another. In every kind of work it cannot fail to happen, and actually it does happen, that the wages of the worker are limited to what is necessary for his subsistence.[12]

This "Iron Law of Wages" was of great comfort to the capitalist. He could amass to himself with a perfectly clear Christian conscience. It was here that the Theology of Power had its capitalistic expression. The Few could amass to themselves through the labor of others and easily achieved a power of command over his hirelings. His personal life was one of leisure and ease as others did his work. But his reach now was much greater than his baronial counterpart of feudalism, he could go beyond the local market and profit from international relations. He could influence supply and demand throughout the world and became a player in matters of war and peace. His achievement and exercise of power would place him in *history*. He could think of himself as being outside the normal conditions of human existence and perhaps "win eternal mention in the deathless roll of fame." [13] His wealth and power allowed him to experience that immaculate feeling of divinity, just as had the man enraptured in the religious experience and the mathematician immersed in the calculus of divine thinking. Augustine and Descartes would have understood well this fascination. For the man on the "outside" though, there could be no such alleviation, his lot was weighed down from dawn to dusk. Whether in the fields or on the march, his life was in the powers of others. Christianity, the New Science, and capitalism are then all of a piece, all but varying strains on the same theme, all achieving for the Few an alleviation in the face of anxiety.

The discovery of America was decisive for the history of Europe. But there were really *two* Americas, that of the South and of the North. Each would take a different course based upon its initial experience. The difference is one of geology. Gold and silver were immediately found in the South. The Catholic Spanish conquistadors came for gold in the name of the Christ.

And now I insist in the name of His Majesty that my principal intention and motive in making this war and the others that I have made is to bring and reduce the said *naturales* to the said knowledge of our holy faith and belief...[14]

The justification for the violence and theft of Cortez in the West was the same as it had been for the crusaders to the East, in the name of the Father, Son, and Holy Ghost. Soldiers of fortune came to cart off the golden artifacts, to be melted down for currency, so that they could live the life of leisure back home. Catholic missionaries quickly planted the cross and the "profits" flowed to Church and State. These were not capitalistic profits but rather the profits of theft. The natives were simply slaughtered for sport. There would be no "sanctity" of life here. The legacy of this destruction is evident today, as the hierarchies of Church were replaced by those of the military *junta*. In the South was established a system of Church sanctioned feudalism where the "individual" was not protected. The consequence is that South America looks very similar to feudal Spain.

In the North a different opportunity would be taken. Gold was not available for the taking but the land was. Those who came were not the male treasure hunters of the South but rather families in search of a place to worship as they wished. Those who came were interested in building a new life, a new community, and were committed to stay. The Puritans were a determined lot that would gut out the long haul. They would build God's rightful social order on

121

earth, the City of the Hill. The Cambridge Platform is published in 1648.

Our Churches here, as (by the grace of Christ) wee believe and profess the same Doctrine of trueth of the Gospell, which generally is received in all the reformed Churches of Christ in Europe: so especially, wee desire not to vary from the doctrine of faith, & truth held forth by the churches of our native country...wee, who are by nature, English men, doe desire to hold forth the same doctrine of religion (especially in fundmentalls) which wee see & know to be held by the churches of England, according to the truth of the Gospell. [15]

These early Americans came with the same intolerance that they had learned so well in Europe, and dissent and contention would not be allowed, but circumstances conspired against them when the Old World methods of Inquisition could not be imposed. There was simply *too much land*. Troublemakers could be sent packing rather than being left hanging. The taste for the blood of the Inquisition was never able to flourish as new colonies could be peopled by those who found their neighbor's opinion unbearable. The land was big and ironically religious intolerance proved to be a spur to further settlement.

The several colonies were settled by diverse Old World peoples, with specific religious views firmly held in mind but, before long, it was not the requisites of dogma but the demands of survival which became the highest priority. The stupendous *abundance* of land gave rise to a unique opportunity. Rather than basing one's interpretation of reality upon the assumption of scarcity, as with Christianity and capitalism, the New World allowed the chance to imagine an interpretation based upon the possibility of abundance. When looking West across the land many a pioneer imbibed such a vision. With abundance, everything would be different. The Ideology of Exclusion would be undermined by the possibility of Inclusion. Hard work, initiative, and effort would bring to the settler an abundant life unimaginable to his relatives remaining in Europe. Of course there was no magic here, as many suffered as before and scarcity continued as their daily fare, but the decisive difference was that the *idea* of a possible better life was in the air and nourished many as they made the total effort to succeed. Out of the reach of king and pope, in a land of stunning natural abundance, without traditions of religious zealotry, with the hope and idea of something better, early America was *a land of opportunity*. As a beacon of hope this vision has attracted millions from hundreds of lands. But, before this could go too far, the laws of the new land needed to be constituted to ensure this liberty of the person.

Legislatively, rules needed to be established, something that would ultimately emerge as the *Constitution of the United States.* Founding Fathers understood the gravity of the opportunity. Thomas Jefferson is famous for having written the *Declaration of Independence*, but his greatest contribution occurred back in his home of Virginia. He wrote the law on *religious freedom*. The document read:

An *Act* for establishing *Religious Freedom*, passed in the Assembly of Virginia in the beginning of the year 1786. Well aware that Almighty God hath created the mind free; that all attempts to influence it by temporal punishments and burthens, or by civil incapacitations, tend only to beget habits of hypocrisy and meanness, and are a departure from the plan of the Holy Author of our religion, who, being Lord both of body and mind, yet chose not to propagate it by coercions on either, as was in his Almighty power to do; that the impious presumption of legislators and rulers, civil as well as ecclesiastical, who, being themselves but fallible and uninspired men have assumed dominion over the faith of others, setting up their own opinions and modes of thinking as the only true and infallible, and as such endeavoring to impose them on others, hath established and maintained false religions over the greatest part of the world, and through all time: That to compel a man to furnish contributions of money for the propagations of opinions which he disbelieves, is sinful and tyrannical; that even the forcing him to support this or that teacher of his own religious persuasion, is depriving him of the comfortable liberty of giving his contributions to the particular pastor whose morals he would make his pattern, and whose powers he feels most persuasive to righteousness...*be it therefore enacted by the General Assembly,* That no man shall be compelled to frequent or support any religious worship, place or ministry whatsoever, nor shall be enforced, restrained, molested, or burthened in his body or goods, nor shall otherwise suffer on account of his religious opinions or belief; but that all men shall be free to profess, and by argument to maintain, their opinions in matters of religion, and that the same shall in no wise diminish, enlarge, or effect their civil capacities... [16]

Eighteen centuries of dead popes collectively turned in their graves. An idea was taking root. The only thing not to be tolerated would be intolerance. Religious freedom here of course entails *all* freedoms, only then would the right to think for oneself be open to the emerging dimension of social self-responsibility. The idea was not an accomplished deed, but the force of the law would humble many a would-be petty tyrant who hoped to tell others what to think. Religious intolerance had not survived the ocean crossing and mothers rejoiced throughout the land that their children would be safe from sectarian harm. By way of contrast, the words of Louis XV of France:

In my person alone resides the sovereign power...To me alone belongs the legislative power, unconditional and undivided. All public order emanates from me. My people and I are one, and the rights and interests of the nation, which some dare to make a body separate from the monarch, are necessarily united with mine, and rest in my hands alone. [17]

The expanse of the American continent and its distance from Europe made it inevitable that the privileges of European kings could not stand. Tradition and custom suggested caution, but finally the king was no longer useful and a different form of government was possible. Royal monarchy would be replaced by liberal democracy.

We hold these truths to be self-evident, that all men are created equal, that they are endowed by their Creator with certain unalienable Rights, that among these are, Life, Liberty, and the pursuit of Happiness. That to secure these rights, Governments are instituted among Men, deriving their just powers from the consent of the governed, That whenever any Form of Government becomes destructive of these ends, it is the Right of the People to alter or to abolish it, and to institute new Government, laying its foundation on such principles and organizing its power in such form, as to them shall seem most likely to effect their Safety and Happiness. [18]

Of course this was *revolutionary*. No government *ever* had sought the happiness of its own people. The principle of equality and the right of the governed to govern themselves would be heresy for all the European tyrants who continued their wars of attrition. The people of the United States took it upon themselves to set a new standard and chart a new course which the rest of the world would be slow to follow, but today it is the *only* standard. *Thinking for oneself*, that is the culmination of a tradition encompassing the Old Testament, Plato, the Teaching of Jesus, Luther, Descartes, and the settlers of the New World, for the first time *would be protected by the law of the land.* The *Preface* to the Constitution reads:

We the People of the United States, in Order to form a more perfect Union, establish Justice, insure domestic Tranquillity, provide for the common defence, promote the general Welfare, and secure the Blessings of Liberty to ourselves and our Posterity, do ordain and establish this Constitution of the United States of America. [19]

Had this not been the case, had another Spain ravaged the North, then the world would be profoundly different than it is today. Privilege will never relinquish its position and can be relied on to constrict economic expansion to its own advantage. Middle class prosperity is not a goal of tyranny. The American Experiment was a radical proposal indeed, for a world steeped in religious fanaticism.

The American experience would prove to be scattered through with failures and shortcomings, the most important of which were southern slavery and the extermination of the native peoples, causing a legacy of great anguish and misery that is simply evil. Additionally, vested interests were established that took unfair advantage, undercutting the rights of individuals and smacking of Old World brutalities. Capitalistic organizations produced huge wealth and anguish alike. But, *for the most part*, when seen in the relative context of the rest of the world, the American Experiment in self-government and human rights was *a spectacular success*. The Odyssey of the Western spirit had achieved a final breakthrough. The individual was left to think and do for himself, releasing him to the greatest productivity that the world has ever seen. The list of forebears is impressive. Homer, Moses, Plato, Jesus, Descartes, Luther, Jefferson naming but the leading lights. Of course this is the odyssey of a spirit that has been imbibed by simply millions in their collective quest to live a better and more honest life. Many would and continue to refuse but the force of the positive is simply greater than that of the negative, if it only chooses to be. The economic engine of this success was the Industrial Revolution.

While obstructing a revolution in the New World, England was engaged in a different one in the Old World. The Industrial Revolution took place under a unique set of circumstances that existed only on this island nation. There occurred a set of conditions that emerged in the light of the New Science that hoped to take theory into practice, take mathematical physics into applied technology.

Why did the Industrial Revolution come to England First? Because England had won great wars on the Continent while keeping its own soil free for war's devastation; because it had secured command of the seas and had thereby acquired colonies that provided raw materials and needed manufactured goods; because its armies, fleets, and growing population could not meet these widening demands; because the profits of far-flung commerce accumulated capital seeking new avenues of investment; because England allowed its nobles--and their fortunes--to engage in commerce and industry; because the progressive displacement of tillage by pasturage drove peasants from the fields to the towns, where they added to the labor force available for factories; because science in England was directed by men of a practical bent, while on the Continent it was predominantly devoted to abstract research; and because England had a constitutional government sensitive to business interests, and vaguely aware that priority in the Industrial Revolution would make England for over a century the political leader of the Western world.[20]

From 1776 to 1900, the Western world experienced expansion on every front. The combination of the introduction of machines, in both industry and agriculture, expanding markets, new products, scientific and capitalistic organization, and the establishment of a general business consensus, all contributed to the greatest expansion of material prosperity in human history. Aggregate statistics sketch a general picture. From 1790 to 1900 the population of the United States increased from 3.9 to 76 million. From 1800 to 1900 coal production went from 3 to 7,643 trillion BTUs. Gross farm production for that same period went from $236 million to $4.298 billion. The number of manufacturing production workers increased from 957,000 in 1849 to 4,502,000 in 1899. A Manufacturing Index was 16 in 1860 and 100 in 1900. The population of Europe as a whole increased from 187.6 million in 1800 to 400.5 million in 1900. [21] The population of Great Britain increased from 8.8 million in 1801 to 32.5

million in 1901. The population in Germany increased from 22.3 million in 1816 to 56.3 in 1900. Coal production increased from 1.3 million metric tons in 1817 to a monumental 149.5 million metric tons in 1900. While these numbers present a rough picture, the obvious fact is that the period leading up to 1900 witnessed an unprecedented expansion in all types of economic activity to the greater general welfare of more and more people. But this expansion was not entirely positive. People were forced from the land and into industrial centers, children were put to work, the environment was savaged, and the prosperity was not equitably distributed. The capitalists took more and more for themselves. General working conditions were poor and dangerous and the common man found himself either manning a factory or manning an army. From Napoleon's March to Moscow at the beginning of the century to Roosevelt's charge up San Juan Hill at the end, a coalition of violence and stupidity conspired to consume any newly created wealth in the fires of ambition and insanity. It is startling that *in spite of* such continual destruction and waste, the economic base continued to surge. The 19th century achieved the first economic miracle but a great price had been paid by many. Social relations would become strained.

Charles Dickens has provided a vivid description of life during this first miracle.

It was a town of red brick, or of brick that would have been red if the smoke and ashes had allowed it; but as matters stood it was a town of unnatural red and black like the painted face of a savage. It was a town of machinery and tall chimneys, out of which interminable serpents of smoke trailed themselves for ever and ever, and never got uncoiled. It had a black canal in it, and a river that ran purple with ill-smelling dye, and vast piles of buildings full of windows where there was a rattling and a trembling all day long, and where the piston of the steam-engine worked monotonously up and down like the head of

128

an elephant in a state of melancholy madness. It contained several large streets all very like one another, and many small streets still more like one another, inhabited by people equally like one another, who went in and out at the same hours, with the same sound upon the same pavement, to do the same work, and to whom every day was the same as yesterday and to-morrow, and every year the counterpart of the last and the next. [22]

The industrialists did not care, as wretched living conditions for their workers was of no concern.

They were ruined, when they were required to send labouring children to school; they were ruined when inspectors were appointed to look into their works; they were ruined, when such inspectors considered it doubtful whether they were justified in chopping people up with their machinery; they were utterly undone when it was hinted that perhaps they need not always make quite so much smoke...Whenever a Coketowner felt he was ill-used--that is to say, whenever he was not left entirely alone, and it was proposed to hold him accountable for the consequences of any his acts--he was sure to come out with the aweful menace that he would 'sooner pitch his property into the Atlantic' yet but, on the contrary, had been kind enough to take mighty good care of it... [23]

Even though the capitalist recognized that he had accumulated infinitely in excess of anything that he himself could possibly need, and that the armies of the poor and downtrodden, those that worked in his factories, could be relieved by a more equitable distribution of goods, notwithstanding, such distribution was thought to go counter to the *design of nature* and was possibly immoral as well.

It is a fact well known to those who are conversant in this matter, that scarcity, to a certain degree, promotes industry, and that the manufacturer (i.e., manual worker) who can subsist on three days' work, will be idle and drunk the remainder of the week...Upon the whole we can fairly aver that a reduction of wages in the woolen manufacture would be a national blessing, and no real injury to the poor. By this means we might keep our trade, uphold our rents (revenues), and reform the people into the bargain. [24]

Or, as more poetically inspired observer would say. "Everyone but an idiot knows that the lower classes must be kept poor, or they will never be industrious." [25] The current justification for those in power shifted from the religious to the assumptions of the New Science. It was no longer God that guaranteed the advantages of the Few but rather Nature. The result was the same. An objective, all-powerful, force was relied upon to sanction the confirmation of things as they were. The authority of science would assure the powerful that their position of privilege was in harmony with the proper order of things. The latest scientific authority, Charles Darwin, was called in to support the cause. His principle of "natural selection" was transformed by others into the principle of "the survival of the fittest," where in the competitive march of history the strong must prevail and the weak must die. The losers must perish by necessity in order to insure the survival of the species. Darwin himself restricted his observations to plants and animals but others would apply it to human society. These "Social Darwinists" established scientific justification for the perfectly free exercise of power by the capitalist to do as he pleased, and that he would not be held accountable for anything that he would do to main and kill his workers. His greed was *stainless,* and the poor *must* continue to go *without* as a matter of *natural design.* To do otherwise, to show Christian compassion and charity, to extend a kindness, to feed widows and orphans, would be to invite the general decline of society and would be a "mortal" sin against nature.

Andrew Carnegie (1835-1919), the American industrialist, had natural thoughts on the matter of the proper relation between rich and poor.

The price which society pays for the law of competition, like the price it pays for cheap comforts and luxuries, is also great; but the advantages of this law are also greater still, for it is to this law that we owe our wonderful material development, which brings improved conditions in its train. But, whether the law be benign or not, we must say of it, as we say of the change in the conditions of men to which we have referred: It is here, we cannot evade it; no substitutes for it have been found; and while the law may be sometimes hard for the individual, it is the best for the race, because it insures the survival of the fittest in every department. We accept and welcome, therefore, as conditions to which we must accommodate ourselves, great inequality of environment, the concentration of business, industrial and commercial, in the hands of a few, and the law of competition between these, as being not only beneficial, but essential for the future progress of the race. [26]

Some individuals would surely suffer but the collective good would be greater as the "race" would prosper as never before. Any wealth expended in the welfare of citizens would be wasted and consumed for no lasting advantage.

There remains, then, only one mode of using great fortunes; but in this we have the true antidote for the temporary unequal distribution of wealth, the reconciliation of the rich and the poor--a reign of harmony--another ideal, differing, indeed, from that of the Communist in requiring only the further evolution of existing conditions, not the total overthrow of our civilization. It is founded upon the present most intense individualism, and the race is prepared to put it in practice by degrees whenever it pleases. Under its sway we shall have an ideal state, in which the surplus wealth of the few will become, in the best sense, the property of the many, because administered for the common good, and this wealth, passing through the hands of a few, can be made a much more potent force for the elevation of our race than if it had been distributed in small sums to people themselves. Even the poorest can be made to see this, and to agree that great sums gathered by some of their fellow-citizens and spent for public purposes, from which the masses reap the principal benefit, are more valuable to them than if scattered among them through the course of many years in trifling amounts... [27]

Carnegie has the odd fortune of being absolutely right and absolutely wrong. As a theoretical and mathematical model of economic production, as statistically sketched by the New Science, this view of all wealth and power to the "plantation master" is perfectly true, but as an expression of the proper way in which human beings ought to treat each other it is perfectly false.

The man of wealth is to be a law onto himself, dictating and commanding to his own strict advantage, as his workers are denied their rightful share of their daily labor. A social reality based on the power of the Few is a tyranny and therefore subject to its either immediate or gradual demise. *A house divided cannot stand.* But Carnegie had his own vision and such a house might remain standing for a little while at least.

This, then, is held to be the duty of the man of Wealth: First, to set an example of modest, unostentatious living, shunning display or extravagance; to provide moderately for the legitimate wants of those dependent upon him; and after doing so to consider all surplus revenues which come to him simply as trust funds, which he is called upon to administer, and strictly bound as a matter of duty to administer in the manner which, in his judgment, is best calculated to produce the most beneficial results for the community--the man of wealth thus becoming the agent and trustee for his poorer brethren, bringing to their service his superior wisdom, experience, and ability to administer, doing for them better than they would or could do for themselves... [28]

Carnegie's final solution:

132

Thus is the problem of the Rich and Poor to be solved. The laws of accumulation will be left free; the laws of distribution free. Individualism will continue, but the millionaire will be but a trustee for the poor; intrusted for a season with a great part of the increased wealth of the community, but administering it for the community far better than it could or would have done for itself. The best minds will thus have reached a stage in the development of the race in which it is clearly seen that there is no mode of disposing of surplus wealth creditable to the thoughtful and earnest men into whose hands it flows save by using it year by year for the general good. [29]

While the theory may sound reasonable enough, in actual practice it failed year after year as advantage piled higher and higher to the one side. The power of the wealthy seldom reached to the common good, the "modest living" of the rich naturally was transformed into a "conspicuous consumption," this "superior wisdom" was confined to more and more sophisticated ways in which to indulge the appetites, and the "ability to administer" was spent refining methods of paternal condescension. Dictatorial and hierarchical fiefdoms, corporations, were established to service the vanity of owners and little more. Devastation was visited upon the land as profits were ruthlessly extracted. Wages were artificially reduced to the level of subsistence, keeping millions over-worked, hungry, and desperate. So Carnegie was wrong, it had nothing to do with the common good and everything to do with the now familiar theme of the Theology of Power, that feeling of divinity when one lifts oneself beyond the normal conditions of human existence, when one feels almost like a god as millions scurry to one's idle commands. Confident of their moral superiority the Few had everything to lose, while desperate of their daily bread the many had nothing to lose. The battlefield rose on the horizon.

Without a major change of attitude, the situation could only

133

worsen, as disparities broadened. The significant increase in wealth of the 19th century would be dwarfed by the colossal gains of the early 20th. Rich men would have sons and grandsons who would become unimaginably wealthy, consolidating their political positions of power, as more and more people were brought under the dominion of their vast operations. The stand-off continued. The rich did not receive the respect which they felt was their natural due and the poor did not receive a living wage to which they felt entitled. Social bitterness and resentment predominated in both Europe and the United States. The 20th century would witness radical change in one way or another.

The individual had advanced greatly since the emergence of the Lutheran "I think therefore I am," that Descartes had brought into the world, but great inequalities and inequities had been imposed. Some few individuals took the lion's share and great hardship was set upon all the rest. People began to think revolutionary ideas and that some sort of social fairness and mutual responsibility was possible. The social and common good would need to be brought to the middle of the discussion.

Chapter Six
The Public and the Idea of Social Welfare

Unquestionably, the most influential social thinker of the 19th century was Karl Marx (1818-1883). His legend in the 20th century would inspire millions to heroic efforts. With both exultation and dread the world has felt the force of his influence. But, there is deep confusion, as much passes under the Marxist banner that has no basis in his writings as the Marxist Revolution in Russia in 1917 quickly became the Leninist Revolution of the Soviet Union. Many "revisions" would need to be made while still maintaining the sanction of his authority.

Marx was fundamentally a critic of the social order that had produced vast riches alongside of equally vast human desolation. The Industrial Revolution had produced a dramatically *unequal* distribution of well being. In the *Manifesto of the Communist Party,* co-authored in 1848 with his life long friend Engels, he attempted to precisely describe the situation and offer a solution. The view was that society had historically divided itself into *classes,* into mutually hostile groups, that could seek only their self-interest. With the 19th century there were but two classes.

Our epoch, the epoch of the bourgeoisie, possesses, however, this distinctive feature: it has simplified the class antagonisms: Society as a whole is more and more splitting up into two great hostile camps, into two great classes directly facing each other: Bourgeoisie and Proletariat. [1]

The owners and the workers had squared off against one another and there could be no working together for a mutual benefit. Power was naturally held by the owners and great social misery inflicted.

The bourgeoisie, wherever it has gotten the upper hand, has put an end to all feudal, patriarchal, idyllic, relations. It has pitilessly torn asunder the motley feudal ties that bound man to his 'natural superiors,' and has left remaining no other nexus between man and man than naked self-interest, than callous 'cash payment.' It has drowned the most heavenly ecstasies of religious fervour, of chivalrous enthusiasm, of philistine sentimentalism, in the icy water of egotistical calculation. It has resolved personal worth into exchange value, and in place of the numberless indefeasible chartered freedoms, has set up that single, unconscionable freedom--Free Trade. In one word, for exploitation, veiled by religious and political illusions, it has substituted naked, shameless, direct, brutal exploitation. [2]

The new order apparently had replaced a more gentle form of human exploitation, of the rural peasant by the baron, with a much more vicious exploitation, of the workers by the owners. Life for the worker had always been hard but it had now gotten grim. A caring overlord had been replaced by an uncaring owner.

The bourgeoisie, during its rule of scarce one hundred years, has created more massive and more colossal productive forces than have all preceding generations together. Subjection of Nature's forces to man, machinery, application of chemistry to industry and agriculture, steam-navigation, railways, electric telegraphs, clearing of whole continents for cultivation, canalisation of rivers, whole populations conjured out of the ground--what earlier century had even a presentiment that such productive forces slumbered in the lap of social labour? ³

For some this described the positive evidence that this "rule of scarce one hundred years" had been an overwhelming success and that it was with these "colossal productive forces" that the destiny of civilization lay. Only by having awakened these "slumbering" forces would it be possible for the human condition to improve. Carnegie, of course, had taken this position, but Marx's criticism cut deeply in another direction. He would see things from the point of view of the workers and not from that of the owners. His concern was not with the *fact* of industrial development but with the unfair distribution of its benefits. The reality of the worker of course had changed dramatically.

Owing to the extensive use of machinery and to division of labour, the work of the proletarians has lost all individual character, and consequently, all charm for the workman. He becomes an appendage of the machine, and it is only the most simple, most monotonous, and most easily acquired knack, that is required of him. Hence, the cost of production of a workman is restricted, almost entirely, to the means of subsistence that he requires for his maintenance, and for the propagation of his race. But the price of a commodity, and therefore also of labour, is equal to its cost of production. In proportion, therefore, as the repulsiveness of the work increases, the wages decreases. Nay, more, in proportion as the use of machinery and division of labour increases, in the same proportion the burden of toil also increases, whether by prolongation of the working hours, by the increase of the work exacted in a given time or by increased speed of the machinery, etc. Modern industry has converted the little workshop of the patriarchal master into the great factory of the industrialist capitalist. Masses of labourers, crowded into the factory, are organised like soldiers. As privates of the industrial army they are placed under the command of a perfect hierarchy of officers and sergeants. Not only are they slaves of the bourgeois class, and of the bourgeois State; they are daily and hourly enslaved by the machine, by the overlooker, and, above all, by the individual bourgeois manufacturer himself. The more openly this despotism proclaims gain to be its end and aim, the more petty, the more hateful and the more embittering it is. [4]

Marx's deep sympathies were for the worker enslaved in a life that was owned by someone else. Some claimed the absolute priority of profits, but he spoke up for the lowly worker who made those profits possible but was himself consumed by the process. The capitalistic regime had done wonderful things in producing more and more but the high cost to its workers had caused absolute misery. Something needed to be done, such a level of human exploitation could not stand. This was nothing more than slavery. Marx's solution was simple. *Revolution.* The workers were the *rightful* owners of the profits of their labor and therefore the capitalist owners needed to be violently eliminated. The workers, the Proletariat, would unite under the flag of a special group who would provide leadership.

The Communists, therefore, are on the one hand, practically, the most advanced and resolute section which pushes forward all others; on the other hand, theoretically, they have over the great mass of the proletariat the advantage of clearly understanding the line of march, the conditions, and the ultimate general results of the proletarian movement. The immediate aim of the Communists is the same as that of all the other proletarian parties: formation of the proletariat into a class, overthrow of the bourgeois supremacy, conquest of political power by the proletariat. [5]

The established power of the owners would be overthrown and the workers would become the new owners of the means of production. The workers themselves were incapable of carrying forth the Revolution, as a special group of practioners would need to take control. These were the Communists who were the theoreticians better positioned to understand the needs of the Revolution. This delegation of authority would have the greatest consequences upon the regime that was actually established under the Communist flag. But of this the *Manifesto* could know nothing. There would be much blood before this was to be fully comprehended. But, with the initial seizure of power, the most heart felt dread of the capitalist would be realized. The ownership of private property, the central basis of all exploitation, would be eliminated.

The distinguishing feature of Communism is not the abolition of property generally, but the abolition of bourgeois property. But modern bourgeois private property is the final and most complete expression of the system of producing and appropriating products, that is based on class antagonisms, on the exploitation of the many by the few. In this sense, the theory of the Communists may be summed up in a single sentence: Abolition of private property. [6]

Personal property could be retained but the ownership of the large systems of mass production would need to be taken over and put under the "ownership" of the Proletariat. To the extent that the worker had been degraded under capitalistic ownership, to the same extent he would be uplifted under common ownership. "In bourgeois society, living labour is but a means to increase accumulated labour. In Communist society, current labour is but a means to widen, to enrich, to promote the existence of the labourer." [7] In capitalist society all surplus is accumulated for the further accumulation of wealth for the owner. In Communist society all surplus would be expended on the current welfare of the worker. Rather than accumulating principle and interest, the workers would be able to spend the interest. Distribution rather than accumulation would be the central difference, which of course would make all the difference. Social relations would be transformed immensely. "Communism deprives no man of the power to appropriate the products of society; all that it does is to deprive him of the power to subjugate the labour of others by means of such appropriation." [8] In another context, Marx sketches life as he imagined it to be in the new order.

For as soon as the distribution of labour comes into being, each man has a particular, exclusive sphere of activity, which is forced upon him and from which he cannot escape. He is a hunter, a fisherman, a shepherd, or a critical critic, and must remain so if he does not want to lose his means of livelihood; while in communist society, where nobody has one exclusive sphere of activity but each can become accomplished in any branch he wishes, society regulates the general production and thus makes it possible for me to do one thing today and another tomorrow, to hunt in the morning, fish in the afternoon, rear cattle in the evening, criticise after dinner, just as I have a mind, without ever becoming hunter, fisherman, shepherd, or critic. [9]

While the vision was descriptively astute and emotionally pleasing, problems and questions immediately arose. Communist society was based upon the assumption that economic production would continue under its rule to produce the great wealth of goods that the capitalists produced. But, without specialization, without the efficiency of standardized production, if instead each man were entitled to be one thing or another, being a fisherman or a critic, surplus production could be reduced if not eliminated entirely. And, of course, the violence of the Revolution left a chill to all but those fully convinced of its necessity. Once there is blood upon the land the misery inflicted is simply immeasurable, but in the happy days *before* the Revolution these losses are not to be calculated. It is the Way of the World that its will be done. Solutions are often not. Before the fall, there was great optimism. The Marxist Program.

...in the most advanced countries, the following will be pretty generally applicable. 1. Abolition of property in land and application of all rents of land to public purposes. 2. A heavy progressive or graduated income tax. 3. Abolition of all right of inheritance. 4.

140

Confiscation of the property of all emigrants and rebels. 5. Centralisation of credit in the hands of the State, by means of a national bank with State capital and an exclusive monopoly. 6. Centralisation of the means of communication and transportation in the hands of the State. 7. Extension of factories and instruments of production owned by the State; the bringing into cultivation of waste-lands, and the improvement of the soil generally in accordance with a common plan. 8. Equal liability of all to labour. 9. Combination of agriculture with manufacturing industries; gradual abolition of the distinction between town and country, by a more equable distribution of the population over the country. 10. Free education for all children in public schools. Abolition of children's factory labour in its present form. Combination of education with industrial production, &c., &c. When, in the course of development, class distinctions have disappeared, and all production has been concentrated in the hands of a vast association of the whole nation, the public power will lose its political character. Political power, properly so-called, is merely the organised power of one class for oppressing another. If the proletariat during its contest with the bourgeoisie is compelled, by the force of circumstances, to organise itself as a class, and, as such, sweeps away by force the old conditions for the existence of class antagonisms and of classes generally, and will thereby have abolished its own supremacy as a class. In place of the old bourgeois society, with its class and class antagonisms, we shall have an association, in which the free development of each is the condition for the free development of all. [10]

The *Manifesto* concludes with a call to action. "Let the ruling classes tremble at a Communistic revolution. The proletarians have nothing to lose but their chains. They have a world to win. *Working men of all countries, unite!*" [11] The vista was big, the cause just, and the way now clearly defined. It was thought that the weight of history itself would determine such a course. As a matter of *historical necessity* the Revolution would inherit the world. Capitalism would die with the birth of the earthly paradise of Communism.

While Marx displayed a compassionate and sympathetic view of the workers in their struggle to survive in a hostile world, his theory had shortcomings and not the least of which was the fact that he was dead wrong about the *individual*. He was a profound social commentator but he was a poor psychologist. He understood little of the nature of motivation and initiative. The theory was simply one-sided. The primary force in human affairs was asserted to be that of *material,* following the materialistic bias of natural science to which he was heavily indebted. The experience of ideality had no validity.

The premises from which we begin are not arbitrary ones, not dogmas, but real premises from which abstraction can only be made in the imagination. They are real individuals, their activity and the material conditions under which they live, both those which they find already existing and those produced by their activity. These premises can thus be verified in a purely empirical way. [12]

While he speaks of "individuals," he does not intend this to mean anything more than as a center of material activity.

The production of ideas, of conceptions, of consciousness, as at first directly interwoven with the material activity and the material intercourse of men, the language of real life. Conceiving, thinking, the mental intercourse of men, appears at this stage as the direct efflux of their material behavior. [13] Life is not determined by consciousness, but consciousness by life. [14]

The experience of ideality, thinking, then is reduced to a highly sophisticated organization of materiality. Ideality is not something uniquely itself but rather simply a special case of materiality. This view is shared by much 20th century social theory but cannot be supported by descriptive evidence. As the New Science reduced living experience, the realm of secondary qualities, to the dead reality of primary qualities, in conformity with the requirements of mathematical measurement, so too, with the social analysis of Marxism and contemporary sociological and psychological theory, the experience of ideality is reduced to the conditions of materiality. Circumstances that resist this conversion are deemed incidental. The prejudices of theory are to be maintained in the face of any evidence to the contrary. The fact that 1+1=2, as an instance of universal truth having nothing to do with materiality, is interpreted away according to materialistic theory with the claim that all truthfulness is but a neurological event in the brain without any merit as to universality. Great damage will be inflicted upon the innocent in the pursuit of this mistaken theory that reduces mentality to materiality. Scientific authority is invoked in favor of the economic efficiency that is possible when man is but *a piece of the machine*. Ironically, Marx's attempt to free the worker from the machines of the capitalist owners resulted in their being more securely enchained to the *workers' state*. When conceived of as a material component part of the machine, the worker is no longer free at all. He simply works.

In all matters involving people there exists an interplay between the individual and the social, between oneself and the larger domain of others. Each of course is absolutely essential to the possibility of human existence. An individual by himself would wither and die as would the social without the contributions of the individual, but, nonetheless, a central priority must be accorded the individual. The experience of scarcity and privation is a matter of the individual's *alone.* Hunger, pain, disease, and death are one's quite personal affair. The crispness of this is not diminished in the least by the fact that *everyone* experiences this identical reality. We may empathize to the fact of our mutually shared type of experience but the experience itself is ours alone. My laughing and crying is as essentially my own as yours is your own. Obviously, then, life can be lived only from the point of view of the individual. This is something that Marx did not fully understand. He felt confident that the social collective could carry the full weight of human existence. This is not to say that life is *only* a matter of the individual, as individuals must come together in order to share a world but, it is in the individual that the social process *begins* and this beginning is rooted in the mentality of thinking that becomes self-consciousness. This is the driving force that will transform material conditions into the Industrial Revolution. Marx took for granted this underlying reality. In the end he had neither use nor need for the individual, it being but a romantic illusion of Bourgeois culture. He was utilizing the physics of his time. The Law of Inertia assured that motion would continue unless otherwise acted upon.

Of course the difficult moment for natural science is to account for the *initial* move, the beginning of motion from a state of rest. But this beginning has never hindered science or Marx as once material forces have been set into motion then the laws of physical nature will apply. The historical momentum that was in place in the world, having been carried forward from feudalism to capitalism to eventual communism, was a force that could be accounted for simply as the impetus of material momentum. Thinking, so it was thought, was not necessary. Yet none of this historical materialism could have taken place without the mental inception that is the conception found in the thinking self-conscious individual. *There is no accounting for this* except as a divine dispensation, but this does not diminish its evidential fact. Something need not be denied validity simply because it cannot be accounted for according to the principles of mathematical physical science. Its absolute fact speaks volumes. *Furthermore,* Marx did not realize the importance of the *continued* force of inception in the momentum of a seemingly self-sufficient material necessity. The metaphor from the Law of Inertia comes apart as in social relations momentum is a matter of *maintenance* that again is possible only within the dynamic of the thinking of self-consciousness. Social momentum needs to be *carried forward* by succeeding generations of thinking individuals. The momentum of a thrown stone is not appropriate to an account of human affairs. Something once set into motion must be maintained at every step on the way. Famine, war, pestilence, religious slaughter, and natural disaster guarantees nothing as human beings must work to build and re-build, again and again, in order for the social to continue. The individual, with the power of inception, must be at the beginning and at every moment along the way. Simple momentum is not enough. The expanse of the industrial edifice had swollen to such a gigantic size that it seemed as if the individual were no longer necessary. This omission is the fatal flaw in the Teaching of Marx. Without the individual the notions of "mankind," "humanity," "society," and the like, are but mere ideas, verbal abstractions, without any reference to reality. Society would surely fail if left entirely to itself.

A crush of circumstances brought together the Teaching of Marx and the Russian Revolution of 1917. Discrepancies of theory and practice were evident from the start. Marx's theory involved the rise of the proletariat against capitalist owners. In Russia there were few proletarians as most people were peasants working the fields of a feudal aristocracy. The working class was insignificant. There was exploitation of peasants by landowners but a long standing tradition of deference to Church and State made the thought of revolution incomprehensible. The peasant could know nothing of this. He merely hoped for some betterment but was resigned to more of the same. Only a few intellectuals were thinking of an overthrown of power and their opportunity came with the collapse of the Russian army in World War I. Russia quit the war and brought revolution home. Lenin would make the situation conform to ideological theory. The Soviet Union would skip directly from feudalism to communism, not needing to pass through capitalism. A "Dictatorship of the Proletariat" was formed, a small group of activists who would take control of the revolution, depose the Tsar, eliminate the landed aristocracy, and take power absolutely in the name and on behalf of the proletariat. Millions of people were headed for grief. The Dictatorship replaced the Tsar at the center of power. This was not a revolution of the Left but rather a *transfer* of power on the Right. The principles of Tsarist Russia would be the same as that of the Soviet Union.

In Russian political life the unacknowledged parallels between tsarism and Stalinism are obvious to the objective observer. Centralization, autocracy, an official belief, police methods unrestrained by law, suspicion and repression of initiative independent of the state--all these have been the rule for old and new regimes alike. Russia's history generated the possibility, if not the necessity, of revolution, while the Russian political tradition invited recourse to old despotic tactics of the revolutionaries. Time and again during the development of the Soviet system from Lenin to Stalin, autocratic Russian experience set the line where doctrine failed to guide. [15]

The "revolutionaries" then were intent upon grabbing *power.* The long tradition of heavy handed tsarist rule had been borne by impoverished students and political riffraff in hovels and prisons throughout Russia. This "intelligentsia" had been denied livelihood and the privilege to which they felt entitled. With a rage and resentment they sought power. Marxism provided the ideological banner, rhetoric enlisted the masses, and Tsarist incompetence and world circumstances extended the opportunity. Revolution was successful and Marxism proclaimed in theory and discarded in practice. Lenin was the new Tsar. "...after smashing the unfinished structure of capitalism, the Bolsheviks found that their only institutional resource was the Russian tradition of centralized despotism." [16] Little would change except the degree of the savagery of the central Authority. The ideology of radical social reform was

146

buried in the debris left by the rush to power.

Marx then has his place in history. His social critique was powerful and proper. He was a man of his time who did not rise above the fray. His reputation is built upon revisions that left little of his original thought. He has come to represent for some all that is evil in the world and yet what is evil is evil itself and not a man who thought long and hard and finally proved to be fallible. As the social and political pendulum swings from one side to the other, from the Left to the Right and back again, Marxism represents a legitimate swing that perhaps served to lay the foundation for a possible balance at the middle, in-between, where the individual and the social are balanced in a harmony that sustains and nurtures both without cost to either. In the West a different road would be traveled towards the middle.

Social reform in 19th century Europe was possible as the economic base continued to expand. Reform had simply become affordable. It was no longer necessary to subject men, women, and children to economic depravation. Laws were enacted in England that limited abuse. The Factory and Mine Acts of the 1840s and the Ten Hour Law improved the quality of life. Revolutionary talk across the continent motivated industrialists to improve conditions *before* this talk motivated their workers to action. The social revolutionaries would be less attractive if the worker saw that greater reforms were possible *without* revolution. If the existing structure could reform itself from within there would be no need for the violence that would naturally follow with any armed struggle. By 1914 workers were protected across Europe. Laws covering workman's and unemployment compensation, health insurance, and retirement security were in place. The long standing polarity between capitalist and worker had been narrowed, as each came to recognize that their respective interests were better served by mutual cooperation. Differences of principle remained, but each was able to more clearly see their common interest.

Social reform in the United States witnessed bloodshed and division, as the industrialists refused to compromise their traditional privilege. For example, Andrew Carnegie, the self-promoting philanthropist, bought the steel works in Homestead near Pittsburgh. His first action was to increase the price that he received for his steel and the second was to decrease worker wages. His profit margins were to be improved. The blatant unfairness of this angered many. A strike was called at the Homestead mill with other mills in the area joining. In a battle with company security and hired guards, there was death and injury on both sides but the strike was crushed and the union broken. Carnegie power was maintained as the sides became entrenched, but finally the unions were too weak and easily put in their place.

At the turn of the century the Progressive Movement brought together people who were outraged by social conditions and the tactics of industry and who sought reform through legislation. A slate of reforms, similar to those already enacted in Europe, became law. Children and women were better protected and working conditions generally improved. Significant legislation was passed which placed responsibility for the injury and death of industrial accidents upon the owners. Often times as an initial condition of employment a worker was made to sign *in advance* holding the factory blameless for any possible accident. Of course little was then needed to be expended for machine and workplace safety as the dead and maimed were taken out and new live bodies brought in. The worker was employed at his own risk. The Progressives were able to enact legislation that held the owners responsible and therefore prone to encourage a safer workplace. Profits then would be greater only with a reduced loss of life and limb. Laws were passed limiting the length of the workday. Owners no longer had the right to work their employees to exhaustion. Great improvements were enacted by the Progressives but the primary difficulty remained that this social reform took place at the *state* rather than *federal* level. The various state courts were called upon to rule one way or another and since there was little legal precedence the owners generally won and reform stalled. Without *federal* legislation, without a law mandating for the entire country, reform was easily circumvented and subject to partial and uneven enactment. The Federal Government would not intervene as it remained it the tow of business. It would take a major crisis in order to force the President and Congress to act on the behalf of the majority of people.

In October of 1929 the stock market collapsed. Business and political leaders assured the nation that all was in good hands and that recovery would be forthcoming. Their optimism was exaggerated. By 1932 unemployment estimates ranged from 11 to 17 million. As people feared for the worst they quit spending and began hoarding, forcing production down further.

From the top of prosperity in 1929 to the bottom of depression in 1933, GNP dropped by a total of 29 percent, consumption expenditures by 18 percent, construction by 78 percent, and investment by an incredible 98 percent. [17]

Millions in the richest land in the world were going without. A generation would be reared on the experience of scarcity. The Conventional Wisdom of business and politics was being turned on its head, as its embrace of unfettered capitalism and governmental non-intervention was now perceived as being the essence of the problem itself.

The events of 1929 made an indelible imprint on the United States. Much of the faith that had been shown in markets, institutions, and politicians would quickly give way to skepticism and a longing for effective leadership. Bankers quickly moved from the pinnacle of public esteem to the bottom. Wall Street legends became symbols of avarice and greed, despised in all quarters. Those who once drew crowds of tourists on their way to work would soon lose those jobs after public inquiry into their affairs revealed corruption and a total lack of interest in public accountability. [18] ...the cold truth is that the individualistic creed of everybody for himself...is not applicable in an age of technology, science, and rationalized economy. [19] The bankruptcy of [Hoover's] leadership in the worst economic crisis in our history reveals the tragic failure of rugged individualism. [20]

Fundamental re-considerations were required. The underlying consensus of opinion had been shattered, as it became obvious that only the Federal Government had sufficient power and reach to begin to address the problems. The belief in a mystical "invisible hand" that guided society to its proper balance was discarded as millions looked to Washington for direction. Ironically, during this time of heightened scarcity and privation, there would be enacted the laws that would establish a new social consensus that would facilitate the more equitable distribution of wealth when better times returned. In meeting the immediate needs of millions, there was established a social policy of long term significance.

Franklin D. Roosevelt (1882-1945) was elected President in 1932. The Conventional Wisdom was put out of office and the new administration set to work. The first "Hundred Days" addressed itself to the immediate needs of the unemployed and hopeless. Relief payments and employment were authorized by FDR, something which the prior Hoover Administration had failed to do. The Civilian Conservation Corp (CCC) and the Works Progress Administration (WPA) set people to work. Money was put into the system that was immediately spent. The overall demand for goods and services increased. The Government was no longer to stand aside but would be at the center of economic affairs. The ineffectiveness and inefficiency of individual state powers was recognized as Federal powers broadened. The Private Sector was no longer to be left managing the affairs of the country, as the Public Sector came to predominance. Of course none of this was clear or certain at the time as the Roosevelt initiatives needed to be ruled upon by the Supreme Court. Principles of constitutionality may have been violated. But, significantly, precedent legislation was enacted and the idea of the *Public* gained in stature. The Securities and Exchange Commission (SEC) was established with the broad powers to regulate and oversee the financial markets. Unfair practices, such as insider trading and stock manipulations, things that were commonly thought to have caused the Depression, were now violations of Federal law and subject to SEC prosecution. The public interest had a defender. The Banking Act of 1935 gave greater powers to the Federal Reserve Board (FED) to regulate private banks so as to insure proper behavior. Through a more centralized control, the Federal Government would be able to more effectively regulate and manage economic activity. Great Depressions could perhaps occur no more.

The Social Security Act of 1935 would have a profound effect on society as a whole. Initially it provided some support for the aged, handicapped, and indigent but has since evolved into a general retirement program. It established a precedence and legitimacy for expanded governmental programs. Both business and the individual, employers and employees, would contribute as a middle ground emerged where most could see the mutually beneficial results. A social consensus was emerging in time for the beginning of the greatest economic expansion that the world had ever seen but the world itself was intent upon one last spasm of destruction and violence, World War II. The *idea of social welfare* gained ground and the collective American experience in the War further enhanced this idea as both the Homefront and the War front pulled together in order to defeat the then greatest affront to civilized society. Depression was overcome at home as tyranny was defeated abroad.

151

By the 1930s the Communists were fully in power in the Soviet Union as Stalin served as "Tsar." In "skipping" from feudalism to the industrialization that would be necessary for communism, Stalin extracted all surplus production from the peasants. With the "collectivization" of agriculture, tens of thousands died outright with millions succumbing to the ensuing famine. State sanctioned starvation was policy and the idea of social welfare was supplanted by totalitarian tyranny. The average Soviet citizen was caught between the sickle of famine and the hammer of the State Police and its Gulag. In Western Europe a similar deterioration of common decency occurred as the 1930s saw the political extension of the unresolved "peace" of World War I. The Versailles Treaty simply served as an interruption as the combatants dug in and hoped for a new war. The killing would be quickly renewed. Germany elevated and worshiped its strongman and the Fatherland would be served by and at the expense of others. At a time of a potential expansion of the economic base, where there would have a possible reduction and alleviation of scarcity, the world chose war.

Estimates place the worldwide dead at between 35 and 55 million, with an additional 70 to 110 million casualties. At the Nuremberg Trial of Nazi war criminals, the Soviet prosecutor listed his country's loses.

...Rudenko began a catalogue of the destruction the Nazis had wreaked in the East: ...1,710 cities and over 70,000 villages almost completely destroyed, 6 million buildings ruined, 31,850 industrial establishments, 40,000 hospitals, 84,000 schools and colleges, 43,000 libraries. He calculated that 25 million people were homeless. And they had starved: the Nazis had removed or slaughtered 7 million horses, 17 million head of cattle, 20 million pigs, 27 million sheep and goats, 110 million poultry. [21]

Some in the West had thought these claims exaggerated as the positioning for the Cold War began, but the agreed upon figure for Soviet war dead is 20,000,000. Encompassed in this number is an incomprehensible misery. Capitulation and geography provided the Nazis with the opportunity to inflict a carnage in the East which was not possible in the West. The French abdicated out of the war and the British suffered from only the German Luftwaffe. The savagery of the Nazi land war was thrown fully at the Soviets from the Baltic to the Black Sea. General statistics complete the story.

The cost to the belligerent governments for war materiel and armaments added up to US $1,154 billion. This represented an outlay of $120 billion for Britain, $317 billion for the United States, $192 billion for the Soviet Union, $94 billion for Italy, $272 billion for Germany, and lesser amounts for other nations. Official reports of expenditures did not include any allowance for damage to civilian property. In the Soviet Union this amounted to at least US $128 billion, in Britain to $5 billion. German losses were at least $50 billion to $75 billion...The British had a third of their homes destroyed or damaged. For the French, Belgians, and Dutch the figure approached 20%. Allied merchant shipping losses were 5,250 vessels with a tonnage of 21,570,000, of which 2,828 were victims of Axis submarines, mostly German. Poland reported 30 percent of all its building destroyed, 60 percent of its school and administration buildings, 43 percent of its art, 35 percent of its farms, and 32 percent of its mines. In 49 of Germany's largest cities, 39 percent of the homes were destroyed or seriously damaged. Central business districts were reduced to rubble. Transportation was disrupted throughout Europe by the destruction of rail centers, locomotives, and bridges. Harbor areas everywhere were subjected to especially heavy bombardment. Agriculture suffered heavily from the loss of manpower, animals, machinery, and facilities. [22]

Compiling a statistical list of the war's destruction is of course more easily done than providing an account of its cause. Any objective account would trace macro-economic and geo-political conditions as one nation is propelled against another but here the account is somewhat different. While these objective forces provide the material conditions for the execution of war, they do not in themselves account for its psychological motivation and subjective beginning.

Following in the lines that have been already drawn here, this beginning has its roots in the General Condition of Human Existence that is defined by the schism between the experience of scarcity and privation and that of ideality. The emotional alleviation that was found in the Religious Experience, in the Denial of living reality and the Substitution in its place of a "reality" that has been idealized through conceptual thinking in terms of the Theologies of Faith and Power, is also to be found in the political arrangement that is called Nationalism. In all of this, in these variations on a theme from religion, to capitalism, to nationalism, what is decisive is the *justification* for the denial of the goods of life to some in order that one's self-selected group is assured more. The history of this Ideology of Exclusion is long. The "Chosen People" assured themselves that they had a warrant from God to exclude the non-Jew, the Christian had a similar warrant from a similar God to exclude the non-Christian, and the "God" of the New Science, Nature, provided a warrant for the economic and political exclusions of capitalism. This legacy achieved its quintessential expression in Nationalism which is the dominant carrier of destruction in the 19th and 20th centuries. It was all natural enough. Linguistic and geographical tribes consolidate themselves as single entities of political and economic power. With power gravitating to the center, borders were established at the edge which established frontiers of military engagement. Special qualities were attributed to "The People" and the "soil" as the Homeland or Fatherland became the sole criterion of value. The Nation was born in the heat of the emotions of the fear and jealousy of one's neighbors. Domestic differences were made to defer to the greater good of a united front against rivals. Mobilization for war would be easily achieved in the mind's of those fearful of the outside. But, finally it was always a play for national gain at the expense of others. The foreign extension of Nationalism is the Colonialism that extracted raw materials and plantation labor from peoples unable to defend themselves. Technical and organizational superiority allowed the British, French, Germans, Spanish, Portuguese, Dutch, Belgian, and Americans to take what they could from the rest of the world but this could never be enough as they would need to square off against each other.

World Wars I and II returned home the colonial wars of exploitation. Each sought for themselves what they could get from others but finally the destruction was visited upon the Homefront. The variations are as endless as they are tedious. *Pax Britannica* or Greater England, *Napoleon* or French snobbery, *Deutschland uber Alles* or the Third Reich, (the American version will come later), are all political, economic, and military adventures of one Nation against another which delivers grief to millions.

Churchill was in Paris to lobby for "an army of one million on a compulsory basis" to send into Russia to fight the Bolsheviks. "I want to build up the nation," Churchill said, "with the gallant men who fought together. I want them to combine to form the basis of a great national effort. I want them to combine to make an even greater England." [23]

The full theory of Denial and Substitution as it is expressed in the ideology of nationalism is present in this statement. At the Treaty Conference to end World War I, Churchill is already contemplating a new campaign of destruction. The exhausted survivors of the army that had been slaughtered in the trenches of Western Europe are to be *forced*, "on a compulsory basis," to fight and die in another war with another nation, Russia. "A great national effort" is to be made so that

155

Churchill and his aristocratic brethren, who will not themselves be put in harm's way, may accumulate to themselves the power that will ensure "an even greater England." The island nation hopes to extract from others to their own advantage in the Name of God, King, and Nation. One's self-proclaimed nationalistic bias prejudices all to one's own advantage. The legitimate needs of others are *denied* value and *substituted* in place is the self-interest of the national tribe, now elevated to the highest priority.

With the Religious Experience, Denial and Substitution is divided into the Theologies of Faith and that of Power, with the many being emotionally alleviated by the one and the Few by the other. When the Nation takes the place of God as the central authority the individual is able to more readily participate and quickly gives his full loyalty and enthusiasm. The idealization of one's country achieves the greatest legitimacy and popular allegiance is easily given. The Nation of the here and now replaces the Heaven of the hereafter as one's belief becomes wrapped in the *flag* and *Leader*. The aspirations of the Nation are brought home to the citizens in the person of the leader who stands shrouded in the flag. The armies are ready to roll. The atrocities of Nazi Germany could not have been carried out without the active participation and complicity of millions of its people. In the rantings of the Fuhrer, in his assertions that the Germans were the Master Race, millions found an emotional alleviation that elevated them above their daily labor and encouraged them on carry out the orders of Holocaust. The Nation was to be served to the final degree. A consensus of alleviation was achieved that ensured the orderly passage of trains to Auschwitz.

World War II demonstrated the folly of nationalism but, at its conclusion, ironically, there was formed the United Nations. The Nation-State was to be retained, although in reality this was but a symbolic gesture as the world was reduced from many nations to but *two* powers. The United States and the Soviet Union squared off in a

Cold War, as all other nations were force to align and pick sides. New animosities were imagined and the world went to work building nuclear arsenals. The post war economic boom was to be squandered in yet another generation of self-interest and disregard for anything but the *national interest*. A re-consideration is necessary.

Part Three

The In-Between:

Transition and Opportunity

Chapter Seven
The In-Between: A Description

The single greatest cultural achievement of the power of mentality and of self-consciousness is the creation of the economic system that has produced the enormous material base that exists today. From the times of pre-historic existence, when gripped by the collective forces of hunger, thirst, cold, disease, and blind ignorance, to the present times of material abundance for millions, there has been an unimaginable transformation of human life. An economic structure has been put into place that is able to produce and distribute more and more fundamental goods and services to more and more people. The general level of material scarcity has been reduced. An increasing percentage of people throughout the world are more adequately housed and fed than at any other time in history. Greater numbers are living lives that are at a increased distance from the extremities of want. Millions in the West take this abundance for granted, not knowing anything else, but this wealth is being achieved throughout the world as well. Even though significant exceptions remain, for the most part, the entire world is moving to create a general abundance. The sciences of biology and medicine are reducing the aggregate amount of pain and suffering, and knowledge in general has reduced the level of ignorance as a whole.

None of this changes the absolute fact of death and the great mystery of existence itself but a *mental place*, if you will, has opened up where human beings can live their lives with less fear and anxiety. One can find a certain comfort that allows one to live a productive and "happy" life where the traditional desperation of immediate scarcity no longer holds as tightly. No longer needing to fight for immediate survival, one is instead allowed the opportunity to live at peace, assured that tomorrow's needs are already secured. With this in mind, a general observation is possible. If the great systems of emotional alleviation from the experience of scarcity, that of Judaism, Buddhism, Christianity, capitalism, communism, nationalism, and, as will be shown, romanticism, are one and all based upon the assumption of scarcity, and if that scarcity is no longer nearly as extreme, having been relatively reduced through modern scientific and technological innovation, *then* it becomes possible to experience the world with less natural anxiety, having been set free, as it were, from the machinery of denial and substitution and the ideologies of exclusion. What could this mean? What would the world look like to the individual if the assumption is no longer one of scarcity but rather of *abundance?*

Fundamentally, *it is possible to change one's attitude.* An entirely different perspective emerges as the urgency for emotional alleviation is no longer as acute. It is perhaps a little like the soldier who with the declaration of peace is finally able to emerge from his foxhole and take a look around, no longer fearing for his life. Of course in war when the shooting stops there is nothing less than absolute elation. But, in taking that look around, one ventures forth with confidence and joy, and rather than looking to exclude so as to grab survival one instead looks to *include* and share the happiness of the existence itself, pure and simple. The extreme polarities of the past can be set aside, the divisions between black and white, good and evil, God and the Devil, right and left, night and day, Jew and non-Jew, Christian and non-Christian, East and West, capitalism and

162

communism, love and hate. In acknowledging only black and white, the entire spectrum of color is not seen, interpreted away, as the overwhelming desire for emotional alleviation forces one simply not to see. But, of course, there is a middle ground, there are colors of the spectrum, human fallibility between God and the Devil, a place between right and left, God-fearing people other than the Jew or the Christian, interests other than that of the East and the West, a mutual benefit between capitalism and communism, and certainly, friendship and respect between love and hate. *The In-Between* is here the term which encompasses the general experience of this middle ground, this place were the emotions are at ease and one freely chooses to see for oneself the world as it is. The essential moment is to bear witness to the *pulse* of the world without needing to reduce it to the judgment of ideology. It is the hope of being fully oneself in a free regard to the spectacle of existence itself. A great difference is possible.

One begins in breathing. A simple exercise will do. Put out of mind for a moment all else and focus upon the fact of respiration. Find a quiet that allows for an undivided attention to the ebb and flow of air as it flushes one's inner being. Breathing deeply, in and out, one is able to narrow one's attention to oneself alone. Rather than being oriented to the outside one can re-orient oneself to oneself as such. There one can feel the inner tempo of one's life, a simple flow of time, the passage of the moment as ever new moments flit by. Time passes but the essential structure of time does not. The Now is always an ever new now yet remains exactly Now. Astoundingly, time is not an objective thing in the world but rather an expression of one's inner life itself. Time is not objective but rather subjective in origin. But this subjectivity of time is not an "I" or a "me" but rather simply itself. *Who* I am is of no concern with this exercise, simply *that* I am as an example of the possibility of this awareness of inner time. In all of this one becomes self-conscious, aware of oneself as to the possibility of full self-consciousness. It is here that one *thinks*, here

163

that one finds oneself as the condition for a life among others. This experience of inner time serves as the basis for any possible world with others. Even though this recourse to the experience of inner time is ours alone it is equally everybody else's alone as well. The seeming isolation of inner time immediately gives way to a community of others. One retains oneself in the community of other selves with the choice to return at any time again to that isolation of oneself. This is the basis for the possibility of personality among others. Society and its general institutions are possible only in the interaction of a free interchange between the subjectivity of oneself in inner time consciousness and the objectivity of the world that is the *place* where this interaction occurs. It is at the intersection of space and time, place and inner consciousness, that individual life becomes social. This special moment of self-awareness can quickly be engulfed in the affairs of the world as one returns to the business of one's life, but the opportunity is always present to return to oneself and take another look around, to renew the perspective of inner time consciousness as it lays at the foundation of the possibility of any world whatsoever. One can easily get "caught up" in the world and *most* easily when one relies on an *ideological* interpretation of the world to limit the possibilities of this recourse to inner life. When once fully convinced that such and such is the case, that all questions have been perfectly allayed, then the life of inner time consciousness can have no purpose. When ideologically convinced, there is no *need* to return *to oneself.* The wars of the world begin with the choice not to make this return. But the greater choice is to return and the experience is simply a miraculous event that serves to enhance existence as a whole.

A clarification of the obvious is necessary. Our personal existence must exist in a world that includes others, as pure isolation is only a fiction of the philosophers. Our natural social connection could be termed the "biographical situation." [1] One is born to parents at a particular place and time that situates one with respect to both the living and the dead. Implicit at any time and at any place is all of world history. One's inner life can be played out only in the context of others, the revelation of inner breathing must be consummated through the act of social participation. In sharing a world we must participate as builders. The positive force of one's own being needs to brought forth within the context of one's biographical placement among others. There are few the moments of personal clarity when this is seen to be absolutely true. In order to comprehend this one can simply do all that is necessary in order to see for oneself or, more directly, it can be witnessed in the eye's of one's own child, in the innocent being who is one's perfect responsibility. The child is the cause of one's greatest participation of oneself in the welfare of the world. There are no ideological supports here, one must see it for oneself. Without an emotional reliance upon ideas concerning an "afterlife," without concern for one's "personal salvation," it is possible to recognize the greatest positive force as that of being oneself in the free regard and responsibility towards others, here and now. We are not in this alone, and nothing could be more.

This awareness of oneself within the context of others creates a choice. Within the grasp of the prior scarcity, the world and everything about it was judged to be negative, in a word, evil. Striving for alleviation, it was necessary to *deny* that world of any natural meaning and value and then *substitute* in its place a fiction of an idealized world in the hereafter. Life and the living were depleted of positive value as only the afterlife and the dead could encompass the yearning for alleviation. All of this no longer need be the case. With the awareness of inner time, as the reality of oneself in living space, it is possible to accept the world as it is without recourse to anything negative and instead recognize that *the living* world is only of the highest value. This *Highest Good* can then become the benchmark of one's life. One can choose the Good and forever relinquish the selfish indulgence in the negative. It is simply the

165

absolute difference between something and nothing.

The recognition of the reality of the *In-Between* allows one to re-think what is involved in the "religious experience." The fire and brimstone, and clank and clutter, of denial and substitution, the violence and bloodshed of the ideologies of exclusion, and the chronic disruption of everyday life by religious division, can be set aside in favor of the personal awareness of the beauty and grandeur of the greater world. To recognize that we participate in this grander world, that realities and mysteries pace ahead of our ability to comprehend, that the morning light is a spectacle to which we are a witness, all of this can become the focus of our "religious belief." We need no longer brood over contending visions of Doom, no longer slaughter in killing fields of one assertion rather than another, no longer sulk in the fury of resentment and jealousy so that oneself and oneself alone attains a belief in one's personal salvation. Evil is simply all of this, the pursuit of emotional alleviation through the machinery of denial and substitution, the enforcement of ideologies of exclusion, *regardless* of the damage to anyone else. One seeks to serve only oneself. Any amount of violence and terror to others then has already been sanctioned and sanctified by the God of one's choice.

The Religious Experience in respect to the recognition of the In-Between is something entirely different. It recognizes life for its own sake as the highest value. It understands in the passage of time the very condition of existence and is no longer entranced by the spectacle of salvation and the eternity of immortality. A hard lesson is at hand. Life is not horrible and meaningless because we die, but rather it is only because of death that life has any meaning at all. The highest reality is not the idea of living forever through a personal salvation, but rather the experience of having *ever* existed at all in the full self-conscious awareness of inner life. The slightest glimpse of this personal awareness is infinitely greater than the possibility of any eternity. The "religious experience" is the revelation that in every moment of life there is expressed the divinity of all of existence. It is for each of us to see for ourselves as to whether or not this is true.

It is now possible to turn to the experience of the world as it presents itself in the full meaning of this divinity, those moments of perfect self-consciousness when we see ourselves in truth undivided, when all pretense is set aside and one is face to face with oneself.

You can't run a place like this, which is all about endings, and ignore the religious thing, whatever you think personally. Generally speaking, most of our residents belong to religions which have strict disciplines which they have never observed. That puts it in a nutshell. They are particular about being registered Baptist, Roman Catholic, C. of E., etc., but that is about all. Or Moslem--we have them now. The minority who observe the disciplines do have a different kind of old age. At the same time--and I have always marveled about this-- because I have always thought that these practising religious people would be anxious to have a minister or a priest with them when they knew they were dying, I am surprised when, somehow, nobody ever asks. I say this who see death as a part of the day's work. *Nobody* has ever said to me on their deathbed, "Send for a priest or minister"--not even the Catholics. I do it. I do it myself. A word, a prayer, a look, a touch. What the old person seems to be asking to be done, I always do. Whatever it is. I have learnt all this through my work in hospitals as well as with the aged. In hospital we would say, "Would you like to see So-and-so?" And they would say yes and no--usually no. No, thank you. Thank you, thank you, the dying say. It means, "Don't say any more, don't ask me anything more, I'm sorry I'm bothering you, don't question me, let me be now." Something like that. "Thank you, dear." Very old Christians get beyond the ministry. Whatever it is they've got to have at the end, it is waiting to be found inside them. Just before they die the old ones seem to understand that they are "beyond all this." They are lying there, breathing and listening, and sometimes talking, but only out of a kind of politeness, you feel! Just being as mortal as possible until the end, so as not to upset anyone, but quite uninterested in it. [2]

On the threshold of death, none of the ideologies of life can any longer matter, one perhaps sees clearly for the first time. Whatever it is it is "waiting to be found inside them." At the limit of life there is no fear of mortality but only a recognition of oneself in a moment of time, a letting go that is rightful and proper.

The greatest reality of human existence then is the experience of time and any account of human reality must begin *In-Between* the inner time of oneself and the objective time of the world. At this interface *our* world become possible. The momentary present of the In-Between can be likened to the flight of the eagle. With perfect ease, the great bird glides upward carried higher by the unseen thermal, banking slightly it hangs *momentarily,* poised for the downward continuation. The slight hesitation, the brief cessation of movement, is the moment that is the Now of the In-Between. This is not a mathematical point but rather an experienced bit of "distension."It is the suspended motion that is not quite fully halted, as the continuity of passage is never lost. The Now is simply the moment of the living. The contrast is stark. A dead and stuffed bird in the very same profile of flight is still dead and stuffed. The transition from the attitude of denial and substitution to that of the In-Between involves the heightened appreciation of the life of movement , the process of existing, the becoming of the world, and the relinquishing of the need to fix into place, to reduce to set ideological formulas, the reality of one's world.

...we must cast away the habits of exile--the self-contempt, the illusion of alienation, the hatred of the past, the sterile existentialism, the fear of the future, the willful imposition of meaninglessness on a universe bursting with meaning. [3]

If choosing to free oneself from the ideological shackles of denial and substitution, if no longer judging from the perspective of one's desire for personal salvation, then it is possible to see *life* in its own terms, as it is. If no longer driven by the anxiety of scarcity and privation, it is possible to look again. What is to be seen? There is the miracle of birth and the mystery of death, the glory of motherhood and the pride of fatherhood, the satisfaction of work and the joy of play, the magnitude of rivers and the grandeur of mountains, the revelation of dawn and the quietude of dusk, the cheer of music and the rhythm of dance, the color of flowers and the flight of eagles, the compassion of friendship and the friendship of compassion, the gaiety of laughing and the anguish of crying, the expanse of oceans and the infinity of the heavens, and the magic of touching and the perfection of embracing. These are the realities of life with which we all participate. There may be temperamental differences of preference, one preferring one thing or another, but the fact remains that the essential structure of life is encompassed in realities of this sort. While as individuals there is the tendency to accent the differences, the fundamental fact remains that we necessarily and absolutely *share* this structure. The greater reality is not that we can find difference but rather that at the center of our being there is this essential sameness. We are different only to the extent that we are already the same. A spectrum of perspectives suggest themselves.

A description from nature expresses this interplay between difference and sameness.

Whether plant or animal, small or large, no living organism can function as an independent, separate entity. To live implies not only utilizing available resources but also being shaped by them, modifying them and thereby achieving a state of intimate integration with the total environment. Living organisms can be understood only when they are considered as part of the system within which they function. This is particularly true of us human beings because all aspects of our lives are profoundly influenced by an immense

169

diversity of physical and cultural forces which shape our bodies, our behaviors and the social structures to which we must relate in order to become fully human. [4]

Variations upon this theme of difference and sameness, as an integrated whole, have been expressed throughout the world. The following examples are taken from the regions of music, motherhood, nature, the expectation of death, and friendship and compassion.

The playing of music requires precisely constructed instruments.

The modern grand action is a marvelously complicated device, a contraption of wood, felt, leather, spring wire, and small bits of metal that must accomplish a bewildering variety of functions simultaneously. First, it must multiply the motion of the key in both speed and distance: the hammer must move farther and faster than the key does. Second, the hammer will not remain pressed against the strings if the key remains depressed--thus muffling the sound it has created--the hammer must be thrown free from the rest of the action, so that it travels independently over the last fraction of its path and rebounds immediately after striking the strings. Third, the hammer must not bounce back up to the strings with its momentum; the action must catch and hold it as it makes its downward arc. Fourth, because the player will want to restrike a note without waiting for the key to come back up, or without having to lift his finger entirely off the key, the part that propels the hammer must return to its original position, ready to strike again, while the hammer itself and the rest of the action are still in motion. Meanwhile, the damper that has been sitting over the strings, preventing them from vibrating in sympathy, with other notes, must be lifted so the strings can sound cleanly, and must fall back promptly to cut off the sound when the key is released-- unless the player *wants* the sound to continue after the key has been released, an eventually that must also be taken into account. Finally, of course, the action must do all this without making the slightest sound of its own. [5]

The array of differences that are brought together into a single harmony is a technical masterpiece and the result is a symphony of sound.

This technical virtuosity is one thing but the music itself is another, as it resounds at the center of our being.

There is something marvelous in music. I might almost say it is, in itself, a marvel. Its position is somewhere between the region of thought and that of phenomenon; a glimmering medium between mind and matter, related to both and yet differing from either. Spiritual, and yet requiring rhythm; material, and yet independent of space. [6]

Music is the mediator between the spiritual and the sensual life. Although the spirit be not master of that which it creates through music, yet it is blessed in this creation, which, like every creation of art, is mightier than the artist. [7]

Music is the harmonious voice of creation; an echo of the invisible world; one note of the divine concord which the entire universe is destined one day to sound. [8]

Simply, the reality of music is the quintessential expression of the harmony, balance, and inclusion of the *In-Between*.

Childbirth and the miracle of procreation is universally the same in all of its difference.

The subject of birth has, inevitably, its own compelling attraction. No one who has given birth or witnessed it ever quite forgets. Mothers relive it secretly, or reflect on their own experience among each other for many years afterwards. For a story that is, essentially, always the same--the long preparation of pregnancy, the varied time of labor accompanied by varying degrees of pain, the arrival of the child--the essence is always new, always dramatic. The drama stems partly, I think, from an almost inescapable wonder at life, and partly, as with death, from the sheer irreversibility of things. I remember after the birth of one of my children a moment of uncontrollable laughter at the thought of how hopelessly final it all was. This baby who had been provided for so involuntarily inside me was now outside, forcing me into responsibility. Nothing was automatic anymore. Never mind, I told myself--it was the same for Cleopatra, for Marie de Medici, for Anna Magdalena Bach and Sophia Tolstoy and Sophia Loren and-- Eve. [9]

A black woman witnesses this universal from a special perspective.

To me, having a baby inside of me is the only time I'm really alive. I know I can make something, do something, no matter what color my skin is, and what names people call me. When the baby gets born I see him, and he's full of life, or she is; and I think to myself that it doesn't make any difference what happens later, at least now we've got a chance, or the baby does. You can see the little one grow and get larger and start doing things, and you feel there must be some hope, some chance that things will get better; because there it is, right before you, a real, live, growing baby. The children and their father feel it, too, just like I do. They feel the baby as a good sign, or at least he's *some* sign. If we didn't have that, what would be the difference from death? [10]

Evident here is a world without extremes, without accusation, without selfishness and instead the realization that there is a natural goodness about our lives that must be affirmed and nurtured. But across the land there is a similar insight as the theater of nature stages its unending drama.

Wisconsin. Marshland Elegy. A dawn wind stirs on the great marsh. With almost imperceptible slowness it rolls a bank of fog across the wide morass. Like a white ghost of a glacier the mists advance, riding over phalanxes of tamarack, sliding across the bogmeadows heavy with dew. A single silence hangs from horizon to horizon. Out of some far recess of the sky a tinkling of little bells falls soft upon the

172

listening land. Then again silence. Now comes the baying of some sweet-throated hound, soon the clamor of a responding pack. Then a far clear blast of hunting horns, out of the sky into the fog. High horns, low horns, silence, and finally a pandemonium of trumpets, rattles, croaks, and cries that almost shakes the bog with its nearness, but without yet disclosing whence it comes. At last a glint of sun reveals the approach of a great echelon of birds. On motionless wing they emerge from the lifting mists, sweep a final arc of sky, and settle in clangorous descending spirals to their feeding grounds. A new day has begun on the crane marsh. [11]

The naturalist John Muir speaks of the land of the Sequoia.

The creek is very clear and beautiful, gliding through tangles of shrubs and flowerbeds, gay bee and butterfly pastures, the grove's own stream, pure Sequoia water, flowing all the year, every drop filtered through moss and leaves and the myriad spongy rootlets of the giant trees. One of the most interesting features of the grove is a small waterfall with a flowery, ferny, clear brimming pool at the foot of it. How cheerily it sings the songs of the wilderness, and how sweet its tones! You seem to taste as well as hear them, while only the subdued roar of the river in the deep canon reaches up into the grove, sounding like the sea and the winds. So charming a fall and pool in the heart of so glorious a forest good pagans would have consecrated to some lovely nymph. [12]

Here there is a natural poetry when *things are allowed to speak for themselves*, when the gush of existence is allowed its rightful cadence. With the strident rhetoric of the theologies of faith and power, when the threat of violence ensures that only the loudest will be heard, there is lost all respect and consideration that makes us fully human in the best sense. We pay a heavy price for wanting to get our own way. But, of course, it is our perfect choice to be otherwise.

Across an abyss of emotion is to be found a similar insight and revelation of life when freed from extremes.

173

This young woman knew that she would die in the next few days. But when I talked to her she was cheerful in spite of this knowledge. "I am grateful that fate has hit me so hard," she told me. "In my former life I was spoiled and did not take spiritual accomplishments seriously." Pointing through the window of the hut, she said, "This tree here is the only friend I have in my loneliness." Through that window she could see just one branch of a chestnut tree, and on the branch were two blossoms. "I often talk to this tree," she said to me...I asked her if the tree replied. "Yes," What did it say to her. She answered, "It said to me, 'I am here--I am here--I am life, eternal life.'" [13]

In the horror of the German camps of the Holocaust, this woman chose to find within herself a place of sanctity and a moment of inner truth which understood that *regardless* of her own pending doom existence itself, the fact of the world and all its beings, was an undiminished good. There would be no regrets on her account. The Nazis could crush the body but *they could not touch the spirit*.

In friendship and compassion the spirit of one touches the spirit of another. Again the horrors of the camp provide the occasion.

We who lived in concentration camps can remember the men who walked through the huts comforting others, giving away their last piece of bread. They may have been few in number, but they offer sufficient proof that everything can be taken from a man but one thing: the last of human freedoms--to choose one's attitude in any given set of circumstances, to choose one's own way. [14]

Respect and consideration for others is our choice at any time, it is ours to either affirm or not, absolutely.

...the mental reactions of the inmates of a concentration camp must seem more to us than the mere expression of certain physical and sociological conditions. Even though conditions such as lack of sleep, insufficient food and various mental stresses may suggest that the inmates were bound to react in certain ways, in the final analysis it becomes clear that the sort of person the prisoner became was the result of an inner decision, and not the result of camp influences. Fundamentally, therefore, any man can, even under such circumstances, decide what shall become of him--mentally and spiritually. He may retain his human dignity even in a concentration camp. Dostoevski said once, "There is only one thing that I dread: not to be worthy of my sufferings." These words frequently came to my mind after I became acquainted with those martyrs whose behavior in camp, whose suffering and death, bore witness to the fact that the last inner freedom cannot be lost. It can be said that they were worthy of their sufferings; the way they bore their suffering was a genuine inner achievement. It is this spiritual freedom--which cannot be taken away--that makes life meaningful and purposeful. [15]

It is the inner resolve of the person, the strength of self-consciousness to see and act on one's own behalf, and to bear the full consequences. It is the simple choice between the negative and the positive, between groping for an excuse and affirming one's responsibility. At every moment of life, this is the single issue of merit. The virtue here is as heavy as it is light, as difficult as it is the greatest thing of all.

Without the mental and spiritual blinders of denial and substitution, without the prejudice and violence of the theologies of faith and power, without the emotional urgency to see only one's own advantage, without the whole range of attitude that hopes to deny the world as it is and to substitute in its place something else, without all of this, the world is simply *there*. There as the "harmonious voice" that is music, there as the "inescapable wonder" and "sheer irreversibility" of motherhood, there as the "new day on the crane marsh" and the "clear brimming pool" of wilderness undisturbed, there as the "I am here" and the "blossoming now" at the edge of death, and there as "comforting others" and a "last inner freedom" at the center of the unspeakable. The being of the world and the reality

175

of our existence will speak for itself, if we only have the humility and courage to listen.

The recognition of the In-between is at the same time an appreciation of the "religious experience," but now freed of the ideological weight of denial and substitution, now with an entirely different focus of attention. It is possible to recognize divinity in all of the world, in every aspect of existence there is a presence that announces a higher spirituality. There must be a higher force, a supreme being, who accounts for all that is, but matters must be left there. We must simply bear witness and leave it at that. To expect a personal salvation, a personal savior, in order to secure oneself against mortality, cannot be the issue here, as that is the surest road to Hell. Rather it is just to see ourselves from the perspective of existence as a whole and to embrace the privilege of our thorough participation. *That* and that alone can concern us here. We must be enlightened to see things in the proper light of day and to recognize the limits of our own being at the threshold of infinity. One's contemplation of this simple revelation is the consummating insight of one's whole being. From here it is only to *look to the Good*.

An unnatural philosophical distinction now makes its divisive and contentious appearance. Natural experience and common sense assures us that the reality of human life is based upon a material and objective foundation. This is obvious enough and few would think to suggest otherwise. The traditional success of both religion and natural science is based upon the assumption of this objective reality, as God and then Nature are taken as being these first causes. All religious belief naturally defers to this objectivity and the high esteem accorded to natural science is based upon the recognition that mathematical physics is the proper tool in which to measure the physical world and that measurement is taken as being the same as "knowing." This objective reality then is the basis of all else and this is unquestionably true. But, astonishingly, this notion is not only not true, it is the greatest falsehood and prejudice that obstructs the way to a clear understanding of both ourselves and the problems of our world. Millions over the course of millennia have stumbled into bloodshed and agony because of this prejudice. In philosophical terms, it is the war between "idealism" and "realism." Two examples will serve to illustrate this most difficult piece of understanding.

Power in the world has traditionally been understood as being essentially military power, which is organized coercion that dominates the physical body. It is the placing of a "hand" upon another without their consent, it is the inflicting of injury and death in the struggle for tribal supremacy. In the 19th and 20th centuries world leadership has gone to those with the greatest ability to coerce the greatest number. The possibility and threat of this force served as the basis for all relationships. All political, economic, and cultural concerns were but variations upon the single theme of physical domination. Colonialism is an example here as the distant power imposes its demands upon a foreign people. In the name of God and Country, the colonial plantation was set to work for the benefit of the homeland. Military power enforced the extortion. But the situation of the moment is that the world can no longer *afford* the luxury of such an imposition and that force is now met with equal force and that only mutual destruction can be the result. Organized military power has finally run up against its natural limitation, its use is no longer just death to others but death to oneself, as murder and suicide can no longer be distinguished. It is all the same.

There is only one alternative. Rather than relying upon the imposition of force, it is necessary to see that only a consensus of mutually beneficial intentions can save us from our self inflicted destruction. This is possible only as an expression of a mental state of affairs that recognizes the ideal nature of all such intentions. Physical force is the failure of self-consciousness and it is our responsibility to transform that failure into a world of cooperation.

This is the ideality that must be recognized as the basis for reality and not the presumed reality of traditional military power. Mental consensus of the ideal rather than the physical coercion of the real will be seen as the proper basis for all relationships of the global community.

A second example says the same. Economic relations concern the organization of work for the purposes of the production of the goods that are necessary for human life. Work in the form of slavery defines one end of the spectrum where production is extorted and coerced. The threat of physical harm is imposed in order to motivate the slave to work on someone else's behalf. Lesser degrees of this slavery exist today in the form of a workplace that intimidates its workers and will motivate only on this side of the negative. Mutual benefit is not possible as the employer takes all the credit and the employee gets all the blame. Working in conditions of fear enchains the worker to a place of labor without merit for himself. It has been proven time and again that the most inefficient form of economic production is slavery. The worker works poorly and is intent upon sabotage. The "overseer" or supervisor is lost to any productivity as he must be concerned only with watching his workers. He cannot trust them to do much on their own. The worker and his watcher have little incentive to anything other than watch each other. Little can be done in this workplace of physical intimidation and mutual mistrust. But this is often the way of the world as the priority of the real convinces that nothing else is possible. At the other end of the spectrum is "free labor" or the entrepreneurial spirit. This is when one works for oneself in the free and positive regard for oneself and others where there is established the conditions for the greatest productive effort in terms of both quantity and quality. When work is done from the perspective of mutual benefit nothing is lost to either refusal or sabotage. Quite obviously, this is to be achieved only as a consensus of understanding, as a matter of a mental state of affairs

178

affirming its natural priority. The traditional attitude of extortion, the getting something for nothing, must be seen as the liability that it is, as the case when the "real" debilitates the "ideal."

These two examples together share a general truth. It is not the real and the material but rather the ideal and the mental that allows for the possibility of human reality. It is not real things but rather ideal relations, that are based upon the power of thinking, of seeing, remembering, seeing, comparing, and imagining, and seeing again, that forms the basis of all that is meaningful to us as human beings.

In this war between realism and idealism, a single mis-understanding bolsters the bias towards realism. Looking at the idealist position, the realist assumes that the matter, or "stuff," of the physical universe, the real, must also have been caused by the ideal. This is, obviously, a position that cannot stand. Common sense and scientific doctrine together would naturally refute such a claim. In the immediate euphoria of the discovery of the "I think therefore I am" some philosophers were led to believe that the *absolute* idealist's position was true and that the physical world *really* was but an extension of the ideal but finally this cannot be and the theory was set aside. But a different formulation of the question gets more to the point. To say that the ideal has priority over the real is simply to say that with respect to *the conditions for the possibility of human existence* such is necessarily true but this does not then presume that the physical universe itself is equally a result of a mental state of affairs. The "world" that human beings occupy is distinct from the world of the physical universe itself. The world of human beings is a *constituted* world, an ideal edifice, that has been built up through the agency of mental life. Physical nature is not the absolute cause but rather an attending condition. *Idealism then is the only position that makes any sense.*

The realist has another very different problem. He cannot account for himself. The realist as a thinking thing cannot account for the reality of his own thinking. The scientific materialist theory has no place for the possibility of that theorizing. The physicist can account for the universe but he cannot account for his thinking about the universe, and *that it a problem*. Of course it is a problem that is just ignored and left to itself.

It may be necessary to seek a deeper clarification of the exercise that began in breathing. When the focus upon one's respiration served to isolate the experience of one's own existence, putting out of play for the time being one's natural orientation to the objective world, an experience of an entirely novel kind comes into view. What is most difficult here is to distinguish between the experience of the fact of one's *own* existence and the ideal possibility of that existence as *an example of a more general experience*, that is without any reference to a real self. Step by step, a regression leads the way. Initially, one is directed *towards the things* that make up the natural and objective world. Then one is directed to the *experiencing* of that world, to the conscious awareness of that world. One enters the dimension of *thinking about thinking* that is essentially an awareness of the inner temporality of one's own self-consciousness. The next step is to set aside all qualifications of the individual self and to be directed instead to thinking as such, as an ideal state of affairs that is prior to the possibility of any experience whatsoever. One has entered into a *transcendental* domain[16] where there exists only the universal structures of consciousness pure and simple. This is a "place" where there can exist nothing that is "real" but only the ideal conditions for the possibility of any experience whatsoever. It is from here, upon this transcendental condition, that our world as human beings is for the first time possible. It is from here that our world becomes *constituted*. This cannot be measured by natural science, as it is the place where the thought of all possible measurement must begin. This is the place where our thinking has absolutely nothing to do with ourselves as real human beings. This transcendental dimension serves as the essential common denominator of all that will *subsequently* constitute human reality. This common dimension is what allows for the possibility of any experience whatsoever and is what binds us together as essentially human. This is the source that allows for the self-awareness that extends a free choice to the possibility of constitution and building. It is the formal standard which makes understandable all conceivable differences. Without this we would be lost to ourselves in the eternal night of the merely real.

The In-between then is constituted by the ideality of consciousness and its ability to think which affirms itself within the context of the world as a whole. The real by itself must remain the speechless stone that it always already is. Any material theory simply cannot account for the full range of human experience, and it is only this idealism that is able to provide a description and account of human reality. What this means for the individual in his own life is everything. It allows for the possibility of both self-consciousness and *self-responsibility,* and it is with this that the great matters concerning social life can be addressed.

Chapter Eight
Abundance and Self-Responsibility

Self-consciousness and thinking achieves its greatest power within the reality of the In-Between and this has the deepest consequences for the individual. It is only the individual who can see and then refuse to become involved in the violence of denial and substitution. It is only the individual who is able to look at the world anew and choose differently. It is only through the agency of oneself that self-responsibility is possible. And, it only through the individual that the forces are let loose in the world that produce the possibility of general abundance. Yet, given the overwhelming growth of the gigantic institutions that structure our lives, institutions that form a global network of power and influence, that simply dwarf any single individual's ability to comprehend, it is difficult to imagine any place for the individual at all.

This suggestion of the centrality of the individual would be rejected out of hand as mere story telling, a sort of idle chatter, by those convinced of the "macro" economic realities of the modern world. To think that the individual would be of any significance in a system that involves billions of people and trillions of dollars is sheer madness, yet the claim here is that that is exactly the case. *Still,* notwithstanding this size, it is the thinking person who remains the

183

underlying dynamic force. It is still the direction of individuals that makes all of the difference as institutions become even larger. There remains the *executive* force that must be present for the whole to function. *Accordingly,* the question as to the possibility for real change is a question that lies with the person, as institutions that have been built by human beings can equally be *re-built* by human beings. Inherent to constitution is re-constitution. It is the question as to whether we can intervene to help ourselves as we look at the problems of the world or are we "fated" to let those problems run apace and dictate their rather dreadful consequences.

This does not diminish the magnitude of the problems but we must decide if we are equal to the task of dealing with them on the terms of positive long term resolutions. What are we to do in the face of difficulties that threaten the world itself? The choice here is to act and to act decisively. This may be deemed idealistic pap by some but it is the only view that includes something constructive, as all else simply concedes to the blind inertia of institutional demise. But the choice here is possible only on the strength of material abundance. A re-statement is necessary in light of the massive gains after World War II.

This abundance has set into place the condition for the possibility of re-thinking all of our systems of interaction, from religion and capitalism, to natural science and communism, and this requires a change in attitude and perspective. R. Buckminster Fuller (1895-1985) was a thinker who took upon himself the challenge of such a re-thinking. He saw the need to change attitudes to be in balance with an emerging abundance.

Those in power politically and economically as of 1980 are as yet convinced that our planet Earth has nowhere enough life support for all humanity. All books on economics have only one basic tenet--the fundamental scarcity of life support. The supreme political and economic powers as yet assume that it has to be either you *or* me. [1]

Neither the great political and financial power structures of the world, nor the specialization-blinded professionals, nor the population in general realize that sum-totally the omni-engineering-integratable, invisible revolution in the metallurgical, chemical, and electronic arts now makes it possible to do so much more with ever fewer pounds and volumes of material, ergs of energy, and seconds of time per given technological function that it is now highly feasible to take care of everyone on Earth at a "higher standard of living than any have ever known." It no longer has to be you or me. Selfishness is unnecessary and henceforth unrationalizable as mandated by survival. War is obsolete. [2]

The realization of the power of initiative and effort, as contained within the dimension of self-consciousness and thinking, as that is expressed in the mental edifices of science and technology, has made it possible that so much more can be gotten from so much less. The long history of scarcity and the wars of possession could have come to an end. Material abundance for all is possible if we only quit with the ideologies of scarcity and recognize that cooperative effort is now the only proper course. But these old habits will certainly be difficult to overcome as entrenched interests need to affirm their privileges but, for the world as a whole, the alternative is obvious.

Bureaucracies will panic because all the great political, religious, and--most of all--big-business systems would find their activities devastated by the universal success of all humanity. All the strengths of all great politics and religion and most business are derived from the promises they give of assuaging humanity's seemingly tragic dilemma of existing in an unalterable state of fundamental inadequacy of life support. [3]

Institutional power has always defended its self-interest, but a new possibility is emerging that may change this attitude. When there is nothing but scarcity, that power constricts to its own advantage and perhaps rightfully so, but with imminent abundance perhaps it is conceivable to think it is now *affordable* to break with the past. Business could facilitate abundance rather than control scarcity. Past behavior is no guide but it is possible. But, before moving forward, it is again necessary to go back, back to the thinking self. Fuller describes his method that recalls the revolution of Descartes.

I sought to do my own thinking, confining it to only experientially gained information, and with the products of my own thinking and intuition to articulate my own innate motivational integrity instead of trying to accommodate everyone else's opinions, credos, educational theories, romances, and mores, as I had in my earlier life. I sought to accomplish whatever was to be accomplished for anyone in such a manner that the advantage attained for anyone would never be secured at the cost of another or others. [4]

In this way his method was simply that he could think for himself, take the long rather than the short view, and see the common rather than the special interest.

Fuller's conclusion could be summarize in a word as being *de-centralization*. Assuming scarcity, the institutions of power have profited from the creation of additional *artificial* scarcities. The centralization of power served to create added wealth but then coveted it for its own advantage. But this will no longer do, as these manufactured shortages threaten the world itself. We no longer have the luxury to give so excessively to the Few and to take from the many. We can no longer afford to leave the woes of the many unattended, as the ensuing negative consequences will affect the entire world. It will no longer be possible to isolate misery as it will be delivered to rich and poor alike. *We are in this together*. Acid rain destroys indiscriminately. Polluted air is breathed by all alike. Social strife will tear at the underlying structures of society that support all equally. Violence in the streets will disrupt global financial markets everywhere. It will no longer do to ignore this interdependence and to pretend otherwise. Luck cannot be a factor here. It is a conscious decision to act responsibly in the face of these difficulties but it is our very nature to do so if we only have the *courage*.

General statistics document the obvious. In 1870 the Gross National Product (GNP) of the United States was 7.4 billion. By 1910 it was 35.3 billion. In 1940 it was 99.7 and 977.1 in 1970. By 1986 it was 4,235 billion.[5] GNP had increased by 572 times while population increased by 4.8 times. Per capita income increased from $148 per year to $17,645, or 119 times greater. Another basic indicator of expansion is electrical production which has grown from 5,969 million kilowatt hours in 1902 to 1,639,771 in 1970.[6] All of these aggregate statistics can be represented by the curve of compound interest, the magical progression of accumulating growth. This simplest of curves illustrates with a single glance the opportunity that now exists for the first time. After millennia of mere survival, when there was little possibility to build and accumulate, the point has now been reached when the very opposite is true. The flat line of the past is about to accelerate into the curved line of the future. But there are no guarantees here, as the upward line could flatten again and accelerate into a new scarcity. Our opportunity could have been missed. The high road to abundance could veer onto the low road of a squandered opportunity and civil war.

John Templeton is a futurist who is optimistic.

In 1912 North America had no color film...no refrigerators...no radios...no transcontinental telephones...no fluorescent lighting...no traffic lights...no talking pictures...no plastics...no man-made fibers...Even after the great boom of 1929 there were still no airlines...no Xeroxes...no telefax...no sports broadcasts...no antibiotics...no nylon...no frozen food....no television...no transistors...no lasers...no genetic engineering...no nuclear energy...no

187

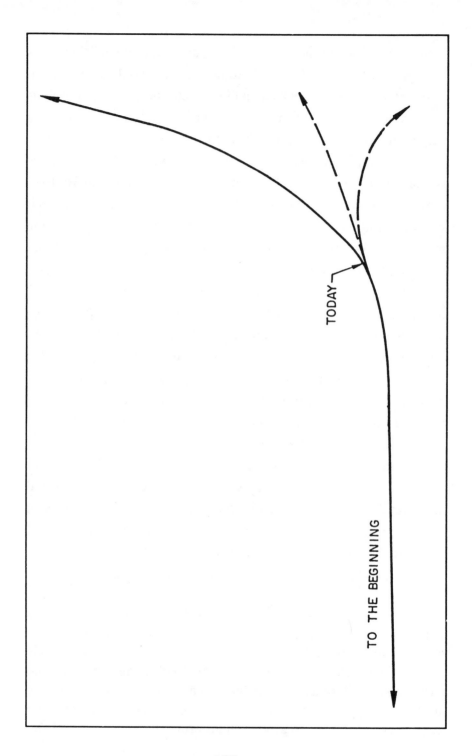

TODAY

TO THE BEGINNING

man-made satellites in space...The people of the world now benefit from using more than a hundred times as much electricity as they did a century ago. Through scientific development enormous improvements have been made in the quality of vegetables and crops and also in the quantity produced on each acre of farmland. Indeed, 50% of all discoveries in natural science have been made in this century. In North America alone more than $160 billion was dedicated to research and development last year. That is more in one year than the total expended on scientific research in all the world's history before my lifetime. Another reason I am optimistic about the future is the steady development in management skills and tools. When I was born there were only two graduate schools of business. Now there are 600 in the U.S. and about 800 worldwide. Life expectancy has doubled in the past two centuries in North America and possibly also worldwide. No longer is humanity terrorized by leprosy, small pox, or a number of other diseases once fatalistically accepted. The number of people in the world who will enjoy the benefit of pensions when they retire is more than a hundred times what it was a century ago. In the past 20 years a smaller fraction of the world's people have died of starvation than in any previous 20-year period. One person starving is too many. But for the first time in world history there are more people suffering from eating too much than from eating too little. The list could go on. The point is that when I was born no one could imagine the variety of blessings that may be in store for our children and grandchildren. [7]

With the continuation of present trends, from 1989 to 2029 the Standard of Living will increase by 4 times, the Cost of Living by 16 times, and the GNP by 64 times. Simply, we are on the threshold of an unimaginable increase in wealth that is possible only if it is shared. Mr. Templeton speaks in a way uncharacteristic of finance.

The laws of love and charity differ from the laws of mathematics. The more we give away, the more we have left. Love hoarded dwindles, but love given grows. If we give all our love, we will have more left than he who saves some. Giving love, not receiving, we automatically

189

and inescapably receive abundantly. [8]

Love hoarded dwindles. Here is a lesson for all that applies in every way. Of course it is for each of us our own responsibility to see this and then to act accordingly. It is for each of us to see the possibility of replacing all ideologies of exclusion with the realization of inclusion. Relinquishing the urgency to serve only ourselves it is possible to adopt the attitude of love about which Mr. Templeton speaks. Centralization and scarcity would be replaced by de-centralization and abundance. It is necessary again to see if this is possible for the individual.

Any change of attitude rests upon the recognition of the force of thinking, as that thinking then expresses itself in the social world through self-responsibility. Rather than presuming an "objective" and external cause, one must see that any cause must originate in mentality. The *intention* to see this is itself a fact of self-consciousness. The common sense assumption is reversed. It is not the objective but rather the subjective that has priority. Great historical forces have been brought into play that now dwarf consciousness but a careful tracing of lineage, of genesis, reveals that the underlying force is thinking, that encompassing reality of seeing, remembering, seeing, comparing, and seeing again. For example, while the edifice of mathematics is no longer comprehensible by a single individual, it is inconceivable to think that it could have *begun* in a way other than with some one individual thinking for himself and realizing that $1+1=2$ as a matter of ideal relations, as a matter of universal truth. From there, this mental beginning, the edifice was built and continues to exist and accumulate as an objective and seemingly self-sufficient structure. The condition for the possibility of these objective structures is established by the mentality of subjective consciousness.

An interesting example of this reality is to be found in the program offered by Alcoholic Anonymous. Its Twelve Step strategy for abstaining from alcohol speaks to the issues of the person.

1) We admitted we were powerless over alcohol--that our lives had become unmanageable.

2) Came to believe that a Power greater than ourselves could restore us to sanity.

3) Made a decision to turn our will and our lives over to the care of God *as we understood Him.*

4) Made a searching and fearless moral inventory of ourselves.

5) Admitted to God, to ourselves, and to another human being the exact nature of our wrongs.

6) Were entirely ready to have God remove all these defects of character.

7) Humbly asked Him to remove our shortcomings.

8) Made a list of all persons we had harmed, and became willing to make amends.

9) Made direct amends to such people wherever possible, except when to do so would injure them or others.

10) Continued to take personal inventory and when we were wrong promptly admitted it.

11) Sought through prayer and meditation to improve our conscious contact with God *as we understood Him,* praying only for knowledge of His will for us and the power to carry that out.

12) Having had a spiritual awakening as the result of these steps, we tried to carry this message to alcoholics, and to practice these principles in all our affairs. [9]

The central revelation here is for the person to recognize the higher reality of God, to emerge from a self-absorption that left one selfish and unconcerned about others. God of course is the most exulted principle of objective reality and it is to Him that the alcoholic is instructed to defer. But a second look at the Steps indicates a reverse theme. "We admitted...we came to believe...we made a decision...we made an inventory...we admitted...we were entirely ready...we humbly asked...we made a list...we made direct amends...we continued...we sought...we tried." When focusing only upon the verbs, it is obvious that one is left with the insight into conscious action, with the possibility of *doing* as a matter of a personal choice. Only on the basis of self-consciousness, on the immediate resolve to do so, is it possible for the Twelve Steps to be put into effective action and to be helpful to the individual. Reference to God is possible only on the basis of the conscious resolve to do so. God can be little more than a witness to the individual's decision and intention to act. It is necessary to invoke the presence of God since alcoholics, as a matter of principle, have refused to take responsibility for themselves and this new found experience of the force of consciousness comes as a profound personal revelation and they do not know what else to make of it. They are so unaccustomed to the experience of personal responsibility that when it dawns upon them, they are ill-disposed to understand it as a matter of their own volition. The shock of this revelation is buffered by the deference to God. But God is important in another way. The divine principle is a standard of truth and honesty, something of course alien to the person committed to drinking to oblivion. Without personal honesty towards oneself, it is impossible to invoke the power of consciousness and thinking. Without personal integrity one will remain entwined in the infinite byways of self-deception and deceit, all of which resolves itself into a rather dim-witted out-smarting of oneself. Without the truth, nothing begets nothing.

Most emphatically we wish to say that any alcoholic capable of honestly facing his problems in the light of our experience can recover, provided he does not close his mind to all spiritual concepts. He can only be defeated by an attitude of intolerance or belligerent denial...*willingness, honesty and open mindedness are the essentials of recovery.* [10]

AA has come upon an insight and strategy which has produced great results. It is the confirmation of the power and force of self-consciousness. While credit is given to God, it nonetheless remains true that the individual can be useful to himself only when he has found recourse to himself in the dimension of self-consciousness, self-responsibility, and honesty. Only then is a *change of attitude* possible. This "model" of psychological transformation, this road to self-knowledge, is appropriate for any question regarding a change of attitude. In other words, the dynamic of this choice is at play with all the great issues of both the individual and society.

The claim is made that alcoholism is a *disease.* Just as cancer, for example, is a disease where the body is subjected to material forces that cause pain, suffering, and, ultimately, death, so too, it is thought, is alcoholism. But it is not a disease at all. It is certainly disease-like, but fundamentally it is a *choice.* The decision, the intention, to drink is always one's own. Now, *once* one has indulged oneself in years of alcoholic abuse there is permanent damage to the body in the form of various diseases, but the lineage is always there back to the choice of the person. AA is clear on this account.

The fact is that most alcoholics, for reasons yet obscure, have lost the power of choice in drink. Our so-called will power becomes practically nonexistent. We are unable, at certain times, to bring into consciousness with sufficient force the memory of the suffering and humiliation of even a week or a month ago. [11]

With respect to any actual disease there can be no sense of having "lost the power of choice..." Alcoholism is disease-like but the fact that it can be brought under control through the Twelve Steps confirms that it is not a disease at all.

A special interest group has sprung up around the assumption

193

of the objective causality of any "psychological" condition. "Professional" help is available to search out the objective causes of one's afflictions. Significant fees are paid in order to keep one from insight into one's own responsibility for the life that one lives, for the attitude that one chooses. Whether it is the abuse of alcohol, drugs, tobacco, food, and so on, it is all the same choice. Some assert that it is all just some disease but it is always the same question of personal honesty and integrity. It is even suggested that psychological depression is a disease. While there may be some attending physical conditions, depression itself is nothing but the conscious understanding and awareness that one is allowing oneself, choosing, to give in to the forces of denial and substitution, into the entanglement of excuses and accusations. One's anxiety and depression appear as one recognizes one's own complicity *without the courage to say so.* One has *let oneself go* and there is no possibility of retrieval. Gambling, too, is claimed to be a disease, when it is perhaps the clearest example of the choice that chooses its own affliction.

Psychologists may be divided between those who aggravate dependence upon the objective and those who recognize the force of self-consciousness, between those who obstruct and those who show the way for the "patient's" revelation of himself. An addiction is simply the attempt to find some sort of relief from the anxiety of one's world, of scarcity and privation, the same relief that is sought in the Religious Experience, Capitalism, and Modern Science. It is all the same as the mistake is to forego the force of personal responsibility in the pursuit of an objective cause, or excuse, or conspiracy, for one's misery. This failure of course only compounds the pain. The notion of "Cold Turkey" is instructive.

Sometimes, sooner or later, *one is on to oneself.* Whatever the addiction, it finally becomes obvious that one is solely to blame, that it is not any objective cause but rather oneself and oneself alone that is the cause of one's choices and final condition. Faced with this absolute certainty, the person is in a position to *choose otherwise*, regardless of any baggage to the contrary. *One simply quits* as a force of one's own now active will power. One goes Cold Turkey. All bogus posturing, excuses, accusations, and easy passivity can be transformed into a positive self-esteem and the dignity of acting on one's own behalf. The sham of anything less is no longer acceptable. Instantaneously, the difference is present. After having passively indulged in a self-inflicted life of unhappiness, it now becomes possible to find the greatest happiness in the simple *act* of self-responsibility. The odyssey of self-knowledge enters upon the high road of accountability and honesty. This is nothing but the journey that travels into the In-Between and discovers the balance and harmony of knowing oneself. This is the condition for the possibility of all balance and harmony for society and the world as a whole.

An interesting corollary to the fact of Cold Turkey is that of the "placebo effect." When the natural scientific medical establishment deems it important to denigrate any positive effect that lies outside of its strict domain of expertise, it is charged to be only the placebo effect. In other words, there is nothing real but only the psychological condition of thinking that something is real. Much more is said here than just to denigrate. If the psychological has the power to transform physical conditions simply by willing itself to do so, this is not grounds for denigration but rather the cause for a deep insight into the power of oneself. Of course since the medical institutions as a matter of principle can acknowledge only material causes, the positive reality of the placebo effect is missed. This effect says much about the narrowness of the medical field and more about the power of mentality to transform itself.

Naturalistic clinical psychological theory also distorts the power of consciousness when it asserts the notion of the unconscious. Significant research has gone into the explanation of this "source of

195

consciousness." Of course this is one more attempt to deny the obvious. In not willing to recognize the power and force of consciousness itself, in not willing to relinquish the emotional satisfaction of personal irresponsibility, clinical psychology has deferred to a "fictitious entity." The unconscious is reputed to involve the same reality as consciousness except that it operates in the dark. This "mystery" shrouds action in a web of unsubstantiated "causes," something of course for which the individual cannot be asked to be responsible. Yet another excuse is hung in the closet, ready, willing, and able to take the fall for any conscious mis-deeds. Much violence and destruction has been suffered by the innocent at this divide. The psychologists then go on to convince the judicial system of the same mistake. Personal irresponsibility becomes institutionally sanctioned. The law stands ready to defend excuses and mis-deeds.

The failure of responsibility is evident throughout society. Professional sports is layered with one failure after another. The whining, rudeness, poor sportsmanship, and violence of these public institutions continues to be tolerated because the individual is no longer held accountable. Poor behavior is rewarded at the expense of decency and the common interest. Athletes are given a reign that simply ought to be curtailed. Arrogance, selfishness, and mean spiritedness need not be tolerated. Both the institutions and the individuals ought to be held accountable. Society pays a steep price for this failure.

All of this need not be the case. A clear and distinct recognition of oneself is possible. The power of self-consciousness and self-responsibility need no longer be crushed under the weight of the failure to achieve true accountability. It is within the strict power of ourselves to act to make the changes necessary. It is possible to change our attitudes on all of this and choose the positive.

There's one thing I don't understand: it has to be black and white, devils and angels. And there's nothing in between. But everything is in between. There's something of darkness, and of devils, and of angels in everyone... [12]

This is the insight of a Russian revolutionary years later. The recognition and appreciation of this middle ground, the dimension of mentality and spirit, is the Rock upon which could be built a sane world.

The change of attitude of the person to self-responsibility has consequences for personal finance. Here too there are great difficulties when the person does not think for himself and instead gives over to various financial institutions the power over his financial well being. Central to this is a simple principle of money, the Rule of 72, the mathematical formula for calculating the time value of compounding money. This is either working on one's behalf or it is not. When one gives over to a financial institution the responsibility of choice, the individual will generally lose. The Rule is as simple as it is profound. Divide 72 by the interest that is being paid upon a lump sum of money and the result will be the number of years that it will take that lump sum to *double* simply on the basis of compound interest. For example, at 4% it would take 18 years to double, as 72 divided by 4 is 18. At 6% it would take 12 years and at 12% it would take 6 years. The numbers are startling. A $10,000 investment can earn at 65 as little as $40,000 and as much as $640,000, a significant $600,000 difference.

Age	4%		6%		8%		12%
29	10,000	29	10,000	29	10,000	29	10,000
47	20,000	41	20,000	38	20,000	35	20,000
65	40,000	53	40,000	47	40,000	41	40,000
		65	80,000	56	80,000	47	80,000
				65	160,000	53	160,000
						59	320,000
						65	640,000

The issue concerns the vehicle of investment. Guaranteed returns, such as that of a Certificate of Deposit or a Whole Life cash-value death insurance policy, will yield at the lesser end, in the range of 4%. Traditionally, these type of investments were all that was available but over the last thirty years the Mutual Fund has emerged as the primary investment of choice. Through the pooling of investors' money a mutual fund is able to efficiently invest in the equity markets where the risk is as high as the reward. The individual investor is able to participate directly in the market, no longer needing a "middle man" to invest for him. The mutual fund charges a fee for its service, while a guaranteed investment, such as a CD or whole life insurance, takes the difference between its own market return and what it has guaranteed. This middle man institution invests in the same stocks and bonds that a person could invest in through a mutual fund. Historically, mutual funds have returned in the area of 12%, or enough to make the difference between the $40,000 return and that of $640,000. Anyone who does not understand the time value of money, as the Rule of 72 illustrates, could easily be talked into investing with a middle man who assures them that a guaranteed return is in their best interest. Of course it is in the best interest of the institution, as they take the lion's share, but it is a financial disaster for the individual. Not taking responsibility to understand the "big picture," the individual is left financing the profits of institutions rather than securing his own financial future. But, a deeper problems insures that the individual loses. It is the question of the death insurance industry.

The greatest concentration of wealth in the history of the world has occurred through the marketing of whole life cash-value death insurance. Fully two thirds of the assets of the United States are held by insurance companies. A stark comparison is possible.

On an overcast afternoon late last February, a 27-year-old real estate salesmen was laid to his final rest in a cemetery outside Baltimore, Maryland. As the graveside service came to a close, and the young widow and her two children walked slowly down the hillside towards the parked automobiles, a friend was heard to remark: "I hope Ed had enough life insurance. They're going to need it." On the same day, across the country in Seattle, Washington, a 27-year-old aircraft design engineer, the victim of a highway crash, was being lowered into his grave. As the funeral procession drove away, one of the pallbearers said to a companion: "Do you suppose he had much life insurance? It's going to be rough on Mary and the kinds if he didn't." Both men, fortunately, did own life insurance. In due time the young widow in Baltimore received a check from the life insurance company whose name and motto are virtual household words. The check was in the amount of $20,000. In Seattle the engineer's widow also received a check from an equally well-known company. The amount was $105,000. Both the real estate broker and the engineer had taken out their insurance within a month of each other, and both had paid an annual premium of approximately the same amount. What was the difference that resulted in one family receiving a death payment of more than five times that received by the other? Why, with everything else being equal, will one family face the future with sufficient financial resources to live a comfortable life, while the other finds itself with entirely inadequate means to replace the earning power that was so abruptly cut off? [13]

The simple answer is that one bought whole life insurance and the other bought term. Whole life is a "bundled" financial product where one is sold death insurance and a savings account together. A single premium pays for both. Term death insurance is a single product that includes only death insurance as there is no attached saving account. By buying the term insurance the man was able to afford $105,000 in protection rather than the $20,000 with whole life.

The life insurance industry in the United States, for its own reasons, has from its early origins de-emphasized the actual purpose for its existence by discouraging the sale of pure death protection. The cases just given shed some light on the reasons for this concealment, for if one company could afford to pay a claim of $105,000 while the other paid only $20,000--and the actuarial calculations showed that each could be paid out on policies calling for the same annual premium-- then there is the matter of an $85,000 discrepancy somewhere. That discrepancy, multiplied by millions of cases over the past century, accounts for the almost unbelievable accumulation of money that is in the hands of the life insurance industry. [14]

The purpose of death insurance is to provide an instantaneous estate for a family whose breadwinner has just suffered a premature death. With dependents still in the home, this "estate" will provide a continuing income, replacing the now lost income of the dead father. A multiple of ten of that man's annual income is used to calculate an appropriate amount of coverage. If he earns $40,000, his coverage ought to be $400,000. A death claim in this amount invested with a 10% return would replace his income and the family could continue to live without any additional suffering due to poverty. A $400,000 whole life policy would cost around $4,000 per year and is easily *unaffordable*. A $400,000 term policy would cost around $600 per year and easily *affordable*. The family is protected for either $4,000 or $600 annually. The obvious comes into view. Buy term insurance and invest the difference in a mutual fund. Get far superior insurance coverage, by-pass the middle man for investment dollars, and receive the full market returns on this investment. Rather than paying $4,000 in premium to have sufficient coverage, the breadwinner can now have that coverage and still have $3,400 to do with as he would. He could spend $1,400 on a family vacation and put $2,000 in a mutual fund. $2,000 per year at 12% for 30 years would accumulate to $482,000. This far out paces anything that a guaranteed return would yield. Rather than lose/lose, poor insurance and a poor investment, the alternative is win/win, where there is superior insurance and a superior investment.

A marketing ruse that the whole life death insurance industry uses is that a person needs insurance for their whole life and that term insurance, which increases in cost every year, would be too expensive in the later years. Yes and no. Term insurance would certainly increase in cost but *it is not needed for one's whole life.* Rather, only while one has debt and dependents is death insurance appropriate. As one's dependents move away and establish lives on their own and as one's net worth increases year by year there is reached the point where death insurance is no longer necessary. When the last dependent leaves home it is time to consider reducing one's coverage to the level of burial needs, if that. If one has accumulated a significant amount during one's productive years, there is simply no financial justification for paying insurance premiums when that money could be better allocated as a further contribution to one's investments.

The death insurance industry is rewarded immensely for its marketing ability that sells a product that pays only itself at the expense of others. Its collective assets as of the end of 1995 are *$2,143,544,000,000.*[15] A very large number indeed. As a middle man this industry has convinced the unsuspecting to bargain with them, except that there is neither good faith nor honesty, only deception and soothing words of encouragement. Interestingly, 57.8 % of this 2 trillion plus pot of gold is invested in stocks and bonds, the very same ownership equities available to the small investor through a mutual fund. By-pass the middle man. Whole life cash-value death insurance is perhaps the most dishonest product ever generally marketed while the mutual fund is perhaps the most honest. An historical parallel that is not strictly coincidental comes to mind.

In the second half of the fourth century, for the first time, we get hints of public complaints against the wealth of Christian clergy and the splendour of its buildings. Some Christian writers took note: "Our walls glitter with gold and gold gleams upon our ceilings and the capitals of our pillars; yet Christ is dying at our doors in the person of his poor, naked and hungry." [16]

Often enough a religious affiliation is used by an insurance company to further enhance the fleecing of the flock. In the simplest terms, the Rule of 72 is used to impoverish and not embellish, as one loses and the other wins, the one retires broke and the other retires early.

Another financial product that needs to be more fully understood by the individual in order to avoid significant losses is the home mortgage. The standard product here is the 30 year fixed monthly mortgage. A $100,000 loan at 9% for 30 years has a monthly payment of $804.62. At the end of the term $189,667.92 would have been paid in interest. An alternative is to re-pay half, or $402.31, of the monthly payment every two weeks. This "acceleration" would allow the loan to be paid in full after but *22 years* with a total interest payment of $129,248.86, or a savings of $60,419.06. A further enhancement would be to pay an additional $50 per bi-weekly payment. The $100,000 loan would then be paid in full after 16 years at an interest cost of $89,077.31, or a $100,590 savings over the original 30 year loan. With this one would have broken free from this "debtor's prison" 14 years sooner, allowing for the re-direction of that loan payment now into a mutual fund. Invest $904 per month, the loan payment plus $100, at 10% for the balance of the 14 years and the accumulation is $331,624. The choice is clear. Pay the monthly 30 year mortgage on time and at the end of the term you will have a document that says your house has been paid off in full. Pay bi-weekly plus $50 per payment and that document is stamped paid in full after 16 years and if the payment is now put into a mutual fund investment at the end of an additional 14 years there would have accumulated $331,624.

In understanding the "magic" of compound interest, the simple mathematics of the Rule of 72, it is possible to do better than if left to the choices of the financial institution. Not knowing the rules insures that they will be used against you, knowing the rules insures at least the possibility of your doing better. The difference is between a comfortable retirement and one subsisting on a Social Security allotment.

The issues concerning personal finance can be easily summarized. Buy term death insurance for the protection of dependents, reducing coverage when dependents leave home, invest regularly into a mutual fund allowing for the time value of money to accumulate in your favor, and then accelerate the home mortgage through the bi-weekly and additional payment strategy that allows for a huge interest savings and a even larger investment accumulation. Of course less of the advantage will be gained if personal debt, primarily credit card debt, is not controlled. One needs to understand the "big picture" and act to implement a plan of action that will return immensely for oneself, as the financial institutions take less. But the general consequences of this are even more dramatic. The vast and overwhelming concentration of financial power in the insurance industry could be reduced and that power returned to the individual with this program of fiscal self-responsibility. With the de-centralization of power, the forces of global sanity and renewal would be enhanced. That would be to the benefit of all, including insurance executives, who still must see the world passed on to their grandchildren.

Abundance and self-responsibility then require the care and concern of the individual person. It is possible to change one's attitude, to go Cold Turkey, and do what is necessary in order to improve the world's chances for continued success. It is possible to take control of one's life and more fully understand the rules that effect the well being of oneself and one's family. It is possible to do better, and that is for each of us to decide for himself.

Chapter Nine
A Change of Attitude: Examples

Obviously, the recognition of the possible transformation from the circumstances of denial and substitution to the reality of the *In-Between* involves a fundamental personal *change of attitude.* The fear and anxiety of exclusion and social division needs to be turned aside in favor of the compassion and concern of inclusion and social consensus. The ideologies of scarcity and privation need to be replaced by the possibility of abundance and plenty. Long standing traditions of exclusion have set into stone the impression that this fear and anxiety is a matter of "human nature" itself. The self-righteous and self-serving boldly assert that things could not be otherwise and that humanity is impelled towards violence from beginning to the end. Human nature is not this tendency to violence at all but rather simply the self-constituting force of consciousness that allows it to be whatever it so chooses. *To be sure,* a strong historical case indeed can be made for continued exclusion, division, and violence, but it is nonetheless absolutely true that the time has come where it is possible to think of something entirely different. The conditions are quickly being put into place to step beyond the legacy of the past and into a global consensus of the future. It may be comforting and assuring to those who will risk nothing, when assuming the worst, as then

205

nothing need be attempted. A self-fulling prophecy assures the rightness of a position that continues the failures of the past. But more is at issue than the emotionally comforting feelings of this as it is now possible to build in a way never before imagined and to choose to make a difference. The "sword" of violence may be broken. The decision is pending.

A series of examples will be offered here to show the possibility of such a changed attitude. Each will present a *before* and an *after,* that is, the example defined by denial and substitution and then as defined by the recognition of the In-Between.

1) The history of Russia and the Soviet Union and its relation to the West is crucial. How was it that the world divided itself into the two hostile camps of the East and the West? While the Cold War may have ended, this issue remains of the greatest importance.

2) The set of associations that reside under the heading of "romanticism" will be shown in its configuration as a matter of denial and substitution and then as something else. The search for personal happiness often fails when one mis-understands oneself.

3) Minority Relations will be shown to be a self-fulfilling prophecy that insures the continuation of the same. In proclaiming the need for change, nothing is allowed to change. A rhetoric of irresponsibility often masquerades as a call for social justice.

4) American Culture, as distinct from any traditional culture, will be shown to be the basis for the free play of the individual within the context of the community. The worldwide attraction to American culture is based upon the recognition that it is the only culture that allows the person to be himself. The "voice" of the multiculturalists will be shown to be possible only as a result of the *accomplishment* that is American Culture, the culmination of the Odyssey of the Western spirit. No traditional culture ever allowed for the "voice" of dissension.

5) Game and Sport will be shown to encompass the

experience of time that is inherent to the experience of oneself. Another look at time within the experience of everyday life will illustrate a piece of philosophical truth.

6) A visual description of the major Washington, D.C. monuments will provide an analogue to the transition from denial and substitution to the In-Between. A close look at the Washington, Jefferson, and Lincoln monuments and then the war Memorials of Iwo Jima and Vietnam provides an example in stone of the historical heritage of recent times.

7) A final example will be the finale that provides a proposal for a political party that would lie In-Between, at the Middle. Under the heading of the *Common Sense Union*, three principles will establish the basis for an agenda of social and political reform. The principles of self-responsibility, the priority of the long over the short term, and the priority of the common over the special interest, will serve to illustrate the possibility of political consensus rather than the politics of extremes and personal power.

The reality of each example will point to the same underlying condition. The experience of materiality and scarcity, that led to various ideologies of denial and substitution, can be transformed according to the experience of abundance and self-responsibility. The future need not be an extension of the bloodshed of the past. Something better is possible. Transition and opportunity defines our moment.

1) *Russia and the West*

The great polarity between the East and the West has deep roots. Long before the Bolshevik Revolution of 1917, there existed a profound mistrust of the one for the other. Depending upon circumstances and autocratic temperament this could easily lead to war. Peter the Great was the first Tsar to open Russia to European influence, himself traveling there on a mission of learning and goodwill. But the Russian experience of the West has been more often one of tragedy and violence than of enlightenment. The West offered technological innovation but little that was useful politically. The empty vastness of Mother Russia left Western notions of culture and commerce ineffective. Moscow and St. Petersburg may boast of some Western sophistication but this was limited to a thin aristocracy whose only task was to maintain the tsar in a position of absolute power over all of Russia. For the millions who toiled upon the earth, anything of the West meant nothing. Life on the land was sufficient unto itself. The eternal recurrence of the same was the foundation of social order. But destruction would be visited nonetheless. Military insanity and political stupidity would devastate Russia with the Western sword. Napoleon, the greatest in a long line of French lunatics, invaded Russia with an army of 300,000. For reasons no better than vanity and arrogance, the dwarfed general marched into Russia, burning and pillaging, on his advance to Moscow. Rather than risk the loss of their army the Russians abandoned the capital city to the French. Napoleon promenaded through the deserted city as if he were the Holy Servant of God Himself. Of course he was not and then *winter set in.* Insufficient provisions forced a retreat. As a gesture of French enlightenment, he had the city set ablaze. Moscow burned while Napoleon fled. He abandoned his troops to their fate of Russian Winter. The attack was nothing but a whim of a madman who thought he owned the world and that others should gladly die for his "glory." The people of France thought to entangle themselves in this tinsel of vanity as that army of 300,000 lay dead and frozen on a line from Moscow to Paris. Less than one in ten returned home.

The effect on the Russian national psyche of this barbarism from the West was natural. Pushed into isolation, the country cultivated self-sufficiency and exclusion. But "geo-political" realities would not tolerate such a simple solution. Territories to the west were coveted as a "military buffer" between Mother Russia and any future Napoleonic type schemes. Eastern Europe, from the Baltic to the Black Sea, would suffer the wrath of this struggle. It was Peter the Great, a full 100 years before Napoleon, who envisioned this buffer, this "Eastern Bloc," as the first defense against attacks from the West. His long battle with Sweden convinced him of the necessity of this solution. But the buffer was yet to have been established and invasions would continue. The Third Reich in due course would send its best against the vast land and it too encountered the brutality of Winter. But the formation of the Soviet Union would dramatically change the tone of the conflict.

Tsarist entanglements in Western political alliances and the exhaustion of Russia in World War I occasioned the "Soviet Revolution." During this period of national crisis, the ruling party of the Romanov dynasty was replaced by the ruling party of the Communist dynasty. Autocratic and centralized power continued as before, as Lenin replaced Nicholas II on the throne of Russia. Little had changed, but the stridency of Bolshevik rhetoric convinced the West that a great new threat to itself had arisen in the East. Calling for an international workers' revolution, the newly formed Soviet Union purported to be in the vanguard of a global turn towards communism. The sacred traditions and principles of Western domination were thought to be imperiled. A Western Alliance was formed for purposes of an invasion of the Soviet Union. It was to be returned to the pre-existing condition of an autocracy under Western influence. The Soviet Union posed a threat to the status quo of existing Western political arrangements. The ill-conceived invading army was easily defeated by the newly formed Red Army. From the very beginning, the Soviet Union was made to resent and fear the West. It drew into itself as power was consolidated at home, with little revolution abroad. Behind this Western interpretation of quickly moving events stood a religious assumption. While Christianity was preached and practiced in Russia, it was the Western version that held the upper hand. As taught in the Bible, reality is to be polarized, split in two, into the white and the black, the good and the bad, the right and the wrong, the West and the East, and capitalism and communism. It was presumed of the West that it uphold the destiny of this will of God. The formation of the Soviet Union was interpreted religiously as the gathering before the ordained firestorm of Armageddon, that last Biblical battle when the forces of good finally vanquish the forces of evil. The Western attitude towards the fledgling Soviet Union was dictated by this Christian vision. The final divide was at hand, the Soviet Union would need to be isolated so as to insure the proper retribution of God. This would make all of the difference in the subsequent American nuclear policy of "containment." Biblical *Revelation,* the most extreme ideology of denial and substitution, would provide the inspiration for much grief to come.

The Soviet Union was isolated and became the "beast" and the "Evil Empire." Under attack, it consolidated at home and lashed out whenever possible. The next Napoleonic madman was Hitler, the true beast of an evil empire. With the rantings of a lunatic, the most "reasonable" nation on earth moved to war and devastated a nation. Ironically, though, the Soviet Union would be aligned against Hitler with the so-called forces of good. The Western Alliance needed the Russians to take the brunt of the Nazi offensive, as Hitler was stupid enough to attack to the east *and* the west.

After the Nazi terror had run its course and the final victory won, the Alliance divided itself again into the "good" and the "bad." But the stakes had risen. In fear of any future unification of the German nation, (the People of Auschwitz), the Western Alliance and the now re-isolated Soviet Union agreed upon a new political alignment. Germany would be forever divided and the military buffer that had been envisioned by Peter the Great was established. The presence of the Red Army on the German river Elbe sanctioned the Soviet Union's possession of Eastern Europe. The Iron Curtain fell as the two powers got down to the business of mutual hostility. There was little acknowledgment in the West of the Soviet contribution to the war, but the Russians now felt a real satisfaction and security from any future attack. The Soviet Union was a superpower in a world where that was the only qualification of importance. But, these newly achieved gains were quickly lost. Western nuclear superiority effectively negated the soldiers on the ground, the territorial gains to protect Mother Russia now guaranteed nothing. Nuclear incineration neutralized any conventional strength. The Soviet Union dug in as the West again forced it into a secondary position. American policy during this time was simply to taunt. Surprisingly, quicker than the taunters could have imagined, the Soviet Union achieved its own nuclear capacity, balancing the Western advantage. But bad blood was spilt daily and, notwithstanding the immense expense on both sides, nothing was to be gained.

The mutual buildup of nuclear redundancy had created an uneasy situation. The geo-politics of old had been eroded. The traditional notion of a winner and a loser in war would no longer apply. Both the victor and the vanquished would be equally vanquished. For the first time it became obvious that a war of aggression could only be murder *and suicide*. Zealots of military "solutions" and disciples of Armageddon would concoct various scenarios to the contrary but the simple truth was as clear as it was distinct, that a general thermonuclear exchange would be immediate global annihilation. The flames of hell would engulf the living and then the dead. The "victor" was already dead, a thought that left the military planners uneasy. A return to the Stone Age could only be humbling. It is necessary to take a closer look at the emotional conditions of the nuclear arms race and the ideology of the Cold War.

The Soviet-American Alliance that defeated Nazi Germany

was based upon the circumstance of Hitler's foolhardy decision to engage in a two front war. Military necessity brought the Americans and the Communists together as legitimate goodwill was lacking. Having already judged the Soviet Union to be the carrier of evil, a legacy of self-fulfilling prophecy was set into place. Every effort was made to see everything about the Soviets as being evil. The decisive moment arrived with the near simultaneous defeat of the Nazis and the test detonation of an atomic bomb. The entire climate of antagonism changed with this dramatic moment of destruction. One scientist perceptively stated the fact when the early evidence suggested a fearful power. "That night there was little doubt in my mind that the world was headed for grief." [1] Hiroshima would become the site.

The streets were deserted except for the dead. Some looked as if they had been frozen by death while still in the full action of flight; others lay sprawled as though some giant had flung them to their death from a great height...Nothing remained except a few buildings of reinforced concrete...For acres and acres the city was like a desert except for scattered piles of brick and roof tile... [2]

In possession of the first atomic bomb, the American attitude towards the Soviet Union was to dictate the terms of the relationship. Contrary to the spirit of their recent alliance to defeat Hitler, this attitude would be none too cordial. News of the test success of the bomb reached President Truman at Potsdam where he was meeting Stalin. A critical moment was at hand.

Stimson left and Byrnes joined Truman for lunch. They discussed how to tell Stalin as little as possible about the atomic bomb. Truman wanted protective cover when Stalin learned that his wartime allies had developed an epochal new weapon behind his back but wanted to give as little as possible away. [3]

The tone was set.

Truman left behind his translator, rounded the baize-covered conference table and sidled up to his Soviet counterpart, both men dissimulating. "I casually mentioned to Stalin that we had a new weapon of unusual destructive force. The Russian Premier showed no special interest. All he said was that he was glad to hear it and hoped that we would make 'good use of it against the Japanese.'" [4]

This apparent calm was deceptive.

If Stalin was not yet impressed with the potential of the bomb, Truman in his private diary was waxing apocalyptic, biblical visions mingling with his autodidact's mind with doubt that the atom could be decomposed and denial that the new weapon could be used to slaughter civilians: "We have discovered the most terrible bomb in the history of the world. It may be the fire destruction prophesied in the Euphrates Valley Era, after Noah and his fabulous Ark." [5]

Rather than seeking an immediate accord of intentions over this weapon of "mass destruction," the Americans forced the issue to coincide with their long standing opinion of themselves as the Biblically mandated carriers of good and the Soviets as equally the carriers of evil. This emerging body of opinion would be quickly set into ideological stone and the nuclear arms race was on.

An author denoting himself secretively simply as "X" published an article in 1947 entitled "The Sources of Soviet Conduct." The new American consensus was stated. The Soviets were caricatured in no uncertain terms. Theirs was the Empire of evil and the West was the citadel of the "free world." Assuming and projecting antagonism, Soviet foreign policy would be characterized in precise terms. It was one of "secretiveness, the lack of frankness, duplicity, the wary suspiciousness, and a basic unfriendliness of purpose." [6] Who is describing whom here? Americans were not to be denied the fulfillment of their self-righteous prophecy. "This means that we are going to continue for a long time to find the Russians difficult to deal with." [7] The cornerstone of the American nuclear policy and the rationale for the Cold War was set into place.

In these circumstances it is clear that the main element of any United States policy towards the Soviet Union must be that of a long-term, patient but firm and vigilant containment of Russian expansive tendencies. [8] ...the Soviet pressure against the free institutions of the western world is something that can be contained by the adroit and vigilant application of counter-force at a series of constantly shifting geographical and political points. [9]

The division that had been originally envisioned in the Biblical terms of *Revelation* would be affirmed in Soviet-American relations.

It is clear that the United States cannot expect in the foreseeable future to enjoy political intimacy with the Soviet regime. It must continue to regard the Soviet Union as a rival, not a partner, in the political arena. It must continue to expect that Soviet policies will reflect no abstract love of peace and stability, no real faith in the possibility of permanent happy coexistence of the Socialist and the capitalist worlds, but rather a cautious, persistent pressure toward the disruption and weakening of all rival influence and rival power. [10]

With the assumption of animosity and having done everything to encourage that animosity, the Soviets would be forced by the Americans into a smaller and smaller range of options. Containment, encirclement, and counterforce would become the buzzwords for the American projection of force at the Soviet Union. Hoping for the worst, the Americans set their nuclear arsenal on alert and looked for a chance to strike. The West would pre-empt the Russians, hoping to do to them what they thought they were to do in return, with one significant difference. The West possessed the capability while the

Soviets did not. The never relinquished superiority of the Americans was always underestimated as Soviet strength was overestimated so as to ensure the escalating march of nuclear weaponry. While charging the Russians with driving the arms race it was always the Americans who lurched ahead. All talk of "missile gaps" was but talk for domestic consumption so as to justify more weapons. The CIA became expert at fabricating military projections so as to justify each new President's need for yet another "buildup." "The Russians are coming, the Russians are coming." Mr. X ends in a flurry and puts everything into proper perspective.

Thus the decision will really fall in large measure in this country itself. The issue of Soviet-American relations is in essence a test of the over-all worth of the United States as a nation among nations. To avoid destruction the United States need only measure up to its own best traditions and prove itself worthy of preservation as a great nation. Surely, there was never a fairer test of national quality than this. In the light of these circumstances, the thoughtful observer of Russian-American relations will find no cause for complaint in the Kremlin's challenge of American society. He will rather experience a certain gratitude to a Providence which, by providing the American people with this implacable challenge, has made their entire security as a nation dependent in their pulling themselves together and accepting the responsibilities of moral and political leadership that history plainly intended them to bear. [11]

The Cold Warriors, at the right hand of God, dug in for the long haul. All personal humility and respect for others would not influence policy as the Americans set about the task of re-making the world in their own self-righteous image. The consequences of this may yet be the global disaster from which the world cannot recover, as piles of nuclear weapons and debris are scattered about with no place to go. The cost has yet to have been fully paid for the damage that these Cold Warriors dumped upon the earth in the name of their own

215

personal salvation.

With the Soviet development of nuclear weapons in the 1950s, the ideological presumption hardened into a specific strategy for annihilation.

SAC's (Strategic Air Command) targeting of "urban-industrial areas" came to be characterized as "city-busting" in the jargon of the new thermonuclear age. LeMay's notion of "bonus damage" was supplemented by the concept of an "optimum mix" of industrial and military targets, whose destruction would maximize the bonus of civilians killed. If war broke out, LeMay intended to drop virtually the entire American nuclear arsenal upon Russia in a single raid. He allegedly told aides that his ultimate goal was a single bomb--one that would destroy the whole country. [12] ...SAC commanders like Curtis LeMay and Thomas Powers made it repeatedly plain...that they considered any deliberate effort to save Russian lives and limit the damage to the Soviet Union as nonsensical--if not treasonous. [13]

With its economic and technological advantage, and its assurance that it was doing the righteous work of Providence, the United States drove the escalation of the arms race and kept the world on the brink of destruction for decades. Domestic opinion was brought into line by a public relations campaign that demonized the "enemy" with every kind of evil. Contrary opinion was rooted out as the United States policed itself with accusation and terror. The "Inquisition" had come home to the final defender of the "free world." LeMay openly taunted the Soviets with his vision and yearning for their annihilation. As the head of the Air Force these taunts were taken to heart. He would go to "heaven" as he sent them to "hell," or so he comfortably thought. As the Soviet Union scrambled to respond, it was accused of pushing the arms race, re-confirming in the twisted minds of the Cold Warriors their original will to power. The world was in a deep hurt as Christian Apocalism pushed on to Armageddon.

216

While LeMay's vision of the future never transpired in the skies over Russia, a more sinister exercise was conducted on the ground. Not being able to directly square off with the Soviets, the Americans found cause to strike indirectly. The country of Vietnam found itself in the cross hairs of the American need to brawl in the name of God. A civil war to rid a country of its colonial overlords was interpreted as being a Soviet inspired communist revolution. A north/south civil war was thought to be an east/west theater of confrontation. Using the propaganda of the struggle for the freedom of the South, "to bear the burden," the United States went into Vietnam as an excuse to flex its muscle at the Soviets. After the debacle of the Bay of Pigs, the young new President needed to express himself. "...Vietnam looks like the place." [14] Encompassed in this simple statement is the death and agony of millions. It just breaks one's heart. There was no necessity, no real threat to American freedoms, with the civil war in Vietnam, there was only the unfortunate opportunity to inflict misery upon the innocent in the name of Providence.

Historians of the future will look back upon the period from 1945 to 1989 as a time of incomprehensible insanity, similar to that of the Crusades of the 12th century, the Inquisition of the Middle Ages, the vicious conquest of the New World by the Europeans, the barbarism of early capitalism, the brutality of Stalinist Russia, and finally the methodical insanity of Nazi Germany. We Americans need not be proud here. But things move on, the way of the world is to forget and remember to suit one's needs. Perhaps it is time to remember more.

Another perspective is necessary, that of the Soviet Union and now again Russia. Under the banner of *Perestroika*, Mikhail Gorbachev implemented significant social and political reforms. Communism had placed a heavy hand upon the individual and initiative and production naturally diminished. Economic growth had

217

ground to a halt. Waging the Cold War exhausted an already damaged economic system. Goods and services were being produced in lesser quality and quantity. A life of standing in line, waiting for shortages, had become normal. Social disintegration was impending. The standard cliches about the superiority of communist society were recognized by a new generation of leaders as being hollow rhetoric. The people knew better and the lies could no longer pass. A change of attitude was necessary and Mr. Gorbachev provided the leadership.

We have come to the conclusion that unless we activate the human factor, that is, unless we take into consideration the diverse interests of people, work collectives, public bodies, and various social groups, unless we rely on them, and draw them into active, constructive endeavor, it will be impossible for us to accomplish any of the tasks set, or to change the situation in the country. [15] Today our main job is to lift the individual spiritually, respecting his inner world and giving him moral strength. We are seeking to make the whole intellectual potential of society and all the potentialities of culture work to mold a socially active person, spiritually rich, just and conscientious. An individual must know and feel that his contribution is needed, that his dignity is not being infringed upon, that he is being treated with trust and respect. When an individual sees all this, he is capable of accomplishing much. [16]

Recognizing the extreme need for change, the Soviet Union disbanded itself and again became Russia, and then let go of its "East Bloc" possessions. *The Communist Party itself was disbanded.* Any remaining Cold Warriors in the West need to more fully comprehend the profundity of this change of attitude. Russia has chosen to opt out of the arms race and the Cold War and chart a new path.

I will never accept the claim--whatever anyone might tell me--that the American people are aggressive toward to Soviet Union. I cannot believe that. There are, perhaps, some individuals who are pleased that there is tension, confrontation or intense rivalry between our countries. Perhaps some people do gain something from it. But such a state of things does not meet the larger interests of our peoples. [17]

Those few persons who would think to gain from continued confrontation with Russia are those who remain locked in the theologies of power and the ideologies of exclusion, those who cannot relinquish the idea of the "Soviet Union" as the Evil Empire because such would shatter their views of the world as understood by *Revelation.* But the larger interests of the world have moved beyond any individual desires for personal salvation. In a truly inspiring way, Russia is critically and openly reflecting upon its problems and looking for constructive and productive reform. This has all come as a shock to the Cold Warriors of the West, but there it is. It took a man of courage from the East to be the first to stand and say No, to say no more to the insanity of an arms race that protected no one.

The Cold War is over. After decades of military brinkmanship and bravado a new day has dawned that is without the need of a Doomsday confrontation. Some sort of genuine respect and cooperation is now possible. But hard habits have petrified into place and old ways continue forward as reasoned policy. The institutional legacy of the Cold War, coldwarism, continues from the sheer weight of bureaucratic inertia. [18] The Cold Warriors refuse to fade away. Old policy continues as if nothing has changed. Perhaps, it is nothing more than a money machine. Corporate interests have a vested stake in the continued production of armaments and refuse to relinquish their easy profits. The rationalizing ideology drones on though, as we are assured of the need for B1 bombers, trident submarines, and Sheath fighters, to name the most expensive and profitable. NATO expands to the East as both an insult and the refusal to see the truth. Yet there is no discernible reason for any of it, history has moved on. No one in the West has stood with the courage to say No.

Two issues stand foremost. What should be the policy regarding nuclear weapons? What should be the status of the American military throughout the world? A single word would answer both questions. Simply, *retract*. It is perfectly foolhardy not to take this opportunity, this dramatically changed global situation, to reduce significantly nuclear arsenals. It makes no sense whatsoever to stand at nuclear alert for an enemy that has vanished. The difficulty is not so much the policy as it is the bureaucracy.

The people of the institutions of the "military-industrial complex" that created these weapons refuse to recognize the obvious. It may be a matter of refusing to acknowledge past errors that have cost the world dearly. By refusing to admit that anything has really changed, they can find justification for the continued squandering of billions. For them the threat is always the same, it is the threat to their own judgments which have now proven to be completely in error. A world of possible cooperation is simply inconceivable for those who can understand only division and mean spirited contention. Some of these Cold Warriors may see the changed political reality but they then choose to do as always and give warning of "the dangerous world out there." Their final loyalty is to the exclusive band of people just like themselves that has saddled the world with monumental problems for which they will take no responsibility. While regional difficulties remain, "strategic" stockpiles can hardly be appropriate to these "tactical" situations. No conceivable regional situation could involve multiple thermonuclear warheads that would be deliverable on ICBMs or B1 bombers or by trident nuclear submarines. It is obvious and necessary to retract to negligible levels. Not to do so would mean that we freely choose to refuse to learn the lesson that is finally there to be learned at an incredible cost to the planet Earth.

Equally important, the American military that is positioned throughout the world needs to be retracted. It is time to bring it all home. The early Cold War ideology of "containment" was the ideological rationalization for a global network of military bases. With no one any longer to contain, it is obvious that the troops may be brought home. There is no longer any conceivable justification for American troops in Europe, Japan, Korea, and Saudi Arabia. Huge sums of money would no longer be wasted for nothing at all. The number of monstrously expensive naval carrier groups could be significantly reduced. Regional situations can be dealt with regionally, the American "big brother" is no solution. The capacity to project military force anywhere in the world at any time is a piece of Cold War ideology that need no longer define overall strategy and policy. But, more importantly, it is time for America to get out of other peoples' affairs. It is time to quit with the self-serving wishful thinking of making over the world into the narrow image of American expectations. While this policy has presumably sought to promote peace efforts throughout the world, its intentions are often stained by ideological self-interest and the maintenance of its own position of unilateral power. American good intentions often reduce to empty rhetoric when compromised by its own hidden agenda. The problems of others throughout the world ought to be left to their own solutions.

For example, American intervention in Somalia simply raised the level of violence to a higher magnitude. Nothing is to be done there yet American conceit pushes its own bloody solutions. In Saudi Arabia troops are put down in a hostile society, welcomed only by the King and his entourage. Casualties will follow. This type of thing must be brought to an end. The killing must stop. When so much is committed to the ready military option it becomes the option of ready use, either directly or indirectly. Its persistent threat becomes the dominant diplomatic tool. "Either do as we say, or else." As a legacy of the triumph in World War II America has come to feel entitled to this attitude of intimidation but this is no longer acceptable. It is time to quit with the legacy of the "ugly American." The lessons of the last 50 years have yet to be learned by the Taskmaster.

2) Romanticism

Matters of love and romance naturally refer to the fact of the sexual difference between man and woman. The physical difference of course is significant as the one penetrates and the other is penetrated. In the name of equality this dramatic difference is often overlooked. It is a matter of activity and passivity, between needing to take the initiative and needing to await the other. Man and woman come together in this tension of difference that often leads to much confusion.

Even when she is willing, or provocative, it is unquestionably the male who *takes* the female--she is *taken*...the male seizes her and holds her in place...In this penetration her inwardness is violated, she is like an enclosure that is broken into. The male is not doing violence to the species, for the species survives only in being constantly renewed...but the female, entrusted with the protection of the egg, shields it also from the fecundating action of the male. Her body becomes, therefore, a resistance to be broken through, whereas in penetrating it the male finds self-fulfillment in activity. [19]

But the difference is even more profound as the respective sexual experiences themselves are entirely distinct.

The woman's sexual experience is determined by the clitoris which is predominantly an occasion for a neurological event. Her pleasure is primarily of the mind. The act of being penetrated is consummated in the "global" experience of orgasm. There is simply nothing quite like this explosion of pleasure at the center of one's being. "The white ecstasy of frictional satisfaction." [20] It will become the defining experience that will constitute her life at its core. The man's experience is essentially something else entirely. Rather than being a neurological event in the mind, it is a vascular event at an extremity and, while there is great pleasure, "a zesty tumescence of

222

fact," it is discernibly less than that of the woman.

Male sex excitement is keen but localized...it leaves the man quite in possession of himself; woman, on the contrary, really loses her mind; for many this effect marks the most definite and voluptuous moment of the love affair, but it has also a magical and fearsome quality. [21]

There is a difference of degree and quality that has significant consequences for the respective perceptions of life.

A description of primitive life allows for an insight into this that remains essentially true.

The woman who gave birth, therefore, did not know the pride of creation; she felt herself the plaything of obscure forces, and the painful ordeal of childbirth seemed a useless or even troublesome accident. But in any case giving birth and suckling are not *activities,* they are natural functions; no project is involved; and that is why woman found in them no reason for a lofty affirmation of her existence--she submitted passively to her biologic fate. The domestic labors that fell to her lot because they were reconcilable with the cares of maternity imprisoned her in repetition and immanence; they were repeated day to day in an identical form, which was perpetrated almost without change from century to century; they produced nothing new. [22]

The necessities of the body required a passivity that defined the woman's experience, as "she passively submitted to her biologic fate." But the joy of motherhood left her with a solace that gave her occasion to affirm herself, but the central fact is that it remained a passivity in contrast to the activity of the male.

Man's case was radically different; he furnished support for the group, not in the manner of worker bees by a simple vital process, through biological behavior, but by means of acts that transcended his animal nature. *Homo faber* has from the beginning of time been an inventor: the stick and the club with which he armed himself to knock down fruits and to slaughter animals became forthwith instruments for enlarging his grasp upon the world. He did not limit himself to bringing home the fish he caught in the sea: first he had to conquer the watery realm by means of the dugout canoe fashioned from a tree-trunk; to get at the riches of the world he annexed the world itself. In this activity he put his power to the test; he set up goals and opened up roads toward them; in brief, he found self-realization as an existent. To maintain, he created; he burst out of the present, he opened the future...Their successes were celebrated with festivals and triumphs, and therein man gave recognition to his human estate. Today he still manifests this pride when he has built a dam or a skyscraper or an atomic pile. He has worked not merely to conserve the world as given; he has broken through its frontiers, he has laid down the foundations of a new future. [23]

Invoking the powers of mentality, he is intent upon *constituting* a world to his own benefit. The man and the woman see the world differently. Through a network of associations, the woman finds her priorities in life to be determined by her enhanced sexual experience, or at least the idea of it, the *romance* of it all. She moves "inward" to the reality of emotion and feeling and finds her place already defined. The lesser sexual experience of the man establishes a different set of associations that project him outward into the world, into the experiences of ideality, power, science, and war, as well as romance. The man's view of the world achieves a diversity of interest whereas the woman's resides upon but one. (None of this is absolutely true, as exceptions will arise as *persons*, but for purposes here the general distinction stands. This will be de-constructed in due course.) In contemporary literature is found an example of this stereotype.

Young, unmarried girls were nearly as difficult for him. Though they might offer richer possibilities for a lasting relationship, most of them viewed him solely as a potential husband. They all seemed to follow

224

the same scenario: the gentle entrapment of Mr. Right. This began with their prying into his life--which they perceived as a necessary condition for both openness and closeness. They wanted to make certain that he was still single; that he did not have a live-in girl friend; that he intended at some not-too-distance time to settle down with one woman, as opposed to, say, joining up with a bunch of swingers; that his financial prospects--or, since he was still a student, the financial prospects of his family--were good; that he could be easily domesticated and made a father soon; that his personality was flexible enough to share everything with a wife; and that he had never been in love--really and truly in love--before. The scenario always grew more complicated by the end of the first week of the relationship... [24]

A specific strategy is put into play in order for the woman to secure for herself the romantic vision. Her whole being is put to the task of achieving this success. Nothing else will matter much at all. If the man were to resist this "gentle entrapment" there is no greater sin that he could commit in her eyes. It is easily understood how this so easily fails. But there is more here, as fundamental emotions are never quite fully open to view.

This, then, is the reason why woman has a double and deceptive visage: she is all that man desires and all that he does not attain. She is the mediatrix between propitious Nature and man; and she is the temptation of unconquered Nature, counter to all goodness. She incarnates all moral values, from good to evil, and their opposites; she is the substance of action and whatever is an obstacle to it, she is man's grasp on the world and his frustration; as such she is the source and origin of all man's reflection on his existence and of whatever expression he is able to give to it; and yet she works to divert him from himself, to make him sink down in silence and death. She is servant and companion, but he expects her also to be his audience and critic and to confirm him in his sense of being; but she opposes him with her indifference, even with her mockery and laughter. He projects upon her what he desires and what he fears, what he loves and what he hates. And if it is so difficult to say anything specific about her, that is because man seeks the whole of himself in her and because she is All. She is All, that is, on the plane of the inessential; she is all the Other. And, as other, she is other than herself, other than what is expected of her. Being all, she is never quite *this* which she should be; she is everlasting deception, the very deception of that existence which is never successfully attained nor fully reconciled with the totality of existents. [25]

The inequality of difference, the contrast between activity and passivity, the desire for more and the reconciliation with less, the opacity of emotion and the failure to see the point, all contributes to a "war of the sexes" that is swept away in yet another hope for the romanticism of love. By both default and necessity the man turns to the objective world, to career and sport. The confusion of undetermined emotions leaves him without reasons. But a deeper level desire is at work here. Since the general condition of human existence is necessarily the same for both man and woman, each sharing the same conditions of mentality and materiality, and each needing to achieve an emotional alleviation in the dimension of ideality that originally encompassed the Religious Experience, which was re-constituted in the objectivities of the political, economic, and scientific, then it is true that the experience of *romanticism* functions in the same way. It too is a version of denial and substitution, a denial of the world as it is and the substitution in its place of a world ideally purified. The reality of everyday life is transformed into a perception that hopes to achieve "love" at a single glance. Romanticism is a reality that is without time, it is an ideology that hopes to achieve an instantaneous immortality in the perfect embrace of a love complete. Of course none of this is possible in fact. As a set of ideas, romanticism has nothing to do with people living in the world of life and death, it is but a failed abstraction. Romanticism entices with a

226

worldly "heaven" that exists nowhere. As the Religious Experience purged the world of scarcity in its idealization of Heaven, so too the Romantic Experience purges the world of interpersonal relations from similar scarcities, as there is left but a hope for a consummated fullness of being. Of course it is just an idea and can never be anything more than a fiction. Nothing else has self-inflicted more personal misery and unhappiness than this failure of expectation.

The romantic ideology is nurtured and sustained through musical expression. Any love song is always but a rendition of something or other from this ideology. One example will do. "Cherish" by the musical group *The Association* was enormously popular and influenced many in their yearnings for romantic love. As defined in the Oxford English Dictionary, *cherish* means "to hold dear, treat with tenderness and affection; to make much of. To entertain in the mind, harbour fondly, encourage, cling to a hope, feeling, design, etc." It is to "harbour fondly" as a possible vehicle of personal alleviation. The lyrics describe.

Cherish is the word I use to describe, all the feeling that I have hiding here for you inside. You don't know how many times I've wished that I had told you, you don't know how many times I've wished that I could hold you, you don't know how many times I've wished that I could mold you into someone who could cherish me as much as I cherish you. Perish is the word that more than applies to the hope in my heart each time I realize that I am not gonna be the one to share your dreams, that I am not gonna be the one to share your schemes, that I am not gonna be the one to share what seems to be the life that you could cherish as much as I do yours. Oh, I'm beginning to think that man has never found the words that could make you want me. That have the right amount of letters, just the right sound, that could make you hear, make you see that you are driving me out of my mind. Oh, I could say I need you, but then you'd realize that I want you, just like a thousand other guys who'd say they loved you with all the rest of their lies when all they wanted was to touch your face, your hands and gaze into your eyes. And I do cherish you. Cherish is the word.[26]

The song is written from the male point of view. He is actively in pursuit of her who passively awaits the attention of both him and others like him. Ironically, while she passively awaits, she retains the right of final judgment, she will chose the one for her, the one whose performance suits her needs. He uses the word "cherish" to describe his "feeling," his desire, that through her he will achieve his *own* happiness. Selfishness runs deep in all matters of romantic love. It is a special feeling, though, "hiding inside," especially for her. There will be no end to the lying and deception in this pursuit. He is obsessed, "many times" wishing that he approach her, take her, and finally "mold" her, conform her, into someone who would be able to fulfill *his* vision of *his* own happiness. As he thinks that he cherishes, so too she is to be *made* to cherish him. One is easily set up for a fall of one's own choosing. He then proclaims his misery if he should be denied in his intentions. He will *perish*. Overstatement is common. It is all or nothing, life or death, me or else, as his extortion of "love" will be successful or he will die of rejection. Proclaiming her responsibility for his possible death, in the suicidal tradition of unsatisfied love, he hopes to extort a decision of compliance that will conform to his expectations. Any contrary judgment would leave his blood on her hands. But, alas, he feels his chances are slim, as they always are. He thinks that someone else will get the positive nod and take away from him the possibility of any happiness at all. Of course we've already been assured that he will perish, so perhaps that's a bluff. His self-righteous and self-inflicted agony continues. Now, it is someone else's fault, some objective reason that he is to fail. It is because "...man has never found the words that could make you want me..." It is a failure of civilization that this woman finds him disagreeable. Then he consoles himself with the "insight" that it is only "words," that one can be talked into accepting the responsibility for the fawning love of another. Verbal expression alone is the final criterion of acceptance. Of course the larger matters of personality, temperament, kindness, consideration, and respect can have nothing to do with the imposition of romantic love. He recognizes his odds and resigns himself to the bluster of the martyr. He gets bitter. He accuses his competitors of being after her only for rather carnal gratification, of course his intentions are pure, at least to start. He will get down to business in due course. He assumes his own feelings to be naturally superior to the others, he rightfully is most deserving. By its proper name this is nothing more than a "power play." His final plea. "Cherish is the word." The fascination with a word or *The Word* as a substitute for reality has a long tradition. "In the beginning there was the Word." Words may be necessary for an understanding of reality, but when they are forced to be realities in themselves, abstractions, there will be much heartache and confusion. The machinery of denial and substitution will have done its work.

The song had great appeal to both men and women alike. The male romantic vision of pursuit and conquest of the "beautiful woman" is as strong as the female romantic vision of being pursued and the idea of her possession of the winning suitor. Each has denied the world as it is and hopes to find personal happiness in another world apart. But problems immediately arise. Conquest can become a "fatal attraction" and possession a stifling imposition. When the idea of romantic love is given over to daily life there will be much cause for accusation as the idea necessarily falls short. Sentiments of loving and cherishing can easily degenerate into acts of hostility and animosity. Both had expected a life of "happiness," of alleviation, and when that necessarily fails there is hell to pay. The other is to blame and responsibility for oneself never a thought.

A statement regarding marriage is necessary here. It is the institution that supposedly encompasses romanticism. Its record is rather tortured. Prior to the gigantic economic expansion after World

229

War II, marriage essentially had nothing to do with romanticism and love, as it was an *economic* institution. Desires for personal happiness could be of little concern when material survival was not assured. Arranged and mandated marriages served an economic need and had little concern for romantic sentiment. Only by accident did it happen that people came to love one another. The low divorce rate in times past is taken as a virtue when in fact it was a necessity, things could not have been otherwise. But with economic prosperity comes the desire to re-interpret marriage as an economic *and* a romantic institution. Marriage is now expected to provide economic well being and personal happiness. A burden is placed that is simply impossible to carry. Expecting the other to fulfill oneself, there is the natural failure to recognize one's own implication and responsibility for insuring one's "happiness." Many make the mistake to think that the institution itself will deliver such happiness while one *awaits* its arrival. Of course this would involve immediate failure. Not seeing this complicity, the other stands accused.

Is there an alternative to this ideology of failed expectation? It is as simple to see as it is difficult to achieve. "Know Thyself." Return to the self and see that all of this expectation is without merit and that it is only within the limits of one's own person that any expectation at all is to be considered. This recourse to the thinking person has great consequences. "Misguided love is revealed as such when I return to myself." Rather than passively imposing romantic expectations, rather than seeing the Other as responsible for one's own "happiness," it is possible to recognize the opposite. It is always time to actively engage the world on its own terms, to quit with sitting about, and to go out and do something, be something, as an act of the will that chooses something more rather than awaiting something less. What is involved here is of course *friendship*, that activity of mind that allows a person to engage another on equal terms without expectation and with the abiding desire to mutual kindness. It is the joy of companionship that is perfectly free of the desires of romantic tyranny. People can choose to quit with a forcing of affection that establishes a "ledger," an accounting procedure, that credits and debits any kindness and affection to the glory of one's own greater "good." "If you loved me, you would do what I say!" This formulation of emotional extortion has been used to diminish and belittle throughout the world. "In short, I am a hired servant. I expect my payment at once--that is, praise, and the repayment of love with love. Otherwise I am incapable of loving any one." [27] All of one's actions and minor deeds have been carefully measured in advance in order to produce the greatest advantage to oneself. This is thought to be a romantic "entitlement," where one is just *owed* such concessions. This romantic power play is a dead end that quickly and easily consumes itself in the white heat of desire denied. Expressed differently. "She denied herself her orgasm so that she could hold that against me later too." Friendship is the recognition of the In-Between, the reality of oneself as witness to the miracle that is another. It is the never taking anyone for granted ever again.

Oh, the comfort, the inexpressible comfort of feeling safe with a person, having neither to weigh thoughts, nor measure words, but pouring them out, just as they are, chaff and grain together, certain that a faithful hand will take and sift them, keep what is worth keeping, and with a breath of kindness blow the rest away. [28]

To have relinquished romantic love for personal friendship is of course the greatest blessing of all, nothing less than a "divine dispensation." A sort of trinity of possibility ensues with the choice of friendship and is possible only within the dimension of knowing thyself. The project of self-knowledge stands at the center of any desire to achieve balance and harmony in one's world. And yet ironically we must do this without any regard to one's personal advantage. Knowledge for its own sake is the portal through which

231

we can see that our efforts must give rather than take. We must turn to the larger world of creation and choose to fully participate in its presence. We need to leave ourselves behind and find the supreme being in existence itself. The confines of the self must be expanded to coincide with the expanse of the universe. It is not necessary to become a philosopher, but it may require appreciating the philosophical. Undivided respect and consideration is the cornerstone here to a knowledge that will finally return to the self. A second aspect of this trinity is that the knowledge of another, the knowledge of a man for a woman and vice versa, is a privileged dimension of knowing, it makes an emotional difference that consummates, as it were, one's place in the world. This is the dimension of care and loving without expectation, the quiet recognition of the majesty of our world together without serving oneself. It is here that *grace* enters the world. The final moment of this trinity of self-knowledge is the necessity to *dance*, to leap for joy at the wonder of it all and celebrate the gift of existence. The bodily expression of the fact of our shared being in a world of infinite wonder and charm allows us to comprehend that this existence is the greatest thing of all. We can find our home in all of the universe as the simple expression of friendship and kindness. The natural *embrace* of one and another is the purest expression of this dance.

The transition from the necessary failure of romanticism to the possible affirmation of friendship requires a re-consideration at the deepest level. Normally, it is thought that the male/female distinction is an absolute fact, yet it is only *relative* to a more primary underlying reality, which is the existence of mentality and self-consciousness itself. To this *we are all equal.* There is not a male consciousness and then a female consciousness, two sets of exclusive associations, rather there is but *one* that is then differentiated into *two*. Without this common reality there would be no possibility of any mutual understanding. Man and woman would stare at each other across an

232

abyss of incomprehension. The ideology of romanticism has no use for this common reality, instead being too quickly intent, perhaps for political reasons, upon establishing the absolute distinction between man and woman. In all matters, difference is possible only relative to a common dimension, as pure difference would separate absolutely. But men and women do arrive at an understanding, they do find friendship, and that of course makes all the difference.

If the sexual distinction were allowed to stand as absolute, there would occur the greatest devastation to the possibility of community and shared experience. Communication itself would become impossible. Two separate realities, two distinct sets of meaning and intention, would entail social chaos and personal isolation. Some would hope to gain personally by maintaining an ideology of this division, as it is thought to be emotionally satisfying to profit at the expense of others, but this is only for the few who have chosen to affirm their emotions of rancor and resentment. But, there are not two sets of meanings, but rather a confusion about one. The resolution of this confusion will emerge into the realization of friendship that will finally achieve "love," which is expressly the experience of the embodiment of ideality with respect to others and the world as a whole.

3) Minority Relations

The quite natural assumption throughout history has been that the *cause* of human reality lies in objective existence, in God. He created the universe and therefore created everything about human life. The woes of the world were attributed to the anger of God at the infidelity of his children. His wrath was delivered with his displeasure at human choices. The individual was called upon to do nothing more than obey and worship and then pray to this objective causality. With the development of modern science the object of worship was shifted from God to Nature, yet the principle of objective causality remained in place. This deference to objectivity has specific consequences in terms of minority relations.

Both sexism and racism assume that the cause of the difficulties of women and blacks is the objective causality called white-male culture. It is thought that an orchestrated white-male conspiracy exists to impose limitations upon the woman and the black. While some of this may be true, for the most part, it is not. Assuming the "conspiracy" theory of sexism and racism, the woman and the black *wait* for the white-male world to rectify the situation by removing past practices of limitation. Women and blacks can only await the outcome, just as the Chosen People awaited God. Nothing more is to be done. White men will be "assholes" and "racists" until they chose to act to give to women and blacks what they think has been denied to them, that to which they are *entitled.* A smug self-righteous attitude easily falls to those who have chosen to await the action of others. A significant misunderstanding is at work here. By assuming the sexist and racist cause of their lives, the woman and the black fail to appreciate the general adversity of everyday life that has nothing whatsoever to do with sexism and racism, but is *a quality of the things themselves.* Life in general has inherent adversity that must be understood on its own terms and not interpreted away according to various theories of entitlement. For example, the woman or black is not promoted in the workplace. Each is quick to charge sexism or racism, and each fails to understand that it is their respective feelings of negative judgment, their smug self-righteous attitudes, that lost the promotion and not anything conspiratorial. Being so concerned to smell out any acts of bias, they become less productive and then unworthy of promotion, and simply undesirable. Of course, some of the time they get the promotion through the extortion of this accusation, as the employer fears a discrimination lawsuit more than an overpriced and unproductive employee. The question is one of attitude, that of entitlement and that of empowerment. A more preliminary description is necessary.

For the most part, differing attitudes are brought to the workplace by men and women. The male's could be characterized as "sportive," that is to say, just as in sports proper, there is a game to be played and that an attitude of playfulness is often appropriate. One wins or loses, succeeds or does not, and *regardless* of the results, moves on to play again. There is always another day and another opportunity to play. Natural to any productive activity is the interplay of success and failure, advance and withdrawal, profit and loss, reprimands made and reprimands taken, and all of this is absolutely essential to the productive activity itself. It could not be otherwise. In these variations of setting, the sportive attitude allows one to prosper, to take one's feeling none too seriously, and just to move forward with the task at hand. In the rough and tumble one can always "land on one's feet," and most importantly *learn from the negative*, allowing adversity to be one's primary teacher. "The greatest pleasure in life next to winning is losing." The lesson is to learn from the negative and go on to create the positive. The sportive attitude then is a willingness to learn at every opportunity, a refusal to take oneself so seriously, and a sense of humor that shares in the productivity of all together. Much would get done here.

Contrasted to the sportive attitude is that of the personal. Here there is little humor, as any criticism or setback is taken as a personal insult that must be returned in kind. The natural adversity of productive activity is misunderstood, as any negativity at all is interpreted as being *sexism*. There is no *tolerance for adversity*, not to get one's way is grounds for the accusation of conspiracy. When feelings are accorded such a high value, the personal attitude is ill-equipped to work through the negative and instead goes off to pout. Venting ones' emotions is a response that seeks to accuse the "asshole" responsible. One does not look to the process of productivity to determine the reasons for the situation, evaluating objectively, rather it is more comfortable simply to sulk. The self-righteous accusation of sexism seals one off permanently from the positive experience of learning. At the very moment when there is the most to be learned, the personal attitude leaves one elsewhere. The *next* setback will find one in the very same position of inability. Co-workers can only become frustrated as others are forced to take up the slack of lost productivity. Nothing gets any better, as the absorption into personal emotion stifles any advance. As one becomes less and less useful, with promotions passing one by, the natural feeling is to accuse sexism, and charge others with the fact of one's own failure. The comfort of the sexist conspiracy insures that one will never learn a thing. When the courts support such a failure, there will be hell to pay. But there is probably no conspiracy at all, only an unwillingness to learn anything at all, a humorless and personal response to all adversity, and an attitude of accusation that leaves one thoroughly unlikeable. Promotion is understandably slow. In a more and more competitive world, businesses are less and less able to wait for her to dry her tears in order to get on with the job at hand. The sportive/personal distinction used here does not exclusively break down into the male and the female. Many women have come to appreciate the sportive and many men seek refuge in the personal.

236

Exceptions abound, yet as a working hypothesis, the distinction stands. It is for the individual to choose for himself or herself the sportive or the personal. In some respects, the personal is the choice to try to get something for nothing, to get someone else to be responsible for one's failure and yet to reserve for oneself the sanctimonious attitude of accusation.

The difference is probably created at the very beginning. Feeling is a *state*, a self-contained structure, which feeds on itself and is the very opposite of process and development. To be sad is to be sad, fully in itself. To feel anger is to feel anger, absolutely. If feeling is allowed to be the primary attitude in one's life then the fact of process will be overlooked. The person simply chooses not to see that much more is involved than the ever vigilant defense of one's feelings. Nothing is to be ventured from this position. Perhaps feeling jealousy towards those who act upon their own accord and achieve greater success, the person locked into their own feelings resents the other's freedom and retracts even further. The personally constructed prison of feeling, that so easily charges sexism, is the failure and unwillingness to invoke the great personal resources of self-consciousness, self-responsibility, and productivity. It is to remain wedded to the passivity that awaits the action of another and in the mean time consuming oneself in a misplaced rage and resentment. It is the failure to suspect the power of self-consciousness and the exhilaration of self-responsibility as one goes out to meet the world of one's choosing. It is the choice to settle for less.

A similar misunderstanding enslaves black consciousness. Black leadership systematically cripples its youth by preaching the gospel of racism, by paying homage to the universal accusation of white responsibility for black failure. To be sure, there has been racism, but now is the time to move forward, to quit with the accusation and to rise from an attitude of passivity and dependence. Without this, failure is predictable, as no one, so it is preached, can confront the white conspiracy alone, therefore all that one can do is to *await* the arrival of redemption, to while away one's time in the empty pursuit of nothing, and only then achieve one's entitlement. All adversity is interpreted as racism The young student's difficulty with a mathematics problem goes untested as an attitude is learned that it must be something to do with racism. Faced with the challenge of learning, the disciple of racism simply quits and never experiences the joy of accomplishment, the achieving on one's own terms, the finding something out for oneself. His elders have taught him instead to march in the army of accusers that will accept so much less for nothing rather than risk the effort and responsibility of more. Feeling entitled, they settle for very little indeed, but never relinquishing the satisfaction of thinking others are to blame. Rather than challenging their children to learn, to try a little harder, to love to read and write, they instead enlist them in the army of downtrodden which becomes so as a matter of course. The message to black youth is to "hang out", wait until all racism is eliminated. Of course in the meantime, they are educationally left behind, without the basic skills of productive activity. All of this is done from a presumptive moral high ground, as white guilt is assumed to be absolute and therefore to be redeemed forthwith. Nothing is accomplished, nothing will be done, as the lost youth are left to the streets, drugs, violence, and finally incarceration. The desire to learn to read and write, the need to accomplish for oneself, to feel the power of thinking for oneself, is not something that will be received after due course, rather it is something that one must do for oneself. When racism is the issue yet another generation will be lost to the joy of adversity and the satisfaction of learning to be useful to others.

Of course the opposite is necessary. Even if there would be sexism and racism, refuse to be led into the emotions of its accusation and realize for oneself that there will be no such excuses. Adversity and the negative present the single greatest opportunity to learn and to learn to be productive with others. But this is the choice of a positive attitude and the refusal to blame anyone, anywhere and anytime. There will certainly be instances of sexism and racism but the responsibility is to ignore them and choose to act on one's own behalf *nonetheless*. Waiting for someone else to act merely aggravates the existing difficulties when much already could have been done.

A comparison of successful and unsuccessful people highlights a few essential characteristics. Successful people as children respected their elders, learned to read and write at the proper time and were encouraged to do so, learned and respected the rules of society and gratefully participated, and understood the need to defer to both others and to the future. They will refuse to blame others for anything and will act to do the best that they can. Unsuccessful people do all of the opposites. They respect nothing but worship themselves, they fail to learn to read and write, they defer to no one, they refuse to participate, they violate the rules of society, they indulge in immediate consumption of everything now, and they self-righteously blame others when all of this quite naturally fails. This is not a male/female or a black/white distinction. It is simply the general rule of success. Anyone whatsoever who does the one will succeed while the other can only fail.

A young black entrepreneur gets his business started. Feeling confident to expand more quickly he applies for a loan at the bank. The white banker denies his request. Two distinct attitudes are possible. The immediate and easy one is to charge racism and throw up one's hands in rage and quit, confident of the moral high ground and the righteous of one's fury. One has been denied by the system and nothing now is to be done. The other more difficult attitude is to closely review the basis for the loan refusal. Insufficient collateral, underdeveloped market, and a high debt have been cited by the banker. The man could think this through and establish a plan of action. He could see that the banker was right, that it is too soon to expand and that more time is needed in order to insure success. He will return to the banker in six months and discuss the matter again. Simply, he could either charge racism and happily choose to do nothing, except rant to whomever will listen to his tired and worn story, or he will get to work to do whatever it takes to succeed. Absolutely and without question, it is his choice. He can choose a self-professed life of the downtrodden or he can invoke the power of self-consciousness and refuse to lose. His example to others would be stellar. There are no short cuts.

Another example. A prominent black baseball player enters the ranks of coaching. He boldly asserts that unless he is a major league manager within five years he will quit the game. His implicit charge is that racism will be the one thing to prevent his rise to the top job. He begins his coaching days with an accusation, he shows no appreciation for the process of "moving up," the paying of one's dues, of working within the system, as one's opportunity may or *may not* come about. Many a person has done all that was needed or asked and did not find that final opportunity, it is the way the "game" is played. But he understands none of this and lays down his ultimatum. He displays none of the respect and modesty which is essential in working with others. He thinks he will be denied because he is black yet ironically expects nonetheless to be promoted *because* he is black. The double edge of racism quickly cuts both ways. As a leader within the black community he has reiterated once again the gospel of racism and convinced yet others that the conspiracy is in place. He rants and raves with neither kindness nor charm. He feels entitled and appreciates nothing.

For many women and blacks, it is easy to understand the truth here and to choose a more productive and responsible life. Many refuse passivity and develop the power of individual self-consciousness, but the rhetoric is so easy and the advantage often simply there for the taking that it is difficult to show restraint. The guilt and duplicity runs deep. The bias of the times supports the prejudice. The ideology of "civil rights" silences their voices but finally the obvious becomes evident. Something for nothing is very little indeed and the deepest cost is paid with one's self-respect. The choice is always there and, as free individuals, choosing is our sole responsibility.

4) American Culture

American culture has admirers throughout the world and for very good reasons. It concerns the general distinction between a traditional culture and that of the culmination of the western spirit which is American culture. Any culture other than that of the west is traditional precisely because *tradition* is absolute. Social and personal relations have been determined *in advance* as the rules of society have already been set into stone. There is no place for the *person* as a thinking entity, as someone onto himself, that thinks and chooses accordingly. Tradition will not tolerate any deviation from the established social structure. Any person is what he has already been determined to be by prior rules of arrangement. There is no leeway for choice. Any boy born into tradition will be exactly like his father, as any girl will be quickly married into place. Religious veneration sanctifies this tradition and nobody knows any different. There is established a closed system of interpersonal, religious, political, and economic relations that moves inward. Society is self-sufficient and *totalitarian*. There is a perpetual recurrence of the same that is held into place by a tyrant who rules through the threat and fact of violence. Every traditional culture anywhere in the world follows this general profile. One is born into a rigid social structure that is based upon strict control. Nothing is to deviate from the past.

Only in the West, only on the basis of the "tradition" of the Western spirit, does this rule of tyranny become broken. For reasons

241

philosophical, historical, and accidental, the cycle of traditional recurrence was broken. Within Greek culture, the original seeds were germinated that would lead to the recognition of the individual as a force *outside* of the structure of tradition. There was always the tendency to be re-engulfed by continuing traditional forces, but the impetus was put into play to resist and achieve a place for the individual on his own terms. From Greek culture to the Teaching of Jesus, to the mathematics of Descartes, to the discovery of the New World, to the final emergence of American culture, there comes to be established a heritage that runs counter to traditional tyranny. The discovery of the America proved to be monumental, as it would be the *place* where something else would be ventured. Finding itself free from traditional tyranny, from the beginning, an experiment in free institutions could be considered. European culture had returned to the conservative forces of tradition and its heritage of the possibility of individual thinking had been reabsorbed into society. Traditional forces always held the upper hand. America allowed for something different. Free institutions were established, in the north at least, and a new "tradition" of freedom and individual rights was accorded the opportunity to be the law of the land. Traditional tyranny was not allowed.

This is not to say that there were not excesses of violence and destruction in the name of this new freedom. The conquest of the New World is a somber story indeed but perhaps it could not have been any other way. The simple fact is that the power of the West was greater than any traditional society could have thought possible and the imposition of that power was just the *way of the world*. This power was clearly understood by a Sioux warrior accepting defeat.

We are poor compared with you and your force. We cannot make a rifle, a round of ammunition, or a knife. In fact, we are at the mercy of those who are taking possession of our country. Your terms are

242

harsh and cruel, but we are going to accept them, and place ourselves at your mercy. [29]

A Stone Age traditional culture could not resist the force of the Western spirit. A fundamental consideration that must resist the temptation to moralize is that it is only the Western spirit that has produced an economic system that has the potential to produce in abundance. All traditional cultures are limited by the fact that structural abundance is not possible, that tradition itself refuses to allow for economic prosperity. A Stone Age culture is necessarily in the midst of perpetual scarcity. While in hindsight it may be possible to romanticize a culture of tradition, in fact it is a life of privation and tyranny. It is possible to take for granted the accomplishment of the Western economic system but then one will fail to recognize that all talk that hopes to condemn that system is possible only as a result of the success of that very same system. Any *voice* of condemnation is itself possible only as a result of the system it chooses to condemn, as in any traditional culture such a voice of complaint would be neither allowed nor tolerated.

A crucial insight is involved. The multiculturalist agenda claims that all cultures are equal, that every culture is entitled to a respect and consideration that recognizes an intrinsic value. All cultures *are* equal *except that of the West*, all cultures are equally totalitarian regimes that allow the person no rights or civil protections, they all function equally in their absolute denial of anything but the "rights" of the tyrant, and they all harbor fundamental scarcity and privation as a matter of perpetual recurrence. While the West has perpetuated brutality and violence, and its crimes are not to be condoned, it nonetheless is the only option that broke free of the cycle of tyranny and the world today is better for it. Western violence has been no more vicious than any traditional tyranny both past and present. Much remains to be done but the accomplishment of the Western spirit is the *only* avenue to general prosperity. The multiculturalist may hope to tear away at this fact, hoping to have the prosperity of the West pay for the support of traditional cultures everywhere, but fundamentally this is an error. The multiculturalist hopes to be the first beneficiary to a system that he is intent upon destroying. The irony and tragedy is that these hopes are being made good and the Western system is paying off those who wish its demise. Little is it understood that the failure of the West would be a return to an absolute brutality of tradition.

The issue here is one between being and doing. A traditional culture is always already satisfied with the *being* that is tradition. Nothing is needed to be done as it is inconceivable that it be otherwise. In the West this tyranny of recurrence has been broken and the power of self-consciousness brought to bear upon the conditions of life itself. One is empowered to do, to act, on one's own behalf. Value is to be achieved in the accomplishment of doing rather than in the complacency and passivity of being. There is little value in simply *being* such and such, as only in *doing* such and such is prosperity possible. Its a hard lesson to cultures of tradition, but it is their choice to either participate or not, to either accept the Western spirit or forever be consigned to poverty and desperation.

The United States then is the place where the Western spirit was given its greatest opportunity. The rigidity with respect to the individual of a traditional culture was replaced by a "tradition" where that individual was accorded the freedom to choose. A constitution was enacted and laws legislated that established the limits beyond which the individual could not go without risking prosecution and penalty, but the latitude left to him *within* the law was greater than anything that the world had ever known. A delicate balance was emerging into the light of day. The demands of cultural organization and structure were being limited by the opportunities that were now available to the individual. The freedom of opportunity was to be

244

balanced by the legitimate requirements of the community. The 19th century pioneer setting out from St. Louis had in his mind the desire to find his own way, to build a home and provide for his family but, just as importantly, he hoped to go West to build a community with others. He wanted to be his own man but respected among others. This is easily taken for granted in hindsight and the South American experience provides a stark contrast. There the same natural advantages did not lead to free institutions but rather the tyranny of Catholicism was fully imposed. The starkest example is the formation of a plantation prison by the Jesuits which left nothing to the individual and took all to the overlords. Power would reside only at the top where was seated either Churchman or military strongman. Only recently has the South been able to rid itself of the military junta.

What was learned in the North was that the free individual is not a threat to stable government. Of course, the perceived threat of the individual in the Old World was not to government but rather to autocratic government. The monarchies of Europe perpetuated their traditions so as to consolidate and maintain their power of privilege. The common man was only a threat to central power. While it is true that traditions and families of power were established in America that acquired far in excess of their rightful share, nonetheless a monarchy was never established, a Bill of Rights insured individual freedoms, and the requirements of the vast land necessitated that the natural initiative of the person be preserved and nurtured. A single man, doing as he saw fit, in the harmony of community, is a force of great economic value. It is the fact of this force that has created the economic abundance of the United States. With awe, envy, and jealousy, the rest of the world recognizes the miracle of American economic power.

Abundant in natural resources, saved from the devastation of war, and left free to develop its liberal institutions, American culture has produced more than a strictly material abundance. It is to this since the end of World War II that the youth of the world have looked for music, attitudes, values, and principles of self-esteem. Much of this gets consumed in the vapors of the moment, but much remains to inspire. Traditional ways and values suddenly become chains when seen in the perspective of individual choice, expression, and initiative. The rest of the world also looks to America as a political and economic model for a replacement to the increasing irrelevance and continued poverty of their respective cultures. Men no longer want to be forced to do as their "shepherd" fathers have done for centuries, living in isolation and scarcity, rather they want the choice of something different.

"We love our (former) country and the families and friends that remain," says Ray Daniels, who grew up in a town 300 miles north of Baghdad. "But we are first and foremost Americans. After all, this is the country that allows us to be who we are." [30]

The traditional culture could only determine *what* a person would be while only in America was it possible to be *who* one would choose to be.

America is not without its problems. Its great wealth is often wasted, inequities are allowed to stand that could easily be corrected, its world leadership is often confused and self-serving but, finally, for good reason, it leads the world.

5) Game and Sport

The single quality of human reality that creates the greatest rub is the fact of *time*. Curiously, we are both *in* and *out* of time. We must certainly live *in* time as we witness its passage, moment by moment, but we are also *out* of time to the extent that as a quality of thinking it is possible to stand removed. Examples of this include all of the experiences of ideality, of mathematics, religion, science, and the simple experience of "I think therefore I am." This is the experience of the *identity* of oneself across a duration of time. I am I regardless of the fact that I remain within the context of the passage of time. It is the question of identity in difference, a difficult philosophical question that will not be answered here. But this duplicity of experience, this being both in and out of time, is not brought together. A natural harmony of the two is difficult to achieve. Traditionally, it has been the case that a distortion is imposed that confuses the short and the long term. The machinery of denial and substitution distorts the experience of time in a significant way. It is always a denial of the Now, the living, breathing present. An ideality of the past, the Deity of original creation, is asserted as the criterion of value, the standard that degrades the Now and makes it meaningless. In place of this loss is substituted an ideality of the future, the idea of eternal sameness. The Now of living experience is crushed between the past and the future, between Arcadia and Utopia, between visions of perfection in the distant past and visions of perfection in the distant future. A yearning for the past and the future effectively annihilates the present. Being the temporal dimension of scarcity and privation, there is little incentive to have it any other way. The Now, which one carries along at every moment, is the single obstacle to a "life" free of anxiety. No one would mourn the ideological destruction of the present. The recognition of the reality of the In-Between, the recognition that abundance and plenty lessens the experience of anxiety, involves a re-interpretation of time. The present is to be accorded an appropriate standing between the past and the future. The present becomes the *place* in which to live, to act, to think, to do, and to be. Its value needs no longer to be denied and substituted for by the religious pretensions of the past and the future. Examples of chess, fishing, and baseball will attempt to clarify this re-interpretation of time.

The chess board defines the limits of the time and place of the game. Given a set of shared rules, which have been developed over the course of thousands of years, the game may begin. But the actual playing never discloses the full extent of the game itself. Having learned to play over an extended period of time, one develops experience and an expertise. In learning the game one is never confined to a single game, yet in the playing of a single game all of that experience is brought to bear. Consequently, any playing of a game involves all of one's personal experience as well as the history of the game itself. With each move there is essentially involved the entire reality of the game itself. But one can only play one game at a time, one move at a time, and that is the quality that gives it its charm. The enhanced experience of the Now stands forth in the greater context of the expanse of the past and the indefinite reality of the future. Here the Now is not the mathematical point of modern physical science, but rather the experienced duration of our living now as a human being. The love of the game is the appreciation of the presence of the whole of oneself in the greater context of time itself. The past and the future are maintained in a perfect balance as the Now is given its fullest expression. The violence of denial and substitution is not entertained.

Fishing, too, follows the contours of this positive experience of time. Again, the limits are defined in advance by the circumstances of the underwater world. The "rules" are established where rod, line, hook, and bait are used to lure the fish out of his world. This activity is dramatically defined by experience, the accumulated knowledge of fish and their world, that can be acquired only after long days on the lake. Past experience then is crucial for success now. This Now is an extended duration of time that circumscribes one's interest. When fishing, that is all that matters, as the rest of the world recedes before the prominence of the task at hand and that is simply all that there is now. It is this that makes up its enjoyment, the realization of merely abiding with the passage of time, the quiet witnessing of existence itself without any desire for anything else. Denial and substitution is denied. Let it be.

Baseball too has a special relationship to time. Its long tradition is it greatest fascination. As a spectator, as a fan in the seats, one witnesses the unique pace of the game, where nothing is to be hurried, everything in due course, as this is but one game in its storied past. The World Series offers a special experience that again enhances the experience of time. After an immense season of 162 games, the field is reduced to but two teams. This is a culmination in the perfect sense of the word. Great effort is implicit in each moment. In the seventh game of the Series the distension of the Now takes on heightened proportions. Each moment is a gasp of indecision until finally it is decided. Lost in the throes of the final innings the Now simply bursts with meaning, as the pulse of the Now enthralls to the end. If the final hitter should drive the ball over the fence to win then there can only be complete satisfaction all around. One was a witness and is better for it.

These positive experiences of time serve as a standard for the negative, when the necessary balance between past, future, and present is skewed to one or the other. Drug and alcohol abuse hopes to achieve an enhanced Now but must necessarily collapse in the wake of the morning. The temporal balance is lost and it is hoped that the Now will simply be forever. The obsessive pursuit of pleasure, in whatever form, also raises the Now only to have it crash down upon

249

one's head sooner than one would have thought possible. In this regard, after but a flicker, tomorrow is already here. This is the surest road to disintegration.

Something in this respect may be said about teenage suicide. It involves a misunderstanding of time. Increasingly, parents have relinquished the responsibility for the care of their children to "society," which means day care and the schools. The schools being ill-equipped and ill-designed to handle such a task, the children turn instead to popular culture, meaning primarily, television, music, and movies. It is there that many kids find what they need. What is projected through this media is an "idealistic" and perfected vision of reality as it is to be. What is created in the child's mind is an expectation of personal perfection. Perfect friends and clothes, perfect opinion and self-righteous disdain for others, and sufficient support from permissive parents who give credence to this expectation. There is developed neither tolerance nor patience for adversity. Plan A is in place when Plan B comes knocking. Presumed personal perfection fails in respect to the realities of the world. Vision does not square with lived experience. The child is not prepared for this inevitable disappointment and lacks the flexibility needed to move forward. Plan B leaves one clueless and immediately death is thought to be the only choice. Nothing is there to counsel otherwise. With no context, no experience, the child has loaded everything into the Now and then it must fail. The Now is thought to be able to stand alone but it cannot.

The appreciation of the reality of the In-Between requires the appropriate understanding of our experience of time. If one continues to distort it to the extremes of either the past or the future or only the Now, there will necessarily be much heartache. Making peace with time is to have made peace with oneself.

6) Washington, D.C. Monuments in Architectural and Historical Review

Visitors from throughout the world come to our nation's capital in order to witness the central architectural monuments of American democratic institutions. The White House, the Capitol, and the Supreme Court are buildings that will be seen along with the unending array of administrative buildings, as well as the great collection that is the Smithsonian Institution. Washington, D.C. is a monumental city of power and being built of stone it may last a millennium.

For purpose here, focus will be made on the "historical" monuments, that of the Washington, Jefferson, and Lincoln, as well as the Iwo Jima and Vietnam Veterans Memorials. An historical interpretation will be offered that will allow the visitor to view these great structures within the broadened understanding of their place in the grand scheme of the American spirit and history.

Naturally one begins with the Washington Monument. In its central location it dominates the skyline and is in the architectural style of the Egyptian obelisk. [31] A gigantic piece of linear stone points heavenward. This symbolizes divinity and the recognition of God as the Supreme Being. As God is the first cause of the Universe, so Washington symbolizes the first cause of the Nation. Washington, the man, is not depicted. What remains is a geometric structure of utter simplicity that represents the divinity of the universal first cause. As the "father" of the country, its First President, he stands for the beginning, the original place and clarification of authority. All that needed to have been done here is the physical enactment of the idea, the form, the principle, that is embodied in the stone of the earth. The human form that will be central to the other Monuments is lacking, it is *the idea of beginning* alone that matters. The affairs of men will come later. A more appropriate structure is unimaginable.

251

252

One moves on across the way to the Jefferson Monument. The rounded dome that encircles the standing man represents one step removed from the abstract form of Washington. The concept of beginning is developed into the task of legislation. The idea takes on human form. A beginning needs to be carried forth into the world. The author of the Declaration of Independence and a man instrumental to the specific constitutional formation of the country stands in a pose of elegant nobility. He is the legislator, a founding father, that will speak of the kind of nation that it will be. Much is at issue here. The individual is to be protected. Religious difference will not be allowed to serve the cause of violence. Men will share power. Privilege will be limited. Each will have an interest in the well being of others. Benefit will recur to those who have earned it and not simply to those who have the power to take it. Aristocratic and autocratic rule will be shunned in favor of democratic institutions. Men in free regard to each other will be allowed to determine their own affairs. Such is the Jeffersonian idea of a free society. Rightfully, Jefferson proudly stands in the name of all this at the center of the perfect geometric form. But the constitution of the idea is not the implementation of its reality. The process is difficult, reality falls short of the idea. As it happens, not all individuals will be protected, religion will spur violence, power will not be shared, only certain men will be free, privilege will not remain limited, benefit will be taken by the powerful, and elements of autocratic domination will remain. Concentrated power will come to limit the free affairs of men. The enactment of the Jeffersonian ideal harbors deep difficulties.[32] This burden would fall to others. Jefferson represents a step beyond beginning but a greater distance remains to be traveled before the reality of the idea can come to fruition. It is time to move on to Lincoln.

The inherent flaws of the enactment of the Jeffersonian ideal burst forth into the nation in violence, in civil war. The architectural

advancement is from the more perfect circle to the less perfect rectangle of unequal sides. The encircled and noble pose of Jefferson is replaced by the anguished repose of Lincoln. The social and political contradictions that had been constituted with Washington and then Jefferson would need to be rectified. It was of course the American Civil War which would decide these issues. Lincoln marshaled the spirit and then the violence that was necessary in order to address these contradictions. In the name of a truer justice, Lincoln was called upon to undercut the ideology of privilege. He mediates the old and the new. The burden cost him dearly, as finally his life too would be lost. He sits burdened and saddened. His Monument perfectly depicts the responsibility which was his alone. The Civil War was fought to preserve and extend the idea of the union of free men in free regard to each other. The special status of the few at the expense of the many was to be denied. If the Confederacy were allowed to stand then the great advantage of equality and fairness would have been negated. Lincoln recognized the importance of the struggle to protect these advantages.

Four score and seven years ago our fathers brought forth on this continent, a new nation, conceived in Liberty, and dedicated to the proposition that all men are created equal. Now we are engaged in a great civil war, testing whether that nation, or any nation so conceived and so dedicated, can long endure. We are met on a great battlefield of that war. We have come to dedicate a portion of that field, as a final resting place for those who here gave their lives that that nation might live. It is altogether fitting and proper that we should do this. But, in a larger sense, we can not dedicate--we can not consecrate--we can not hallow--this ground. The brave men, living and dead, who struggled here, have consecrated it, far above our poor power to add or detract. The world will little note, nor long remember what we say here, but it can never forget what they did here. It is for us the living, rather, to be dedicated here to the unfinished work which they who fought here have thus far so nobly advanced. It is rather for us to be

here dedicated to the great task remaining before us--that from these honored dead we take increased devotion to that cause for which they gave the last full measure of devotion--that we here highly resolve that these dead shall not have died in vain--that this nation, under God, shall have a new birth in freedom--and that government of the people, by the people, for the people, shall not perish from the earth.

America could advance only if it redressed the contradictions of its past and in the great battlefields, such as that at Gettysburg, men died on its behalf. The architectural grandeur of the Lincoln Monument attests to this fact. The Nation does remember.

Ascending the many steps to the Lincoln one glimpses the greatness of the task. The Nation had put itself to a dreadful violence in order to preserve itself. It had been tested and its sacrifice was equal to the burden. A politically segregated America would have done the world no good. A divided nation would have implanted the same divisions as those in a war weary Europe. Standing at the level of the seated Lincoln, one can turn and look across the reflecting pool to the obelisk of Washington and recognize the distance that has been traveled. The Nation had come of age through the sacrifice of many. The carnage of the battlefield had advanced the cause of justice for all. Another Civil War participant spoke clearly on the matter.

So we must not grudge what our dear country has required of us, but must give more, and take her infinite compensations--give all she asks, and needs--give ourselves and our dearest--and give on, and to the uttermost, till she is redeemed, rehabilitated, re-enthroned. [33]

The heroic ideal stands, the individual offers his sacrifice, and the Nation is preserved. The ideality of the just cause is remembered and the Lincoln Monument may be the greatest of all.

The contrasting shades of stone in the Washington Monument confirms that nothing needs to be taken for granted here. The monument's construction had been interrupted by the Civil War and when work was resumed later it was necessary that a different colored stone was used. A different victor at war's end and the structure would not have been completed. A triumphant Lee at Gettysburg and the principles of the Nation would have been vanquished. A slight shift of color then represents the greatest difference of historical fact. Quite easily, free democratic institutions could have been eliminated from the world. Once lost there would have been nothing to summon a return.

But more wars were to be fought. Other generations of men would be called upon for the ultimate sacrifice. Rather than stepping to the left in the direction of the Vietnam Veterans Memorial, it is necessary to cross the Potomac River and witness a last attempt to memorialize the heroic. The United States Marine Corps War Memorial (Iwo Jima) stands for the brave deeds of the Marines in World War II. The war's objective had been clear. Tyranny on both sides of the world would need to be defeated. With righteous belief and clear conscience American youth died for a cause greater than themselves. The Iwo Jima Memorial captures the essence of the enthusiasm of the collective effort to wrest land from tyranny. The cause was just, the effort noble, and the outcome never in doubt. Tyranny would be vanquished, but the totality of the destruction, the 55 million dead, the obliteration of Europe and the East, cut deeply. Something would begin to afflict men's minds. A contradiction became evident. The technology of war had outpaced acceptable limits of destruction. The advent of nuclear weapons changed everything, but old minds clung to old ways.

At the end of World War II the two great allies turned on each other. The providential righteousness of America was not to be shared. The United States and the Soviet Union squared off against each other in an ideological confrontation. The Cold War ensued that was fueled by unnecessary ill-will and resentment. While the Cold

260

261

Warriors proclaimed the advantages of thermonuclear annihilation, it became obvious that something was amiss. Nuclear war would annihilate everyone and then everything, the planet itself. These Warriors too would die. Simply, at the height of its unilateral power, it became clear to some that the very exercise of that power would be suicidal, sheer madness. But World War III, the war to end the world as we know it, was not ignited. It is time to return across the Potomac and take the path that leads away from the Lincoln. It is time to witness the revelation that is The Wall.

Approaching, it is necessary to look closely. Where is it? The monumental size of the others leads one to assume something equally large. The tree lined stone path gives way to black marble slabs to the left. Names appear, one reads the first few on the beginning slabs. Gradually one descends as they rise vertically. More names are inscribed, more and more and more. The slabs now extends far overhead, the names blurring in the distance and height. With descent, quiet conversation among the onlookers gives way to silence. One sees but does not believe, the named dead are just too many. At the lowest level, at the center, one needs to look high overhead to see names that no longer can be read, they extend into the sky. There are thousands of names, full slabs of thousands. A slight turn to the right and ascent begins, the slabs narrowing as the names become fewer and fewer until there are no more. Looking back across the way, it appears as a gash upon the earth. There are no more heros, only dead. One now notices the tears, the people standing along the way in quiet anguish, weeping. It then becomes worse. The numbers here must be multiplied. The 58,000 names become millions when one considers all the people involved, all the family and friends, that suffer this agony, those who will never get over their loss that is absolute. It is a matter of perfect disbelief, incomprehension. Then consider the three million now nameless Vietnamese who are equally dead and the acres of slab that would be needed to inscribe their names. The

262

anguish and tears continue, it is so sad, so agonizingly sad. In the end it was not a war at all, but a proxy fight, a battle between men in Washington and men in Moscow, who cared not a whit about the misery that they inflicted. It was not a war of heros but of ghosts, of men far away imposing violence upon the innocent in the name of nothing more than their own inability to see the truth.

At a distance of some years, attempts are made to rationalize one way or another but nothing is to be done, the dead are still the same dead. The life sized statue of the three soldiers that stands at the entrance to the Wall hopes to find meaning in the otherwise meaningless. Its "heroic" pose is meant to uplift those whose sacrifice continues to be lived daily. Perhaps the saving grace of the defeat of tyranny that found expression in the Iwo Jima Memorial will be found here too. But Vietnam was something else entirely. There is no saving grace, there is only the dead and then the living casualties that find no relief from their inscribed anguish. It is not external tyranny but rather the self-righteous belief in one's presumed superiority that was defeated. The enemy was within. America could have learned a deep lesson about itself. There are rightful limits to its desire to impose its will upon others. The rhetoric of the communist threat was used as cover in order to inflict massive damage upon those who just happen to get in the way. The America that so confidently conquered in World War II did not have a clue as it stumbled through Vietnam. The only lasting meaning is the dead.

As one ascends from the greatest depth of this etched misery, there is off in the distance the monument of beginning, the Washington. The concept has run its course and has come full circle. The high principle of beginning has suffered a difficult and tortured history. The historical and architectural sweep that extends from the Washington, to the Jefferson, to the Lincoln, to Iwo Jima, finds expression in the mournful counting of the dead at The Wall. The progression is from the Idea of God to the fact of human mortality

and death, and then to a renewed appreciation for life.

Leaving behind architectural considerations, it is possible to ask about the historical fact of war. It is possible to achieve a greater understanding of where it is that we now stand. World War I was sold in America as "the war to end all wars." Armies of youth were convinced to march through European trenches on their way to early graves in the firm belief of the moral rightness of the sacrifice. War, of course, did not end, but rather was extended by the Versailles Treaty into the global destruction that would be World War II. Men remained committed to violence as a political strategy. There is a continuity of attitude that extends from the First to the Second, to Korea and then to the Vietnam War, as these last two were an extension of the East/West conflict that remained unresolved. These wars have a single common denominator that is the belief in military destruction as both sanctioned and sacrosanct. But something changed in the aftermath of Vietnam. There was a change of attitude and the emotional experience at The Wall attests to this.

Death in the service of twisted ideological notions will no longer find willing parents. Sons will no longer be offered up for sacrifice. The heroic is no more. Even though there have been more war dead since Vietnam, there is nonetheless a change in attitude in its wake. The desire for vengeance is less. World War I did not change men's minds. World War II left men merely thinking of greater destruction still, but Vietnam may have shown the way to something different. It may have shown that the high moral road is a fiction, that the military option is no option at all, as the dead are always already absolutely dead. The war cries of old need no longer call young men to battle.

I didn't want a monument, not even one as sober as that vast black wall of broken lives. I didn't want a postage stamp. I didn't want a road beside the Delaware River with a sign proclaiming: Vietnam

267

Veterans Memorial Highway. What I wanted was a simple recognition of the limits of our power as a nation to inflict our will on others. What I wanted was an understanding that the world is neither black-and-white nor ours. What I wanted was an end to monuments.[34]

The lesson to be learned comes to America with great difficulty, but there it is.

As it stands, the Vietnam War dead have died in vain, for nothing. The saving grace about which Lincoln spoke at Gettysburg is not appropriate here. But, it may prove to be the turning point in history when men's mind were finally changed, the point at which it is understood that the military option is no option. Stated otherwise, paradoxically, the only saving grace of the Vietnam dead is to see that they did die in vain and, with that, decide to war no more. It remains a question of the future as to whether the Vietnam Veterans Memorial will remain a shrine of mourning or become a place of celebration. The site could become the spiritual center, the hallowed ground, for the final affirmation of the will to end war. As one ascends and the names fade, there is the thought that this simply cannot be allowed to happen again. But serious objections immediately present themselves.

The Bush/Hussein War is not an objection against this new possibility but rather evidence as to the difficulty of the transition. A World War II bomber pilot can be expected to act only as he sees fit, not having been touched by the tragedy of Vietnam. The military option was chosen and power was set against the aggressor. But, finally the "political gains" were infinitesimally small when compared to the loss of life. The world can no longer tolerate these acts of destruction. The imposition of military force will not have the desired effect. The world will not be re-made in the American image. People and countries find ways of their own. Simply put, military force does not work. Somalia will return to its tribal ways as soon as Western interest wanes. Nothing is to be done and the presumption otherwise is our central liability. Balkan petty states will return to their tribal ways as soon as Western interest wanes. Nothing is to be done. It is time for America to re-define its military posture, recognize the limits of its power, and question its presence throughout the world. Perhaps it is time to get out of other peoples' affairs. It is time to come home.

The great ideals of the Nation, of Washington, Jefferson, and Lincoln, will serve the world best when the greatest military power chooses, of its own accord, not to exercise that power when it has been its custom to do so. The devastation of others ought no longer be taken as a matter of pride. American power needs to stand at ease. The issue is one of restraint. The opportunity is at hand.

7) Common Sense Union

The American social and political system is in crisis. Consensus has broken down as special interests self-righteously run wild in the pursuit of single issues. Political leaders hawk tired and self-serving ideologies that are beyond all reason. An array of problems escalate out of control on their march to oblivion. But all of this points to an even more fundamental crisis. The system itself is failing as traditional political alignments no longer serve the interests of the nation as a whole. Presidential and Congressional power grabbing has been reduced to the level of political street fighting. Single issue Presidential contenders out shout each other hoping to get the ear of a public which no longer cares to listen. Republican and Democratic squabbling is without any underlying respect or consideration. Public principle is overrun by blind group loyalty that recognizes only its own. Special interests are in it for themselves, period. The far Right and far Left both push forth agendas that lack balance and reason. Furthermore, media requirements demand immediate reaction as objective analysis is no longer allowed.

269

Sustained, reasonable, and balanced discussion can find no place in this atmosphere of political chaos where the hunt for national power consumes all energies. Special interest groups then line up with their deep pockets and are promised that others will be called upon to pay for the benefits to which they feel entitled. In a world of such mean spirited contention it is perfectly logical that nothing is done. Fundamental problems are left to fester and then quickly get worse. The average person here is without cause for optimism. But, we are all party to this destruction and must consider our own responsibility.

How can we think about these things? The problem is that there is very little thinking at all. Politicians are thinking about the next election and that is all. The personal desire for the power and glory of elected office is simply too great and intoxicates like a drug. Political party operatives are thinking about getting their man elected so as to maintain their position in the bureaucratic hierarchy. Political think tank thinkers are thinking about the virtues of their own thinking. Academics are thinking about whatever vague generalities come to mind and wish to converse only with others like themselves. Journalists are hurrying from one story to the next and have little time to think about anything else. In needing to showcase the events of the day, there is neither the time nor the inclination for any broader understanding. And the rest of us must think about making a living as personal issues take any remaining time and energy. By default, as it were, it is left to the politicians, operatives, think tankers, academics, and journalists, the opinion makers of the world, to do our thinking for us. Of course we get what we deserve here and a crisis is now upon us. This existing state of affairs is inadequate to the task of fundamental structural reform. Something radically different is required, something that will create positive change and enlist people throughout society to the positive task of re-consideration and renewal. Irresponsible, special interest, and short term "thinking" cannot be allowed to continue if disaster is to be averted. It is time to think about an alterative.

Under the heading of Common Sense Union (CSU) such an alternative will be offered. Without altering political institutions, with only a shift in attitude, it is possible to envision a radical change in the political process. A simple formulation will serve as a beginning. On the basis of agenda and policy, center Democrat and center Republican have more in common with each other than each have with their respective extremes. Accordingly, it would be possible to build on this taken for granted consensus as the basis of a Center Party. At this middle ground, think through a political agenda that would no longer be polarized by the fringes of the Left or the Right. A diagram can best illustrate this simple notion.

COMMON SENSE UNION

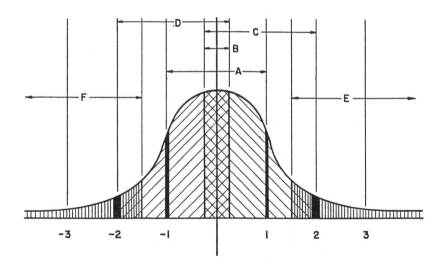

A	COMMON SENSE UNION
B	BI-PARTISAN CENTER
C	REPUBLICAN PARTY
D	DEMOCRATIC PARTY
E	RIGHT WING FUNDAMENTALISMS
F	LEFT WING SOCIALISMS

271

The political spectrum from the far left to the far right can be represented with the curve of general distribution. The area between the curved line and the horizontal axis represents the general distribution of any given statistical group, political society as a whole in this case. The curved line extends both to the far left and right. Area C extends from -1/4 to +2 and represents the Republican Party. Its agenda begins to the left of the center line and then extends far to the right. Area D represents the Democratic Party and reverses the area of the Republicans and extends from +1/4 to -2. The range from -1/4 to +1/4, Area B, represents the area of shared agenda, the area where bi-partisan consensus is possible. This is the place where Republicans and Democrats quietly agree. Generally, uncontested matters of the "nation" and issues of mutual self-interest would lie at this middle ground.

The range of right wing fundamentalisms are represented by Area E, from +1 1/2 to 3 and beyond. Being aligned to the fringe of the Republican Party, the far right is able to influence and aggravate agenda and policy to a much greater extent than its electoral numbers could ever justify. On the other side, the range of extreme socialisms, Area F, from -1 1/2 to -3 and beyond, aligned to the far left of the Democratic Party, are able to influence and aggravate more than they could ever justify. The proposed political party of the CSU would break with this traditional alignment of polarization and look instead to the middle. It would build upon the natural consensus of the *Bi-partisan Center* and encompass the area designated as A. Center Democrat and Center Republican would be re-oriented towards each other and their fringes would be cut loose to begin life on their own. The large and often silent majority of concerned human beings would see that their best interests as both an individual and as a member of the larger society are better served with this agenda at the Center, *in-between* the Left and the Right. With the isolation of the political extremes, this newly constituted majority could lead with authority and confidence. Fundamental decision making would again become possible.

Traditional attempts to understand social reality have been based upon the relative importance of the individual with respect to the social, or the larger world in which any individual must live. Some theories place the highest importance upon one and some on the other. Some give the individual the final say, whereas others give that to the social. Politically, the Right purports to give the highest value to the individual and the Left does the same for the social. The political strife of recent years has been caused by either one or the other imposing its interpretation of this division. Balanced somewhat equally, the net effect has been that neither has gotten its exclusive way, resulting in the virtual disintegration of consensus government, a gridlock of political impotence. Locked in the grip of this ideological fight, there has been a breakdown of the ability to govern. The Presidential Veto has become the symbol of leadership, as all that remains is to say No to everything whatsoever.

Suggesting a possible break with this tradition of division, the CSU would recognize the *equal* importance of both the individual and the social and would look to the relative balance of each with respect to the other. The individual is the primary basis of human life yet there are absolute social requirements to which the individual must defer. The individual must be free onto himself but the social must have the right to limit any behavior that is in conflict with the natural rights of others. The primary principle of the balance between the person and the encompassing world of others is that of *self-responsibility.*

As an agent of free action, being capable of personal initiative and effort, the person can both create and destroy. Simply, the individual is responsible for his choices and the consequences of his deeds. He must share in the results of positive achievement as he must suffer the consequences of negative behavior. Law must be written that encourages the one and discourages the other. Fashionable sociological-psychological theory will disclaim the validity of self-responsibility, claiming instead that no one is free at all as there are only the material forces of nature. Obviously more is involved, specifically the reality of self-consciousness and choice. Everyday we make our choices and live with the consequences. We either make an effort or do not. It is this alone that defines the highest aspect of humanity. Without choice there is only animal existence, that peaceful unconcern about anything at all, that mindless chewing of one's cud that relives itself the very same, day after mindless day. In freely choosing, we decide to build, to create, to think about tomorrow and yesterday. We are able to fashion a world other than the one that we now inhabit. In the act of choosing, we are able to build a future that is better and different than the one of the past. Sociological-psychological theory cannot account for this astounding and marvelous difference. The inertia of material force can produce only more and less of itself, but nothing different. The denial of self-responsibility is just the hope to offer an "excuse," to become a victim, so as to avoid the consequences of failed responsibility. The social, economic, and political system pays a dear price for these excuses. Positioned at the middle, the CSU would constitute true accountability, balancing the individual and the social, the one and the many, so that neither is able to enforce its narrower agenda.

Complimentary with self-responsibility is the principle of the priority of the common over the special interest. No individual or group of individuals can have the right to benefit at the expense of the common interest. Special interests cannot be entitled to enrich themselves at the expense of others. Special interests often market themselves as if the common interest is served with their advantage but it is necessary to judge carefully and first see what serves whom and decide in the favor of the common interest. The difficulty here is that in effect there are only special interests. No one speaks from outside of the fray. When all agenda is exaggerated to fit the emotional needs of fringe elements then of course there are only special interests competing for power. With the move to the Center this will be seen in a new light. There is a common interest distinct from special interests.

Linked to the principle of the common interest is the principle of the priority of the long term over the short term. A perfectly clear criterion is at work here. Given any issue, simply project 20 years and decide if the "numbers" would be tolerable or even conceivable. If Federal debt went from 1 to 5 trillion in sixteen years then in another 20 it will have escalated to over 30 trillion. We will be well on our way to economic collapse. Is this acceptable? Are we helpless in the face of it? If not, something must be done now regardless of short term consequences. If acid rain continues to increase at the present rate, will the earth be inhabitable in 20 years? Effective action needs to be taken now. At its current rate of increase, will health care be affordable in 20 years to anyone at all? The principle here is as obvious as it is irrelevant in current practice. Politics of today are exactly that, of today only. Locked into the politics of irresponsibility and special interests, the long term good is sacrificed to the greed of today. Short term posturing masks the ever worsening conditions that surely will spell disaster for tomorrow and the next generations.

Three principles then stand at the center of the CSU; self-responsibility, the priority of the common over the special interest, and the long over the short term interest. What justifies these three principles? They are simply self-evident, obvious in a way that common sense would easily recognize. But more can be said here. Everything that makes personal life worth living is the result of one's self-awareness and then the ability to act in a responsible way. If this is denied, then human life remains at the level of the animal, simple and immediate existence. But through thinking, self-consciousness, and self-responsibility, one is able to place oneself in one's world as a free individual, free to think and do as one sees fit. The great cultural edifice of society itself is rooted in the collective deeds of thinking and responsible human beings. Only when so many seek excuses for their irresponsible behavior does it seem as if that is the rule but it must always remain the exception. Fundamentally, then, free political life is meaningful and coherent only when the responsible person stands at the center and when social relations are maintained that support that person. The individual must harvest what he sows, be that the positive or the negative. While the truth of this is obvious, much existing legal and social practice cuts in the opposite direction. Much "law" is written to protect the individual from the consequences of his misdeeds. Excuses can always be found after the fact. This must come under critical review.

Necessarily, each person must participate in a responsible way but general welfare is possible only in the context of social reality as a whole. One must act as an individual but can live only in the greater reality of social relations. Accordingly, the common interest must take precedence over the special interest of the individual. Now, certainly, the individual must be protected from the possible overreach of the common interest, but when matters of policy are considered the common interest must have priority. No individual is bigger than the group.

The final self-evident principle concerns the long term interest versus the short term. Without the broadened view of the longer term, it is difficult to see anything at all. Without perspective, things may appear more or less other than they actually are. Without an understanding of longer term trends, when concerned only with the immediately available, with only "press reports," it is difficult to have a clue. The long term view allows the sort of planning that distinguishes humanity from all other creatures. With these three principles in mind, the task of articulating specific policy is possible.

Agenda and Policy

The specific policies of the CSU agenda would naturally divide into the three areas of international relations, social relations, and budget and taxation.

A) International Relations

Central here is the status of the American military. As has already been stated, it would be *retracted* from its forward positions throughout the world and brought home. The United States needs to get out of the business of running the world, it should leave regional problems to the local players, and quit intervening where its objectives are both confused and self-serving. A role remains as a cooperating partner but it can no longer bear either the cost or the responsibility for the difficulties and failures of others. Generally, then, the policy of the CSU towards international relations would be one of fairness and economic cooperation in a context freed of the military option. The attitude of the unilateral would be replaced by that of the multilateral, the maintenance of a center of power would be replaced by its de-centralization, and the United States would seek to find its appropriate place in the world rather than being determined to fix into place all others. America could display world leadership by relinquishing its attitude of global domination. Changes in Eastern Europe and the former Soviet Union do not mean that the "West has won," but rather simply that conditions in that part of the world have come to require courageous restructuring. A point all too easily lost is that a similar restructuring is called for elsewhere and that the United States too needs to redefine itself. Smug self-assurances in the wake of the troubles of others is no agenda for leadership and positive contribution. The United States then should retract its over-extended military position throughout the world. It should bring its troops and

277

equipment home. It should recognize that the military option is no longer acceptable or appropriate. The billions of dollars that would be saved would accelerate positive transformation elsewhere.

At the same time Cold War bureaucracies need to be eliminated. The Central Intelligence Agency (CIA) was created as a Cold War institution and, true to its mission, it has produced "documentation" that supported every step that has escalated tension. The CIA has a history of "inventing the numbers" for any President who felt moved to "contain" Soviet power. With the collapse of the Soviet Union, it has become obvious that CIA estimates were always exaggerations and intent upon continuing the stalemate. The CIA no longer serves a legitimate function and ought to be abolished. Simply, send everyone home and padlock the gate. [35]

Another Cold War institution that needs to be abolished is Foreign Aid. The United States has bestowed its largess upon others only to try to influence foreign events to its own advantage in the Cat and Mouse game of Cold War intrigue. Most of this was military aid and has created stockpiles that are now being consumed in civil warfare throughout the world. It is a legacy for which America ought to be ashamed.

With the retraction of nuclear arsenals and military personnel, the role of the Pentagon bureaucracy would be greatly reduced as well. Having been in charge of the military implementation of the policy of "containment, counterforce, and counterinsurgency," all of which no longer has any place in global relations, the Pentagon ought to be scaled back proportionately. The Cold Warriors need to be retired as a group before their biased views infect more policy decisions. The dead vision of division needs to be buried.

How does this policy of military retraction square with the three principles of the CSU? In being more faithfully responsible to itself, the United States cannot take on the failed responsibility of others. Tribal conflict throughout the world is the responsibility of

278

those involved, it cannot be mediated through Washington. It is not the United States' responsibility to correct the problems of the world, as it is hard-pressed to address its own. Secondly, the common interest is best served by the retraction of the United States military. The wasted billions here could be allocated elsewhere. Some budgetary relief is the first positive. The military bureaucracy itself has become a special interest which hopes to perpetuate itself at the expense of others when its "mission" has become obsolete. One could legitimately ask, what are all those people doing anyway? Thirdly, retraction easily serves the long term interest. To continue to waste resources on pointless military structure into the future would be perfectly insane and would accelerate economic dislocation everywhere. No longer needing to play the part of a military superpower, it would be possible to re-direct resources to the task of building a better world for all. It is difficult to imagine a more appropriate or attractive alternative.

B) Social Relations

While the global posture of the American military would undergo fundamental change, domestic social policy would be virtually revolutionized. Here the principle of individual self-responsibility necessitates a dramatic change of perspective. The central piece of all social policy would involve health care reform. It is here where tremendous resources are being consumed and where changes to individual behavior would result in the greatest benefit.

Health care reform must begin with a single payer system. Private health insurance companies are not able to deliver efficient health care management on a universal basis. The profit motive of private companies establishes two principles that run counter to quality-inclusive care. Profitability is based upon the exclusion of as many people as possible and the denial of as many claims as possible.

279

Locked into the mentality of exclusion and denial, private insurers cannot achieve the level of care and efficiency that is necessary. Since private health insurance companies contribute nothing to the actual health process, concerning themselves only with the collection of premiums and the payment of claims, a single payer system would be vastly more efficient. Premiums would be paid as payroll deductions and claims would be paid directly based upon established criteria. Equally, the "profit" of private insurers is better allocated to health care itself. Some existing health insurance companies would be purchased and their facilities and staffs converted to the single payer system.

The concern over health care touches upon many aspects of social life but everything here starts with the individual. It is crucial that each individual contribute to the cost of care as only in this way does protection become affordable for everyone. The individual would pay a percentage, say 3%, of gross income as a payroll deduction in the manner of the Social Security payroll deduction. The employer would match that percentage contribution. An annual deductible would apply. In this way business would be freed from the fury of uncontrollable and unpredictable health care cost increases and yet would contribute a reasonable amount to general health care costs.

Adverse individual behavior would be charged an additional premium payable by the individual alone. For example, tobacco users would pay an additional 1 to 3% of gross wages. Convicted alcohol related motor vehicle violators would pay an additional 1 to 3%, depending upon the severity of the offense. A higher deductible would be paid by those already paying higher premiums for adverse behavior. Simply, a health care partnership would be enacted where the cost to the individual would be determined by that individual's choices. Adverse behavior would pay more because it costs more and responsible behavior would pay less because it costs less. People would be encouraged, not forced, to chose the better and less expensive habits. When the financial incentives are sufficient perhaps there would be reason to pause and re-consider. The smoker may decide that the misery of his addiction is no longer worth the added cost.

The principle here though is that of self-responsibility as the person is left with the choice. Through these kinds of financial incentives the individual would be encouraged to make healthy life choices. This would influence behavior for the better but would primarily be a way of collecting money from those who will end up costing more to the health care system. A whole range of dis-incentives could be considered. The principle here is that adverse behavior, for which the individual is responsible, would be charged an additional premium. When "bad" behavior costs significantly more some may find within themselves the motivation to change. In comparison, the present strategy of suing tobacco companies for damage done to willing smokers, while emotionally gratifying, is ludicrous. There may be some corporate responsibility here, but it is obvious that it is the person who possesses the final responsibility. The choice to smoke is the person's alone. After the fact, after years of self-inflicted damage, one need not hold anyone else responsible. Only a befuddled legal system would entertain even the possibility of this sort of suit. To be sure, tobacco companies have made handsome profits in the marketing of death but it is the person who must be held accountable for their own adverse behavior. Much higher tobacco taxes would address this question and put smoking further out of reach of youth.

General health care strategy would change. The health care dollar would be shifted from cure to prevention. Modern medicine has led people to believe that any medical condition will find a cure within the health care system. There is a high-biotech solution to every problem, so we are led to believe. Implicit here is the assumption that modern medical science will be able to "cure" all ills. People have come to expect and feel entitled to such a result. This medical strategy distorts health care resources. Vast sums are sunk into programs of cure when much less is done at the level of prevention where relatively little could do so much more.

It's a matter of record that health care costs in the U.S. are up to around one trillion dollars a year. Of that horrendous figure less than 2.5% goes for prevention and an even smaller amount--a mere 0.5%-- goes for health promotion; leaving approximately 97 cents out of every health care dollar for treatment; which is about everything from basic first aid to extremely costly intensive care. Nothing is spared to treat the injured and diseased. [36]

Coupled with this are the huge sums of money which are spent on people within six months of their death. Machine assisted terminal warehousing is merciful to no one. No good can come when the natural limits of life are artificially extended and the personal dignity of the individual violated. People must be accorded the dignity to die when that is their only hope.

The health care industry itself, the doctors, hospitals, and support services, would remain structurally unchanged. New guidelines in the direction of prevention versus cure and the elimination of terminal warehousing would affect in some manner but the industry as a whole would remain essentially the same. Equitable maximum payable fees and rates would be established. Doctors and hospitals could work as before with little interference. Malpractice law would be changed. Malpractice settlement limitations would be enacted and truly incompetent doctors removed. Paying millions to single individuals makes no sense when the effect is to limit care to many others. The recent attempt to reform the health care industry sought fundamental change while hoping to change nothing. The special interests were left in place and obstructed reform to their own advantage. Nothing was allowed that would have improved anything for anybody. The special interests congratulated themselves as the system was allowed to continue its breakdown.

The so-called War on Drugs is an absolute failure. It dispenses more death and destruction than the drug use itself. It is simply overkill. The cure is worse than the disease. As a different strategy of control and prevention, drugs would be legalized. Illegal drug use is essentially two problems. It is a matter of crime and use. The high profits drive the criminal element, whose presence transforms cities into battlefields.

Legalization of drugs would reduce crime in the ghetto, and much that is positive would follow. The vast majority of the crime network ought to crumble. The importance of that cannot be underestimated.[37]

Violence on American streets would decrease, as that violence is destroying more lives then the drug use itself. Drug sales would be heavily taxed, creating revenues for programs of prevention and cure. Simply, by taking the profit out of the sale and "pushing" of drugs, the problem of social violence would be lessened. By breaking the drug problem into two parts, it would become easier to control both. Criminal violence would be lessened and forthright programs of prevention would decrease use.

The only thing that keeps drug prices high is that drugs are illegal. When legal, the marketplace will soon dictate the proper price. That people have been willing to pay outrageously inflated prices for drugs indicates they would also be willing to pay outrageously inflated taxes on drugs. Yes, some people will abuse drugs (as they already do), and drug abuse will have its costs to society (as it already does). Drugs, however, unlike cigarettes, will be able to pay their way--and create a significant amount of government revenue. [38]

Tough militaristic type talk in the end simply justifies government sanctioned violence. The rhetoric of "drug war" and "czars" is empty and deadly idle talk.

The goal of legalizing drugs is to bring them under effective legal control. If it were legal to produce and distribute drugs, legitimate businessmen would enter the business. There would be less need for violence and corruption since the industry would have access to the courts. And, instead of absorbing tax dollars as targets of expensive enforcement efforts, the drug sellers might begin to pay taxes. So, legalization might well solve the organized crime aspects of the drug trafficking problem. [39]

With legalization would come the enactment and enforcement of mandatory drug testing laws for the workplace. It would be a person's right to use drugs but an employer's right to have a drug-free work environment. Drugs would be legal to buy but their use would jeopardize a person's livelihood. Simply, legalization, the elimination of the criminal element, treatment, and incentives for its non-use would greatly limit the debilitating effect of drug use on society as a whole. Furthermore, the current "War on Drugs" is not worth the life of a single more policeman or enforcement officer. Legalization would go a long way towards protecting those whose job it is to protect others. It is asking far too much for these people to risk their lives in the pursuit of murderous drug dealers. Drug use would be reduced through proper management. Those who choose to get their "fix" can do so without that entailing massive expenditures for interdiction. Give the addict his daily dose for $5 rather than $500 and the level of burglary and assault would naturally plummet. The problem could be contained in a way that its current profitability does not allow. Adequate treatment for those interested in freedom from addiction would be made available. At its worst legalization could not be any more damaging than the present "war" and it would cost much less.

An intriguing result of the legalization of drugs is that marijuana, or hemp, is an immensely useful and beneficial plant.

Whereas trees--currently our primary source of paper--take twenty years to grow, hemp can grow to be twenty feet tall in a single season. Warm climates can produce three hemp harvests per year. This, obviously, makes hemp a far more efficient plant for producing paper than trees. In addition, making paper from hemp--unlike wood pulp--doesn't require acid, so all hemp paper is 'acid free' and thus lasts for hundreds of years. Hemp could supply virtually all of our paper, cardboard, and other packaging needs. [40]

As farmers look for new products, it is possible that they grow hemp for the vast papermaking industry. Precious forests would no longer need to be leveled.

The medicinal value of marijuana is well known.

Marijuana is the best medicine for reducing nausea in people being treated with chemotherapy. Marijuana is also an excellent treatment for glaucoma, which is responsible for 14% of all blindness in America and affects 2.5 million people. Marijuana has also been proven effective in treating asthma, epilepsy, MS, back pain and muscle spasms, arthritis, cystic fibrosis, rheumatism, emphysema, migraines, reducing tumors, and in promoting appetite. [41]

While hysteria and special interests have claimed the addictive nature of marijuana, the evidence points elsewhere. There is simply no proof that it is addictive even though some of its users will go on to others drugs. The critical fact here is not its presumed addictiveness but rather the choice of the individual to use some other drug, for which that person is absolutely responsible. Simply, with the legalization of just marijuana a productive, beneficial, and tax paying industry would have been created which would replace the War on Drugs. Use would not be any greater and the cost to society would be dramatically less.

The principle of the legalization of drugs has far reaching social consequences. It raises the question of the criminalization of all acts between and among consenting adults. There is no authorization for the jailing of these "criminals" from either the United States Constitution or the Bill of Rights. A crime is an act that violates the rights of either a person or his property or, simply, an act that has a victim. "Crimes" of consenting adults have no such victim and, consequently, the highest law of the land prohibits governmental intrusion into these affairs and activities. If Constitutional principles are to stand, then all "crimes" of consenting adults must be repealed. Laws against gambling incur the added factor of hypocrisy. It is simply a person's right to do what he wants with his own money, if there is no violation against someone else. The media carries the betting line and many games of chance legally prosper yet a certain few bring police, lawyers, courts, and prison. Again, the gains to society with rational legalization as compared to a hypocritical and spotty criminalization are immense. The process that finally ends in prison is infinitely more costly than a process that immediately pays taxes. Let the gambler have his Constitutional right and he will gladly chip in to the public coffers. The hypocrisy would be less. Some estimates claim that 350,000 people are currently in prison for committing acts between consenting adults. An additional 4,000,000 arrests are made yearly. [42] The numbers are astounding in terms of what could be saved if the "government got off the back of the people."A recent Senate "Crime Bill" carries on the hypocrisy. It can "think" only to put more police officers on the street and build more prisons. It should, instead, empty the prisons of 350,000, and eliminate 4,000,000 arrests. But leadership is lacking.

Politicians today tend to follow popular beliefs (even if those beliefs are based on prejudice, inaccuracies, and myths), repeat the popular beliefs back to the populace (thus enforcing the prejudices, inaccuracies, and myths), and make laws to support the popular beliefs (thus institutionalizing the prejudices, inaccuracies, and myths). Some say it's democracy. Actually, it's cowardice. [43]

The criminal justice system as a whole would be moved in the direction of the CSU's three general principles. At the center of this of course is the principle of self-responsibility. Fashionable sociological-psychological theory, which informs judicial policy, deflects responsibility from the perpetrator of crime to various external conditions. All manner of excuse is put forth in order to shelter the perpetrator from taking responsibility for his deed. Heredity, upbringing, social pressures, chemical and neurological imbalances, and the like, are offered as causes for criminal behavior, yet when the trigger is pulled it can only be as a conscious act for which the individual is absolutely responsible. At that moment he could have chosen otherwise. After the fact, when standing trial, he may plead that something else made him do it but it was not by sociological or psychological necessity but only as a conscious act that the murderer becomes who he is. Society has for too long paid a horrible price for not imposing responsibility here. With our presumptive "mercy" the proven violent offender "walks" to inflict pain again.

The logical choice here is to impose the death penalty for violent and deadly crimes but society has not the "stomach" to execute the thousands that yearly would be deserving of this fate. As an alternative to this, life imprisonment without parole would be mandated with the second violent offense. Again, there would be no stomach for the first offense conviction. We pride ourselves on our compassion by extending a second chance but the results of this compassion are more innocent dead. The scandal of recently released parolees killing again need not continue. The prison space will be found with the release of consenting adult criminals.Those who have forfeited their rights in a free society need to be put away. It is too high a risk for a proven criminal to be afforded the opportunity to kill again. Thousands of innocent people would be saved. The denial of self-responsibility on the basis of the excuses offered by sociological-psychological theory cannot stand in a free, open, and civil society.

The explosive issue of gun control would need to be squared with the principle of self-responsibility. The mass production and distribution of all kinds of weaponry is in the interests of no one. The constitutional rights of the responsible gun owner can be maintained while at the same time reducing the arsenals that are inflicting so much damage. The quasi-religious and self-righteous fervor of those that oppose any gun limits refuse to acknowledge hard reality. By owning a gun, presumably for purposes of self-defense against the would-be burglar or rapist, the chances are three to one that someone with no criminal intent will become a victim.

Keep a gun in the house and your chances of getting murdered triple. 'The risks of keeping guns in the home substantially outweigh the potential benefits in terms of safety.'[44]

The life long neighbor who comes to your house late at night having forgotten his keys is gunned down as a presumed burglar. The ten year old child finds his father's weapon and playfully puts a hole in his playmate.

While her date waited for a ride in the driveway of the girl's home, she shot him in the face from about 15 feet away. She said she shot him to prevent him from breaking up with her and getting another girlfriend. [45]

Unintended violence is perpetuated simply because of easy and ready availability. There may be the times when the possession of a gun prevents a crime but your chances are three to one against that possibility. Common sense would be simply bullheaded to go against these odds. Even during a burglary or rape attempt, it is safer to be without a gun. Confronted with an opposing gun, the burglar or rapist easily can be forced to a level of violence that he may not have intended, becoming a murderer too. To have some possessions stolen or to have been raped is better than to be dead. The rights of hunters and recreational shooters can be perfectly maintained alongside of a policy of the elimination of all other weapons. The cry goes out then that only the criminals will have guns. Yes and no. They will gradually have fewer but your odds are still better without you yourself having one. Common sense indicates the necessity of some gun control.

Many things could be done to reduce the volume of weaponry. People have guns that they would prefer to be without. Buy-back programs have been successful and have encouraged many to disarm themselves. The careless father who leaves his guns laying about must be made to understand his flagrant irresponsibility. The gun owner whose daughter uses his gun in order to shoot her boyfriend in a fit of teenage hysteria should face immediate jail time and steep fines. With such laws in place many would be encouraged to remove their guns from easy access by their children. Most significantly, the use of a gun in a crime would more quickly bring life imprisonment. Weapons and ammunition that can have no purpose other then the killing of human beings would be illegal. Prosecution would target manufacturers. Society pays too dearly when it maintains the unlimited right to bear arms. The Second Amendment remains intact.

Free society is possible only on the basis of work.

At the base of this democracy (Ancient Greece) and this culture lies the production and distribution of wealth. Some men can govern states, seek truth, make music, carve statues, paint pictures, write books, teach children, or serve the gods because others toil to grow food, weave clothing, build dwellings, mine the earth, make useful things, transport goods, exchange them, or finance their production or their movement. Everywhere this is the foundation. [46]

Through the ages the issues remain the same. It is only through work that sufficient goods and services are produced and distributed for the well being of all. Through productive work a person achieves a self-respect that entitles him to the esteem of those around him. Equally, it is through work that one can better oneself and then enjoy the resulting rewards. Work is the criterion of modern industrial society. It has specific rewards for those who do all that they can, those who do as little as they can, and those who do nothing at all. Not to work is to invite the vices of excessive time. Alcohol and drug abuse and related criminal activity finds its primary cause in the effort to *kill time*, in the tedious effort to get through the boredom of yet another day of nothing. Furthermore, the activities of doing nothing impose a penalty on productive work. Not to work is to incur a social cost that with each passing year has becomes more and more difficult to pay. As is obvious, many social problems begin in the idle of unemployment.

The Federal government would adopt a policy of full employment. In the fight against inflation, the immediate effect of policy at the Federal Reserve Board has been to increase unemployment. When prices move upward general interest rates are raised by the Fed causing a higher cost for doing business. This higher interest cost "cools" the economy by causing a recession. Business activity is less, capacity reduced, and unemployment increased. Upward wage pressures are eliminated as the pool of workers without jobs increases. Higher wages though are but one of the elements of inflation, among others such as higher health care costs, higher resource costs, and higher cartel managed energy costs. But the Fed's fight against inflation is directed solely at the wage element of the equation as the other factors are presumably beyond its grasp. In other words, the social misery of the unemployed and underemployed is deemed the appropriate cost for a democratic society to pay in order to restrict inflation. So as not to erode the purchasing power of the wealthiest citizens, those who are least able are called upon to make a total sacrifice. So that the few people with a million dollars will not lose some percentage points of their money to inflation, the many people with little or no money are forced to lose whatever they may have left. Fed policy gives to the takers and takes from the givers. It rewards unearned income as it penalizes earned income. The Fed has never considered the social cost of its monetary policy and simply imposes its "economic model." One sector of society pays dearly for the compounded comfort of another. The Fed's rightful mission is to manage the value of money and the raising of interest rates is one of its legitimate tools, but its fight against inflation extracts a very high social cost. The middle ground of a modest inflation would better serve the interests of the majority. Fed policy has simply been too extreme in targeting one social group for the total cost of inflation control. But the problem here lies much deeper. It lies with America's image of itself as it goes about the world. It concerns the nature of international trade and the balance of power.

As the United States came to predominance following World War II it reversed its policy on trade from one of protectionism to what has come to be called "free trade." As countries were lined up in the grand strategy for the defense of the Free World, the many separate national economies were forced to play by the new rules of development, which meant open markets. Small closed markets were opened to the force and presence of American corporations. The result was predictable. The small got smaller and weaker and the big got bigger and stronger. This new system of trade proved to have little about it that was free. There was a specific and key exception to this development where the domestic market was never opened and instead was able to export unilaterally. Japan sells 4,000,000 cars in the United States and buys 40,000 in return, or 1% of its export. The Americans in their near-sighted and delusionary "wisdom" have allowed their own very important car market to be penetrated to an extent that extracts a huge domestic price. The way in which the "free trade" ideology was allowed to unfold has left a gigantic disparity between the world's two largest trading partners. But this is a matter not so much of trade as of "imperial conquest," something of course a bit odd between trading "partners."

The Cold War implementation of the free trade ideology has allowed a closed market to remain closed as it in turn exports into an open market to its exclusive and unilateral advantage. The one refuses to buy in return and the other is left only buying. A fundamental imbalance has occurred that spells long term economic disaster. The ideology of free trade has to be squared with the necessity for "fair trade." But the Americans persist in their heartfelt vision of the world that will ultimately leave them naked.

Japan has a problem though that it cannot square with free trade. American foods, primarily rice, could be sold in Japan far cheaper than those produced by Japanese farmers, in fact these farmers simply could not compete and would be bankrupted. But, more is involved than just the cost of food commodities, as Japanese culture and traditions are held together by the landownership of these farmers. Simply, to open its rice market to American imports would destroy its own agriculture and much of its cultural heritage. More importantly, this would put the Japanese into the vulnerable position of being a possible economic hostage, something which no country can be expected to do. Certainly Americans would never tolerate this if conditions were reversed. A higher cost for rice has been deemed

292

by the Japanese as the proper price to pay for retaining its own culture. Each country as a sovereign state must be allowed to protect what it sees as its fundamental rights. Yet, while the Japanese can protect their own markets as they see fit, the Americans need not continue to allow huge imports. The free trader's ideology collapses into wishful thinking when there is no reciprocity and with Japan there has been none.

The French farmer is also under attack by the global free trader. The natural inefficiencies of French farmers cannot compete against American "agribusiness" that produces on an immense scale. If the more inefficient market is opened its farmers simply cannot compete. The human and social costs cannot begin to compensate for the "cheap wheat" for the general consumer. The concept of free trade is a "mathematical model" that has been conceived in isolation from the real world. It thinks of consumers, producers, prices, and markets as purely mathematical functions that can exist only in the "ivory towers" of its disciples. Yet it serves as the justification for moral judgment. More costly producers, such as Japanese rice farmers and French wheat farmers, are less efficient and therefore "bad" and therefore rightfully put out of business. If you cannot produce cheaply, then you ought to be removed regardless of the fact that the natural order of one's society is undermined and great devastation visited upon the land. The free trader stands firm though, as it is cheaper and cheaper products for himself that he desires at whatever cost to others. In order that the more efficient American farmer may sell 5% more of his product the Japanese and French farmers' production is cut to zero and he is permanently put off the land. In whose world could this possibly be a good thing?

The many proponents of free trade themselves will never suffer the effects of their theory as it is the quickly unseen and permanently unemployed who will suffer this misery. The free traders feel sanctioned to devastate the lives of others. Academic tenure and

293

the high discretionary income of think tankers and politicians protects the free trader from sharing the fate of those that they have impoverished. Two issues are central here. Each country must be allowed to protect its own domestic market and balance its trade with all others. Japanese trade imbalances cannot be allowed to continue and American intrusion into the Japanese rice market cannot be imposed. Each country must be able to protect itself and then export to the level of its imports. Of course, international trade would continue at high levels but each market would have the right to choose whatever it sees as being best for itself. The Japanese and the French must be allowed the right to protect their farmers if they so choose. Universal free trade is not a formula that can be forced on the world for mutual benefit. It's a prescription for big winners and equally big losers.

The issue of free trade needs to be looked at more closely. "Belief in free trade is as common and widespread among economists as belief in God is among clerics of less worldly religions." [47] Some background is in order.

The United States had long ago called for a reduction of barriers to trade and investment throughout the world, on the grounds that humanity at large would benefit if individual producers were free to concentrate on what they could most efficiently produce. Indeed, Americans went farther than that. Wars, they tended to believe, grew out of rivalries resulting from economic nationalism; if nations could become economically interdependent, war itself might become obsolete. (Never mind that their own tariffs remained high throughout most of their history, or that the connection between trade, investment, and economic development was less than clear, or that the historical record suggested little correlation between extensive economic interchange and the avoidance of war.) And, yet, as had often been pointed out, the doctrine of 'free' trade brings disproportionate benefits to the most efficient producer, and the United States happened to find itself in that fortunate position throughout most of the twentieth century. Americans' disinterested endorsement of the 'open door,' therefore, served their self-interested ambition to expand markets, investment opportunities, and profits. [48]

A hypocrisy and deception then lies at the center of the free trader's religion. While the term "free trade" may lead the uninitiated to believe that it must involve equality, freedom, and the benefit of all, in fact, it involves absolute inequality, increasing dependence for most, and benefit to only a few. Those who have historically preached the gospel of free trade have been England in the 18th century and the United States after World War II. Each was then at the height of its economic dominance of the rest of the world. Each sought to use its privileged position to re-make the world in its own image and to its own advantage and profit. Free trade brings to the dominant producer the advantage of cheap materials and easy markets for its surplus. Both of these advantages of course are absolute. A dependent economy will never develop its own productive capacity if a stronger economy sells cheaply in its market. In effect, the weaker will always remain weaker and finally become merely a "plantation" in someone else's scheme of global world order. But an irony of sorts has become evident. America now has characteristics of both the dominant player and the plantation backwater. It hopes to sell to its own advantage and yet allows itself to be devastated by foreign exporters.

While the United States was opening markets in the wake of World War II, its newly acquired taste for global political dominance involved *giving away* its own market as a reward and pay-off for those who were willing to line up on its side in its "defense of the free world." Simply, America gave away its economic advantage in order to stride atop the world as it saw fit. Countries were allowed special access to the American economy to the dis-advantage of domestic producers until the point has been reached where those domestic producers have been destroyed. Ironically, in a world of free traders,

America may lose. The proverbial goose is now being cooked. The consequences of this has been that American workers have been idled or downgraded by the millions. None of this need continue. America may be weaker but it is still strong enough to regain its prosperity if it were but to choose to do so. National politicians often proudly talk of their "job creation" efforts, but in effect it is a matter of downgrading, of the loss of a high paying job that affords a living and the gain of a low paying job that does not. Obviously it is better to keep and protect the high paying jobs that we already have than to "create jobs" that only accelerate the general decline of the standard of living.

When the euphoria of the free traders has subsided a bit over the recently enacted NAFTA and GATT agreements and the compliance phase entered upon, there will be cause for great disappointment and finger pointing. Export driven producer markets simply will not open themselves to foreign goods. It would be economic suicide. Whatever they may say and agree to today will have nothing to do with what they will do tomorrow. It is not so much a matter of dishonesty as it is a playing along with the insistent Americans who so fervently want to re-make the world in their own image. One thing is certain though, when all of this comes to grief the one commodity that will be freely traded will be blame.

Environmental protection would be extended and enhanced. The pollution control and cleanup industries would be expanded, perhaps repositioning some defense industry workers. Acid rain restrictions would be enforced. The nuclear energy phase out would be continued. Technologies of renewable and de-centralized sources of energy would be encouraged. Conversion to natural gas would be accelerated. A Carbon Tax would be levied that would encourage the development and use of alternative fuels and technologies. Through taxation, the cost of carbon based fuels would rise dramatically. Much could be done that now simply lacks encouragement. Protection of water and air would become a first priority. The automobile industry would be extended incentives to accelerate its efficiency. The whole range of environmental policy can be easily visualized, being simply cleanup, conservation, and care.

Many things could be done that would facilitate a policy of conservation. A few examples will suffice here. The tollroad system in metropolitan Chicago creates unnecessary pollution and congestion. Gasoline consumption while idling in line to pay a toll is pure waste and without reasonable justification. Millions of gallons of gasoline would be saved yearly with its elimination. A further advantage of course would be the greater efficiency of travel in an area that is near the limit of concrete gridlock. Another example of easy conservation is reducible to a billboard type adage. "Cut less grass less often." It is simply wasteful to manicure thousands of acres of corporate grounds and homeowner lawns. Minor gasoline savings would be made here but it would be part of a national program to encourage the "green" attitude. Hundreds of energy conserving things mean little or nothing by themselves but when added together with the proper encouragement a great difference could be made. Most people want to do the right thing but find their single efforts to be meaningless. The missing link is coherent national policy and committed leadership.

Of fundamental concern is energy policy. Partisan bickering and special interest positioning over the last effort to raise the gasoline tax by 4 cents showcased poor policy and worse behavior. The purpose of a broad based Carbon Tax is not simply to raise revenue but, most importantly, to encourage conservation and facilitate the transition to alternative fuels and energy sources. The squabble had nothing to say about these benefits and hawked simply the pros and cons of a higher gas tax with respect to the various special interests. In the long term, the move to conservation and alternative energy sources is absolutely crucial. An additional $1 per

297

gallon tax on petroleum fuels, phased in possibly at $.02 per month for 50 months, would create incentives to conserve and disincentives to consume. A tax of this nature and magnitude would make competitive with oil many very productive technologies which now cannot compete with its artificially low price. The extensive network of carbon based special interests need to be convinced that they are welcome to be part of this transition and that their participation in this move to efficient energy policy is in their common interest. A world laid barren is a disaster for all. Furthermore, when calculating costs, such things as the Bush/Hussein War, are not included. Cheap oil is government policy but it is not necessarily as cheap as it seems. The dead and wounded of that war will attest to that.

Another factor is important here. The greatest fear in Saudi Arabia is energy conservation in the United States. Ever increasing worldwide oil demand, led by huge American consumption, is the central leg in the Saudi led cartel to prop up oil prices to a higher than real market level. The United States' policy of deferring to this cartel in order to prop up its own domestic oil market leads to no effort whatsoever to conserve and reduce consumption. The oil cartel that has punished so severely the American economy is supported by American policy. The Saudis of course are quite pleased. A conflict arises though for American society as a whole. By not conserving, the Saudi price for oil is paid by the American consumer, monies which then support huge building and spending projects in Saudi Arabia, a monarchy whose second greatest fear is its own people. By not conserving, the American consumer is depleting the ability of the domestic economy to sustain itself and to continue to provide a high standard of living.

A $1.00 per gallon additional Carbon Tax on petroleum would help to reverse this. A higher tax here would encourage less consumption, thus reducing imported cartel oil. In scrambling to replace lost revenues overextended cartel members would increase production and compete with each other for a shrinking market. The cartel would effectively lose control over market prices. Oil prices would drop dramatically worldwide. Fewer dollars would flow out of the American economy. The real price of oil would drop but the additional $1.00 per gallon tax would be paid to the United States' treasury instead of into the King's purse. By conserving and taxing itself, monies would remain in the American economy for its own benefit. The net effect is in the common interest. The real price of oil would be less worldwide, aiding struggling economies everywhere, which often end up seeking American money to make up for their shortfalls. Alternatives to petroleum energy would be encouraged and a new generation of energy saving devices brought to the market. Monies would be kept in the United States to fund American projects instead of building palace cities in the sand of Saudi Arabia. Finally, the gross aggregate of petroleum based pollution would be less. All of this for $1.00 per gallon, a bargain by anyone's estimate.

Of course, there is nothing special about this tax at the round number of $1.00 per gallon. What is crucial is that oil be taxed to the point where incentives for change take effect, where various alternative energy technologies become competitive, and then the necessary behavioral changes will be brought into play. The tax could be more or less then $1, but at whatever rate, everyone with a stake in the American economy would be an overwhelming beneficiary.

Environmental policy could be best summarized by the words of the renown English fisherman Izaak Walton. "To strive for the purity of water, the clarity of air, and the wise stewardship of the land and its resources; to know the beauty and understanding of nature, and the value of wildlife, woodlands and open space; to the preservation of this heritage and to man's sharing in it."

An Equal Rights Amendment would be enacted into law and Affirmative Action abolished. A policy of equality cannot be implemented through a program of inequality. Mandatory sentences for child abuse would be imposed. The adversarial system of justice would be re-evaluated. Arbitration would be encouraged.

Abortion would be a matter of choice. The only thing worse than an abortion is an unwanted child. For this decision the woman must decide for herself alone. To criminalize abortion is simply to make it bloodier, as then it will be performed under primitive medical conditions. Whether legal or illegal, abortions will be performed. The remaining issue then is the conditions of the operation. The stridency of the anti-abortionists indicates a hidden agenda. Proclaiming the Word of God, they assure themselves of serving the Lord yet the ultimate justification is not the saving of the unborn but rather the saving of themselves. In thinking to do the work of God on earth they hope to find personal salvation in heaven. Tainted personal motives need not inform public policy.

Liability law would be changed. Those truly responsible would pay and not simply those involved with the most money. Settlements would be capped. The payment of unspendable amounts of money helps no one when the rest of society underwrites the major portion. The frenzy to sue, to find someone else to blame, in order to get something for nothing, is a tradition for which America is famous and about which it ought to be ashamed. When one fails in the self-consciousness of one's self-responsibility it becomes convenient to proclaim the special rights of the "victim." Without accepting any blame for oneself, someone else stands accused. Listening to the voice of phoney victims encourages more of the same.

For the many other issues of social policy, there would be established the criterion of the CSU's fundamental principles of self-responsibility, and the priorities of the common over the special interest and the long over the short term. Rather than throwing these issues into the piranha bowl of special interests, recourse would be made to objective public principle.

C) Budget and Taxation

The Fiscal Affairs of the United States need to be put on a new footing. Years of irresponsibility, mis-management, and political bad blood have led to a situation that cannot be allowed to continue. An immediate goal must be to reduce and balance the federal budget. While potential military savings would seem to suggest that ready cash is at hand to fix the budget, something much more profound is required. Fundamental and systematic changes need to be made.

Fiscal responsibility must be borne by those standing at the top. The President and Vice President would be paid the average national wage, about $25,000. Members of Congress would be paid through the charity of taxpayers and not from tax revenues. Presidential, Executive, and Congressional pensions would be cut by 75%. Those who sat in attendance and oversaw the escalating hemorrhage of irresponsible public policy ought no longer be the cause of further losses. It is no longer the responsibility of the public wealth to underwrite pensions of those whose service has been so poor. Presidential, Executive, and Congressional level pensions are simply too generous relative to the pensions of others and the "labor" expended. Once having been in Congress ought not to entitle one to an extravagant lifetime maintenance. No other group has such privileges at the public expense. Military pensions would be cut by 15%. Having served their country in the past, and enjoying the advantages of early retirement, it is now time for these veterans to contribute to their country's effort at economic survival. In being asked to do their duty once more, most military pensioners would understand the necessity. Government pensions would be scaled back to be more in line with those of the rest of society. These service and pension reductions signal only the beginning. Tax policy as a whole would strive for greater equity. Privileges at the expense of the U.S. Treasury must be curtailed.

The question can be expressed in terms of taxation. In recent years Republicans and Democrats have danced cheek to cheek as they together orchestrated an unimaginable run up of the Federal debt to the tune of 5,000 billion at the expense of the middle class and to the incredible advantage of the upper class. The modern equivalent of the Divine Right of Kings is Supply Side economics. Give more to the rich and they will bestow upon everyone else the blessings of their advantage. One is assured that this is simply the way that it was meant to be.

Reducing tax burdens for the wealth holders is a political program that will reward some citizens and penalize others. As an economic program, it does not yield the increased savings and investment and faster economic growth that the conservative logic promises. This is not entirely a secret. Conservative economists have pored over the numbers for years, searching for evidence to confirm their conviction that taxing the wealthy lightly benefits everyone else. In theory, they are sure it is right. Only they can't find much in the way of facts. [49]

The tax savings to the rich that are to be re-invested and spur the economy on to new and better jobs for everyone else never appear but instead are pocketed for purposes of greater personal consumption. The general advantages that were to be created are converted instead into the particular pleasures of personal leisure. The Supply Side solution is not only wrong but it is the very cause of the problem.

In other words, Mellon (a major proponent) had it backwards and so do later generations of his apostles. A growing economy with widely distributed incomes and full employment creates the effective demand that leads investors to increase capital investment--new factories and more jobs. Capital will not build new factories to make goods that no one can afford to buy. [50]

The few wealthy cannot create sufficient general demand, something that is possible only by meeting the needs of the many who are not wealthy. Not on the Supply Side but on the Demand Side will general prosperity be found. The religion failed, although the High Priests continue unabated to preach the salvation of the faith. An obvious lie can be maintained as the truth simply by being repeated over and over again. But something more is at issue here. It concerns the psychology of power.

While the possession of sufficient money allows one to no longer experience the anxiety of a possible scarcity, having "stockpiled," as it were, it also allows for a real power over those who are without. The experience of the rich is at its most satisfying when it involves a power to determine the conditions of those that are necessarily under their dominion. It is a great satisfaction to draw the distinction between one's own culture of leisure and the culture of one's workers. It is the difference between finding every door open to one's touch and finding no doors at all, between living at ease and working under duress. It is the difference between the privilege of access and the fact of none at all. This difference lends style and class to a life of leisure that is obviously distinct from the noisy hubbub of everyone else. Simply, the rich take great pride in being what they are and expect respectful recognition from everyone else. Two pillars then hold up the ideology of privilege, the Divine Right of Kings that is expressed in Supply Side economics and the exquisite experience of privilege and condescension itself.

A brief comment regarding greed is possible here. A simple definition will do. Greed is the taking from someone else who will go without while one has more than one could possibly ever use. Greed is corporations which underfund their agreed upon pension funds. Greed is an employer taking all the credit and giving all the blame in order to restrict wages. Greed is the Federal Reserve Board unemploying millions in order to protect the wealthy from modest inflation. Greed is corporations moving "offshore" in order to boost profits at the expense of the unemployed. Greed is corporate "raiders" dismantling productive organizations because they can be sold in pieces for an immediate profit. Greed is the act of intentionally making someone else's life worse simply for the sake of it or, as is often done, simply for the sport of it. And greed, finally, is being in a position to be a positive force in the world and choosing instead the greater personal profits to be made elsewhere. In a word, it is selfishness. In a world that is shared by us all, this imposes a liability that is more and more difficult to sustain. The Ancient Greeks understood this well.

> Show me the man who asks an over-abundant share
> Of life, in love with more, and ill content
> With less, and I will show you one in love
> With foolishness.
> In accumulation of many years
> Pain is in plenty, and joy not anywhere
> When life is over-spent. [51]

Something has emerged which has fundamentally altered the terms of the equation between the rich and the rest, between privilege and daily labor. The economic base has expanded to the point where there may be enough to go around and it is no longer necessary to covet beyond possible need. As the tax code is written and re-written, this fact is not introduced, as the old assumptions continue with new ferocity in the face of better evidence to the contrary. Various commentators, intent upon emotional titillation and hysteria, reduce the issue to the single aspect of taxation. Everything else is made to ride on this one issue. What is lost of course is the entire context of social life, the relationship between expectation and reality, between social costs and benefits, between human beings and other human beings living in the same world. What is lost is the notion of balance in the play of equally valid concerns. What is lost is simple respect for one's fellow man. A tax policy could be enacted that would strive to establish that missing respect to the benefit of all. Simply, it is not the amount of tax that one pays that is important, but rather the kind of world that remains. What is important is the standard of living that one's remaining income will sustain with respect to the world as a whole.

Complimentary to a regressive Carbon Tax would be added a progressive "bracketed flat tax." Current tax reform proposals are split between either the existing system of deductions and brackets or a flat tax with no deductions and a single bracket. Both have virtues that are lost when it is the choice of either/or but when combined an attractive and reasonable alternative becomes evident. The greatest virtue of a flat tax is the elimination of deductions. It is here that is found the greatest source of political corruption and payoffs. It is here that votes are "bought" and powerful special interests "feed" from the public Treasury. The less powerful with equally legitimate claims can be ignored, as their role is reduced to paying for the "entitlements"of the powerful. By eliminating this hodgepodge of deductions there would be a simplification that would "level the playing field," disallowing the powerful undue access. But a flat tax would unjustly favor the wealthy if set in the range of 12 to 18%. The net dollars left over to higher incomes would be unfair to those of lower incomes, therefore brackets would be established. The election year flat tax issue was a cover for a tax cut for the wealthy and a tax increase for the less so, something which a bracketed flat tax would correct. This fundamental revision of the tax code then would benefit in two ways. It would be a fair way of collecting revenues and it would greatly reduce the potential and opportunity for political favors and deal making that could favor only the selected few.

A National Sales Tax of perhaps 2% would be enacted. This would be levied on all purchases, including equity and financial market transactions, real estate, and general consumption. Again, by making all of this taxable there would be eliminated the potential for political deal making as well as it would simplify and ensure the collection process. This would naturally function as both a regressive and progressive tax, as everyone, of whatever income, would be taxed the same but since the wealthy spend so much more their tax bill would be more. Summarizing, then, these numbers could be revised depending upon general budgetary needs, but the principle is in place, regressive consumption taxes would be combined with a progressive bracketed flat tax.

In general, then, the principle of a greater tax fairness would be imposed, expanding the tax base so as to reduce the liability for any given individual. Budget surpluses would be targeted to debt reduction. Sustained lower interest rates would be a spur to the financial and business markets. People would profit through business initiatives rather than through the manipulation of tax laws and financial deal making. Real economic productivity rather than financial sleights of hand would produce wealth. Long term capital gains would be rewarded at the expense of short term profit taking. These sweeping modifications of tax policy would eliminate traditional privileges that can no longer be tolerated in the face of Federal bankruptcy. Too many take for themselves in the name of an "economic theory" that simply shifts the burden to the unprivileged majority.

The issue of Social Security requires a detailed consideration. Current recipients are entangled in a hypocrisy which their self-interest refuses to acknowledge. The generation that fought and won World War II came home to experience the greatest economic expansion in history. A world devastated by war was the necessary foundation of this prosperity. An escalation in real wages and real estate values created new wealth. Simply, this generation will go down in history as the most privileged. It is unlikely that any other will ever experience such a broad based accumulation of wealth.

306

Wages paced ahead of inflation and significant profits were returned on the sale of two or three homes. Equally significant, as this group aged they became a dominant political force. Age votes, youth does not. In appealing to this bloc, politicians continued to promise and deliver increasingly generous benefits that were beyond legitimate actuarial projections. They were getting far more than their contribution could justify. A gigantic special interest was constituted that could dictate its own terms. In a budgetary climate of lesser competitors, the grandparents would win. But the win is hollow, as it is bankrupting the next generations. Without any central consensus each group gets what it can and then these privileges are wrapped in the romance of entitlement. "We just deserve it and don't forget to include my 10% discount." But the hypocrisy now becomes evident.

The affluent generation that dotes on its grandchildren, sparing no expense in their welfare, has deeded a debt in their name that is simply unpayable. A generation that may be the luckiest in history has chosen to bequeath to its heirs a lesser world simply to maintain a retirement that refuses to spend any accumulated principle. This is the height of irresponsibility by those who know better. But their lobbies chant and they chatter and prior to the final collapse no one will think any different. But it is clear that the excesses and greed of the grandparents will be visited upon the children and grandchildren. Equally, though, this need not be the case. A political realignment towards the consensus of the middle would be able to address these issues without bombast and exaggeration and the majority would recognize that enough is enough and that some reduction in benefits is both possible and necessary without causing undue hardship. They would also understand that this is something that should be done and the proper vote ought to be cast. They would choose to end the hypocrisy and finally square their love for their grandchildren with the world that will remain with their passing.

The far reaching transformation of society that is here

envisioned is possible only when based upon the principles of self-responsibility, and the priorities of the long and common interest over the short and the special. Obviously the many changes being contemplated would effect every special interest, but the effort must be made to resist their intrusion. To let one interest influence the general question is to let two, then three, and then all the rest. The net gain would be reduced to zero. A clean break is necessary. It is better to legislate on the basis of general principle and "let the pieces fall where they may." Only then would it be possible that the net gain be greater than nothing and only then would fundamental change for the better be possible. Something must be done and nothing less than this will do.

The fundamental solution must originate with citizens outside Washington, for it requires nothing less than to change the political culture itself. Politics has to develop a fierce, new governing impulse to displace the old one--a skeptical perspective toward the reigning assumptions about how government is supposed to govern. Only the people can bring this into the arena and impose it on the governors.[52]

Perhaps the most important significance of the social and political philosophy of the CSU, the agenda of the middle ground, is that it would enhance the middle class. The policies of both the rich and the poor do not serve the common good but only their own. The rich want to keep all that they got and the poor want to get as much of that as they can and neither care to work. The result can only be destructive. Only the middle class that is based upon individual labor can support society as a whole.

...it is plain, then, that those states are best instituted wherein the middle classes are a larger and more formidable part than either the rich or the poor...whenever the number of those in the middle state has been too small, those who were the more numerous, whether the

308

rich or the poor, always overpowered them, and assumed to themselves the administration of public affairs...when either the rich get the better of the poor, or the poor of the rich, neither of them will establish a free state. [53]

As Aristotle says so well, the best interest is served at the middle.

What would the "numbers" be with such a shift to the CSU? Precision would be impossible here but a simple test will do. Given any particular change, is it positive or negative with respect to the budget? Virtually every change would be positive. Less military spending, both here and abroad, no CIA, a health plan that pays for itself, fewer billions on the War on Drugs, fewer unemployed and more gainfully employed, a stronger economy, less waste and pollution, more taxpayers, less cost of government and, overall, a policy of "paying your own way." While all of this may seem to be imaginary, perhaps delusionary, nonetheless it is possible.

...the old order is failing and people everywhere recognize it. The next step must be to mobilize the political imagination--and courage--to construct a new order in its place. [54]

The CSU agenda would involve comprehensive change. Many special interest groups would be encouraged to go out of existence, for their own good. Industries would undergo major transformation and people would be dislocated for the time being. Hopefully, the long list of affected would include everyone. Defense contractors and their workers, white collar labor servicing high finance, religious and tax-exempt groups, insurance companies, the medical and legal professions, the tobacco industry and its smokers, polluting and nuclear industries, the interests of traditional power suppliers, drug dealers and their bankers. Equally, Affirmative Action beneficiaries, Cold Warriors and the Propheteers of Doom and Apocalism, the disciples of rage and resentment, the practioners of double-talk, and those intent only upon themselves would need to change if the agenda of the CSU were to be enacted. All special interests would need to defer to the general good. But in an electoral system the majority could vote this special interest out of power. Many would think the trade-off to be unacceptable, being themselves unwilling to change, having decided that the old is better than the new. Everyone would have to weigh for themselves the benefits versus the liabilities, responsibility versus irresponsibility, common versus special interest, the long versus the short term. The defense industry worker that loses his job because of a changed world that no longer needs his products may recognize this to be a net personal gain. His children then will have better prospects for the future. Another job would be made available to him, perhaps building smokestack pollution control systems. The resources re-allocated away from defense procurement would spur great economic expansion, producing more and better jobs than those lost in the short term. Of equal importance would be the freeing up of creative people, the designers and engineers of weapon systems, who then would become available for much more positive activities. The health care industry would be transformed and made into a single system of care with a significant improvement in well being. The standard of living would increase, people getting more for less.

The list of trade-offs could be amplified in endless ways, but the final judgment would concern the benefits for all of a greatly expanded economic base and a balance among international and social affairs and budget and taxation. Each individual would be faced with a personal choice but, when seen within the overall context of a general improvement of society and the standard of living as a whole, it is not a mere fantasy to believe that the majority of people would choose to forgo the past and to affirm the future. There would be a resounding Yes vote for the principles and agenda of the Common Sense Union. Following the contours of the Bell Curve, this would mean that the middle seventy percent of the electorate could lead with effective authority, leaving the remaining minorities at the Left and the Right to grumble among themselves. Effective and comprehensive change could be carried forth without their intrusion.

Nothing is likely to change until people decide to change it. This is a truism of democracy, but it has special application to the deterioration of the Democratic Party and, ultimately, to the deeper dimensions of decay in the governing processes. If the public's voice has been lost, it cannot be restored without a political party to speak for it. Citizens cannot hope to rediscover their connection to power without exercising the collective power that is available to them through elections. None of the deeper problems of government...whatever plausible solutions may exist, are likely to be addressed until this sort of political development occurs. Someone will have to invent a genuine political party that takes active responsibility for its adherents. This is an awesomely large project, of course, for it literally means trying to construct piece by piece, in the fractured modern society, the personal and institutional relationships that might draw people back into the process of democratic governance. [55]

A full understanding of the issues here requires a look at the most deep seated and persistent error in human judgment. This concerns the nature of causality. This can be approached only through examples. The Great Pyramids of Egypt stand forth in absolute objective and material majesty. Their physical presence simply dwarfs any possible human comprehension. Yet, the initial cause of their existence has nothing of the objective at all but rather is a result of human subjectivity, after all they are man made. It is not the objective but rather the subjective that defines the possibility of their objective reality. It was only as someone's conception, someone's thought, that they were conceived and then built. The inception of the idea can only be a matter of human thinking or consciousness. The implications of this are nothing short of astounding for our world today. Our great institutions and bureaucracies possess an objective reality that is equally overwhelming as that of the pyramids. In the same way, these structures must trace their existence back to a subjective reality that conceived of their possibility and then began the work of their objective and material construction and maintenance. All great organizations entail a similar original causality, a similar mental tradition. In someone's thinking, in conjunction with others, was conceived the idea that was brought to bear in the objective dimension of space and time. The point of this is decisive. Rather than needing to remain overwhelmed and even intimidated by these structures, standing in place as if powerless, it is possible to see that their initial causality is based in subjectivity and therefore subject to change. What was once built can be re-built, what was once constructed can be de-constructed or, simply, to be constituted is to be re-constituted. In other words, when confronted with the objective structures of existing social and political institutions, the impression is felt that nothing can be changed, that their very objectivity is resistant to human intervention and that we are powerless to do anything different. Nothing could be further from the truth. The force of subjectivity and self-consciousness is simply the greatest force on earth. The institutional legacy of special interests and privilege can be changed. It is within the rightful power of mentality that it can do, re-do, and do again. It is only through the unwillingness to recognize this fact that it seems that nothing can change. Examples abound. Cold War institutions can be changed if we so choose. Social and political institutions of irresponsible short term special interests can be changed is we so choose. *Nothing stands in our way but ourselves.* This is the negative power of nothingness. It is only the inertia of believing that we cannot that obstructs the path to positive change. Simply, in a world of global institutional forces it is possible to assert the greater force of self-consciousness. We can change whatever we choose if only we choose to do so. That is the decision to be made.

We are all party to this decision. It is assumed that the private individual can do nothing but bear witness from afar. But the matter of these trade-offs, the necessity of understanding one's individual interests and habits with respect to the common good, brings the question of responsibility home. The choice of agreeing to the loss of one's defense industry job, for example, and facing short-term personal uncertainty for the sake of a greater good that is without the need for high technology weapons, is a matter of fundamental individual and personal responsibility. The choice of one's attitude is one's own. No one can be forced to be happy with this. But it is here that the questions of war and peace becomes personal. It is here that one realizes that power is not a matter of political leadership but rather of individual insight. It is here that one realizes that activities at the personal level have global consequences for which one is responsible. Personal participation is required. But this need not be nearly as terrifying when one realizes that everyone is party to this change. It would be so easy to scoff at this "idealistic nonsense" and assure oneself that traditional greed and self-interest will prevail and will not be altered. But to scoff is to overlook one essential fact of human nature. When given a choice, the vast majority of people would prefer the good. It is true that as afflicted individuals, when convinced of being met with greed and self-interest by others, people have chosen greed and self-interest for themselves. But when an opportunity is presented where others act in harmony with one's own best interests, then concerted positive community action would be the overwhelming choice. One would willingly participate. None of this has ever been tried, but if the reality of a better world were to stand on the threshold of realization, then the great positive force of individual persons would emerge in full strength. It is easy, assuring, and self-righteously justifying to say No, but then nothing is to be done. A Yes is a risk, but a risk worth taking. The good is of course infinitely greater than nothing. Such a grand opportunity as we have simply cannot be missed for anything. Whatever short-term trade-offs are demanded of the individual are to be returned in full in the long-term. The individual personally will find no greater satisfaction than having made his own contribution. Willing participation in the building of the good, to have done one's part, is the greatest thing of all.

How is this possible? How would it happen that the Common Sense Union would achieve political power? Easily. We, the people of the United States, are anticipating just such a transformation but the first step is difficult. There is a pervasive frustration with the ways and means of the existing system of political affairs. People everywhere are actively looking for an alternative.

...the political status quo is also highly vulnerable to a concerted electoral assault from citizens. The rising popular resentment aimed at all elected incumbents demonstrates the potential for such an effort.[56]

A wide range of groups and coalitions already have been formed, some national in scope, which are bound by the common desire for positive change. People throughout the country are thinking and doing as best they can in order to move the system forward but success has been thwarted and painfully limited. What is needed is the articulation of general principle and specific policy with a plan of action that encompasses a move to the good and away from the partisans of privilege and self-interest.

The truly difficult part would be to develop focused political objectives that resonate authentically with the army of fed-up citizens--the political ideas that people could call their own and would march behind confidently. [57]

The Common Sense Union here hopes to have presented these objectives. It is a first step and possible catalyst for a second. An initial organization could be formed with the task of clarifying in detail and then presenting this program to the American people. The center 70% of the electorate, the middle class, would quickly see that their own best interests would be better served by the affirmation of the common interest that is embodied in this agenda. Great popular enthusiasm would be forthcoming. People would understand that positive change is possible and that a specific plan is being offered for all to see. Significant contributions would be volunteered and preparations begun for the next election. Seated elected officials would see this enthusiasm and then appreciate the virtue of their "defecting" to the new party. Hoping to retain their seats they would become convinced of the need to switch to the party of the CSU. Political consciousness simply would be drawn to the center and away from the rancor of ideological extremes. Traditional bases of power would be set on a new footing. New candidates would be put forth against those hoping to retain the prerogatives of the past. Fringe factions would be left to their own devices as this program of the common interest would be able to move forward on the basis of an overwhelming electoral majority.

The existing legislative process has sunk to the level of a horse trading of one pork barrel issue against another. One group butts heads with another so as to maintain its turf at the expense of others. Single issue politics reduces reform to piecemeal impotent wailing. Nothing is allowed to change as the momentum of social and political disintegration gains velocity. Congress wallows in its own filth as the Presidency leads from the rear. The spectacle would be humorous but it simply is not all that funny. Prejudice and self-interest are dressed up in the cloth of reasoned argument but when the pretense is removed there is nothing but prejudice and self-interest. Something better is both possible and imminent. The person must judge. The CSU agenda is a single and comprehensive program of positive change. The individual as a person will be called upon to vote Yes or No across the board. Nothing less will do.

This agenda could be implemented in the near term for the common good of all. It will no longer do to prop up personalities in the absence of political vision. It is time to act upon a comprehensive plan of action. The process of renewal will have begun.

Conclusion
Personal Choice

The conditions for the possibility of a transition to a world of consensus and cooperation are in place. Recognizing the need for a change of attitude is at the same time a significant step in that direction. It will be the common rather than the special interest that will make the difference. It is the question of whether we will choose to encourage our incidental differences or our shared experience.

We have a different climate from the West, a different landscape, a different temperament and character, a different blood, a different physiognomy, a different way of thinking, different beliefs, hopes, pleasures, different relations, different conditions, different history, everything different... [1]

This was written in 1917 at the time of the Soviet Revolution but what impresses the most is that all of this difference is with respect to the very *same* world. Difference is only what it is to the extent that it refers to an underlying common reality. Of course this reality is often taken for granted and its significance overlooked. It is within the dimension of our own personal attitude whether much or little is made of this difference, whether we choose to aggravate difference into division or see the difference as a special opportunity in which to more fully appreciate the underlying sameness and potential consensus. "The fact that we are human beings is infinitely more important than all the peculiarities that distinguish human beings from one another..." [2]

All of this has quite direct consequences for the question of war and peace in our time. Is the world ready to make that one last courageous and definite step towards global understanding?

And perhaps the great day will come when a people distinguished in wars and victories and by the highest development of a military order and intelligence, and accustomed to make the heaviest sacrifice for these things, will exclaim of its own free will, "We break the sword," and will smash its military establishment down to its lowest foundations. *Rendering oneself unarmed when one has been the best armed,* out of a height of feeling--that is the means to real peace, which must always rest on a peace of mind...[3]

As we ponder ourselves and our future it is to these questions that we must naturally turn. Are we to choose to reiterate again and again the same tired and worn tradition of self-centered ideologies? Are we to remain wedded to the negative forever? Or, can we choose to break free of this and look to the good in all of our relationships and endeavors? A world at peace is a world able to do so much more.

A peace of the peoples is hardly something that will steal over us unawares. Prepared for by a gradual change in the disposition of dominant groups, the final stroke will come in consequence of a daring, voluntary, and decisive act of breaking the sword. [4]

From all points, circumstances converge to suggest that deep and significant change is not an idle fantasy, but a matter of real possibility. But it needs our care and finally our love and for that it needs our personal choice to say *yes.*

One day in the ripeness of time new leaders may appear who will induce their peoples to take the irrevocable step, an act so bold it will be greatly contagious and compel imitation. Obviously such a deed will not be wholly the work of one man or a small group. The people as a whole must be ready to support the act. But even when large numbers have undergone that inner change of mind and heart...it will still require the most courageous of leaders to break the sword in their name and thus assume responsibility for possible failure. A man will be needed of great simplicity and profound conviction. [5]

A single individual may need to serve as the catalyst for this transformation but that does not diminish in the least the responsibility that remains to each of us to fully participate. As human beings in full possession of our powers of mentality, at the culmination of the odyssey of the Western spirit, there is nothing else to be done than to courageously act on behalf of ourselves and all others and to become custodians of the world that can finally achieve its yearning for sanity and peace.

Epilogue
A World at Peace

Spanning the ages, from the time of the man sitting by his fire considering his broken spear, to Odysseus struggling to find home, to Moses shepherding his people, to Jesus turning his cheek, to Plato receiving a divine dispensation, to Descartes thinking for himself, and, finally, to our own troubled time, there is to be told a story of humanity coming to know itself, of self-consciousness struggling to push beyond temporary limitations in order to find a greater goodwill. The achievement overreaches our limited ability to understand, but there it is. It is time to affirm our blessings and choose to do better than we would have ever thought possible.

Endnotes

Refer to bibliography for full citation.

Preface

1 Obviously this is not a male only affair as all persons regardless of gender participate in this possibility. For reasons of simplicity here the pronoun "his" will be used rather than "his/her."
2 For the general theory of *epoche* confer Husserl, *Ideas*.
3 Husserl, *Cartesian Meditations*, p. 7.
4 As in Plato's *Meno*.
5 Durant, *Story of Civilization*, Vol. 2, p. 242.
6 Homer, *The Odyssey*, translator, Fitzgerald, p. 363.
7 *Odyssey*, p. 364.
8 *Odyssey*, p. 371.
9 *Odyssey*, p. 371.
10 *Odyssey*, p. 373.
11 *Odyssey*, p. 374.
12 *Odyssey*, p. 374.
13 *Odyssey*, p. 377.
14 *Odyssey*, p. 378.
15 *Odyssey*, p. 389.
16 *Odyssey*, p. 402.

Chapter One

1 *Deuteronomy* 28:26-34, Oxford Bible, p. 250-1.
2 *Haggai*, 1:6, p. 1145.

Chapter Two

1 *Readings in Vedic Literature: The Tradition Speaks for Itself*, p. 22.
2 *Vedic*, p. 109.
3 *Vedic*, p. 165.
4 *Vedic*, p. 74.

5 *Bhagavad-gita: As It Is,* p. 216.
6 *Source Book in Chinese Philosophy,* p. 146.
7 *Source Book,* p. 139.
8 *Source Book,* p. 142-3.
9 *Source Book,* p. 154-5.
10 *Source Book,* p. 147-8.
11 *Egyptian Book of the Dead,* p. xcv-xcvii.
12 *Egyptian,* p. lxiii-iv.
13 *Egyptian,* p. lvii.
14 *Genesis* p. 1.
15 *Genesis* 1:14-19, p. 2.
16 *Genesis* 2:4-9, p. 3.
17 *Genesis* 3:14-19, p. 4-5.
18 *Leviticus* 26:3-13, p. 156.
19 *Leviticus* 26:16-20, p. 156-7.
20 *Deuteronomy* 32:40, p. 259.
21 *Isaiah* 26:18, p. 852.
22 *Exodus* 6:3, p. 73.
23 *Deuteronomy* 6:4, p. 223.
24 *Judges* 10:6-7, p. 308.
25 *Isaiah* 37:18-20, p. 866.
26 *Exodus* 20:1-17, p. 92-3.
27 *Deuteronomy* 16:18-20, p. 236.
28 *Job* 34:10-12, p. 646.
29 Plato, *Republic*, 331e, p. 7.
30 *Republic* 332d, p. 8.
31 *Republic* 338c, p. 15.
32 *Republic* 359a, p. 37.
33 *Republic* 433a, p. 111.
34 *Republic* 433b, p. 111.
35 *Republic* 443d, p. 123.
36 *Republic* 443d, p. 123.
37 *Republic* 517c, p. 196.
38 *Republic* 504e, p. 184.
39 *Collected Dialogues of Plato*, 180b, p. 534.
40 *Dialogues* 185c, p. 539.

41 *Dialogues* 186d, p. 540.
42 *Dialogues* 188e, p. 540.
43 *Dialogues* 191a, p. 543.
44 *Dialogues* 190a, p. 542-3.
45 *Dialogues* 190b, p. 543.
46 *Dialogues* 191a, p. 543.
47 *Dialogues* 192e, p. 545.
48 *Dialogues* 193c, p. 546.
49 *Dialogues* 195b, p. 547.
50 *Dialogues* 197c-e, p. 549-50.
51 *Dialogues* 200e, p. 553.
52 *Dialogues* 201d, p. 553.
53 *Dialogues* 202d, p. 555.
54 *Dialogues* 202e, p. 555.
55 *Dialogues* 203e, p. 556.
56 *Dialogues* 205d, p. 557-8.
57 *Dialogues* 206a, p. 558.
58 *Dialogues* 206c, p. 558.
59 *Dialogues* 208e, p. 560.
60 *Dialogues* 209a, p. 560.
61 *Dialogues* 211a, p. 562.
62 *Dialogues* 211d, p. 563.
63 Hamilton, E., *The Greek Way*, p. 15.
64 *The Greek Way*, p. 29.
65 *The Greek Way*, p. 29.
66 Durant, W., Volume 2, p. 242.

Chapter Three

1 Cassirer, *An Essay on Man*, p. 135.
2 *John* 1:1-3, p. 1286.
3 *Psalms* 38:3-8, p. 684.
4 *Job* 25:2-6, p. 637.
5 *Psalms* 23: 1-6, p. 672-2.
6 *Psalms* 34:1-22, p. 679-80.
7 *Psalms* 91:1-10, p. 727.

8 *Psalms* 116:1-4, p. 746-7.
9 *Psalms* 11:4-7, p. 663.
10 *Matthew* 7:21-23, p. 1179.
11 *Matthew* 10:34-39, p. 1183.
12 *Matthew* 22:14, p. 1201.
13 *Matthew* 6:25-34, p. 1178.
14 *Matthew* 3:2, p. 1173.
15 *John* 6:35, p. 1295.
16 *John* 4:13-14, p. 1291.
17 *Matthew* 8:1-3, p. 1179-80.
18 *Matthew* 11:28-30, p. 1185.
19 *Matthew* 9:18-26, p. 1181-2.
20 *Matthew* 16:18, p. 1193.
21 *John* 17:1-26, p. 1312.
22 *Luke* 6:27-36, p. 1251.
23 *Luke* 10:27, p. 1260.

Chapter Four

1*Hebrews* 11:1, p. 1465.
2 *2 Corinthians* 1:6, p. 1398.
3 *Luke* 9:23-27, p. 1257-8.
4 *Revelation* 1:3, p. 1493.
5 *Revelation* 22:7, p. 1513.
6 Haasse, H., *In a Dark Wood Wandering*, p. 146.
7 *Philippians* 2:14, p. 1425.
8 *Matthew* 23:1-12, p. 1202.
9 *1 Corinthians* 7:40, 1387.
10 *1 Corinthians* 9:1-2, p. 1387.
11 *Romans* 8:28-30, p. 1370.
12 *Romans* 15:1, p. 1377.
13 *Acts* 4:32-37, p. 1324-5.
14 *Acts* 5:11, p. 1325.
15 *Romans* 15:25-29, p. 1378.
16 *1 Corinthians* 9:11-12, p. 1388.
17 *Colossians* 3:23-24, p. 1431.

18 *Philippians* 2:1-11, p. 1424.

19 Grillmeier, *Christ in Christian Tradition*, p. 544.

20 Gibbon, E., *The History of the Decline and Fall of the Roman Empire*, Vol. 7, p. 248.

21 Durant, Vol. 3, p. 266.

22 *2 Samuel* 8:3-8, p. 385.

23 *2 Samuel* 7:3, p. 383.

24 *2 Samuel* 6:20-23, p. 383.

25 *Colossians* 2:8, p. 1429.

26 Gibbon, *Decline,* Vol. 2, p. 363.

27 Augustine, *Confessions*, p. 65.

28 Durant, Vol. 4, p. 555-6.

29 Johnson, P., *A History of Christianity*, p. 191.

30 Durant, Vol. 4, p. 587.

31 Gibbon, *Decline,* Vol. 6, p. 288.

32 Durant, Vol. 4, p. 592.

33 Durant, Vol. 4, p. 592.

34 Gibbon, *Decline*, Vol. 6. P. 464.

35 *John* 15:6, p. 1309.

36 Durant, Vol. 4, p. 780.

37 Durant, Vol. 4, p. 772.

38 Strayer, J., *The Albigensian Crusades*, p. 31.

39 *The Albigensian Crusades*, p. 32.

40 *The Albigensian Crusades*, p. 62.

41 Lea, H., *The Inquisition of the Middle Ages*, p. 61.

42 *The Inquisition*, p. 206.

43 *The Inquisition*, p. 207.

44 *The Inquisition*, p. 101.

45 *The Inquisition*, p. 256.

46 *The Inquisition*, p. 256.

47 *The Inquisition*, p. 257.

48 Hale, J., *The Civilization of Europe in the Renaissance*, p. 98.

49 Durant, Vol. 6, p. 22.

50 Durant, Vol. 6, p. 351.

51 Durant, Vol. 6, p. 353.

52 Luther, M., *Three Treaties*, p. 262.

53 Durant, Vol. 6, p. 367.
54 Durant, Vol. 6, p. 422.
55 Durant, Vol. 6, p. 422.
56 Durant, Vol. 6, p. 448.
57 Durant, Vol. 6, p. 472-3.
58 Durant, Vol. 6, p. 634.
59 Durant, Vol. 6, p. 909.
60 Durant, Vol. 6, p. 751.

Chapter Five

1 Durant, Vol. 7, p. 608.
2 Descartes, *Works,* Vol. 1, p. 144.
3 *Works,* Vol. 1, p. 147-8.
4 *Works*, Vol. 1, p. 151.
5 *Works*, Vol. 1, p. 101.
6 *Works*, Vol. 1, p. 158.
7 *Works*, Vol. 1, p. 237.
8 Locke, J., *Essay*, Vol. 1, p. 170.
9 Cf. Husserl, *Crisis*, p. 21ff.
10 Durant, Vol. 7, p. 567.
11 Clough, *Economic History of Europe*, p. 151.
12 Durant, Vol. 10, p. 79.
13 Plato, *Dialogues*, p. 560.
14 Thomas, H., *Conquest*, p. 451.
15 Boorstin, *The Americans*, p. 16.
16 Jefferson, T., *Notes*, p. 223-5.
17 Durant, Vol. 10, p. 92.
18 *Papers of Thomas Jefferson*, Vol. 1, p. 429.
19 Kelly, A., *The American Constitution*, p. 1075.
20 Durant, Vol. 10, p. 669.
21 Clough, *Economic History*, p. 667.
22 Dickens, C., *Hard Times*, p. 17.
23 *Hard Times*, p. 84.
24 Durant, Vol. 10, p. 677.
25 Durant, Vol. 10, p. 677.

26 *Darwinism*, p. 126.

27 *Darwinism*, p. 131-2.

28 *Darwinism*, p. 132-3.

29 *Darwinism*, p. 134-5.

Chapter Six

1 *Marx-Engels Reader*, p. 474.

2 *Reader*, p. 475.

3 *Reader*, p. 477.

4 *Reader*, p. 479.

5 *Reader*, p. 484.

6 *Reader*, p. 484.

7 *Reader*, p. 485.

8 *Reader*, p. 486.

9 *Reader*, p. 160.

10 *Reader*, p. 490-1.

11 *Reader*, p. 500.

12 *Reader*, p. 149.

13 *Reader*, p. 154.

14 *Reader*, p. 155.

15 Daniels, R., *Russia*, p. 18.

16 *Russia*, p. 116.

17 McElvaine, R., *The Great Depression*, p. 75.

18 Geisst, C., *Wall Street*, p. 196.

19 *Wall Street*, p. 197.

20 *Wall Street*, p. 197.

21 Tusa, J., *The Nuremberg Trial*, p. 194.

22 Snyder, L., *Historical Guide*, p. 210-11.

23 Mee, C., *The End of Order*, p. 75.

Chapter Seven

1 Cf. Schutz, *Collected Papers I*, p. 9.

2 Blythe, R., *The View in Winter*, p. 113.

3 Turner, F., "Escape from Modernism," Harper's, 11/84, p. 49.

4 Dubos, R., *Celebrations of Life*, p. 37.

5 Lenehan, M., "The Quality of the Instrument, Building a Steinway Grand Piano," Atlantic Monthly, 8/82, p. 42.

6 Bradley, J., *The International Dictionary of Thoughts*, p. 505.

7 *International Dictionary*, p. 504.

8 *International Dictionary*, p. 506.

9 Sorel, N., *Ever Since Eve*, p. xvi.

10 *Ever Since Eve*, p. 28.

11 Leopold, A., *A Sand County Almanac*, p. 95.

12 *Wilderness World of John Muir*, p. 213-4.

13 Frankl, V., *Man's Search for Meaning*, p. 90.

14 *Man's Search*, p. 86.

15 *Man's Search*, p. 87.

16 Husserl, *Ideas,* p. 63ff. A full account of this view is presented here.

Chapter Eight

1 Fuller, B., *Critical Path*, p. xxiii.

2 *Critical Path*, p. xxv.

3 *Critical Path*, p. xxvii.

4 *Critical Path*, p. 125.

5 *Statistical Abstract of the United States*, 1988.

6 *Historical Statistics of the United States, 1975*, p. 820.

7 Templeton, J., "Basics of Global Investing," World Monitor, 2/89, p. 59.

8 Templeton, p. 61.

9 *Alcoholics Anonymous*, p. 59-60. The Twelve Steps are reprinted with permission of Alcoholics Anonymous World Services, Inc. Permission to reprint the Steps does not mean that AA has reviewed or approved the content of this publication, nor that AA agrees with the views expressed herein. AA is a program of recovery from alcoholism--use of the Twelve Steps in connection with programs and activities which are patterned after AA, but which address other problems, does not imply otherwise.

10 *AA*, p. 570.

11 *AA*, p. 24.

12 Frankland, M., *The Sixth Continent*, p. 259.

13 Reynolds, G., *The Mortality Merchants*, p. 1.

14 *The Mortality Merchants*, p. 4.

15 *1996 Life Insurance Fact Book*, p. 85.

16 Johnson, P., *A History of Christianity*, p. 79.

Chapter Nine

1 Rhodes, R., *The Making of the Atomic Bomb*, p. 292.

2 *The Making*, p. 728.

3 *The Making*, p. 689-90.

4 *The Making*, p. 690.

5 *The Making*, p. 690.

6 X, "The Sources of Soviet Conduct," p. 572.

7 X, p. 572.

8 X, p. 575.

9 X, p. 576.

10 X, p. 580-1.

11 X, p. 582.

12 Herkens, G., *Counsels of War*, p. 37.

13 *Counsels,* p. 81-2.

14 Englehardt, T., *The End of Victory Culture*, p. 170.

15 Gorbachev, M., *Perestroika*, p. 29.

16 *Perestroika,* p. 30.

17 *Perestroika*, p. 211.

18 Coldwarism is a neologism meant to encompass all ideological justification for the nuclear standoff between the East and the West.

19 DeBeauvoir, S., *The Second Sex*, p. 21.

20 *The Second Sex*, p. 223.

21 *The Second Sex*, p. 391.

22 *The Second Sex*, p. 63.

23 *The Second Sex*, p. 63.

24 Kosinski, J., *Pinball*, p158-9.

25 *The Second Sex*, p. 197-8.

26 "Cherish" by Terry Kirkman and the *Association*.

27 Dostoevsky, F., *The Brothers Karamozov*, p. 56.

28 Craik, D., *Inspiring Quotations*, p. 46.

29 Brady, C., *The Sioux Indian Wars*, p. 334.

30 Wood, D., "Iraqi-Americans Rue War, Voice Concern for Homeland," Christian Science Monitor, 1/23/91.

31 An authentic Egyptian obelisk stands in Central Park in New York City. It was a gift to the United States in the 1880s from the Egyptian government. It dates from 1600 B.C.

32 Jefferson understood the contradiction of his position regarding equality and his final will would let his black people go. But the weakness of this seemingly benevolent gesture is its premise that the hard reality would fall to others after his death and that there was finally no place to go. He allowed himself to remain a beneficiary to a system that he knew to be a violation of all the political theories which he cherished.

33 Putnam, G., American Heritage "Civil War Chronicles," Winter, 1993, p.19.

34 *The Wall*, p. 121.

35 Senator Daniel P. Moynihan introduced legislation to abolish the CIA in the "End of the Cold War Act of 1991." Cf. Greider, W., *Who Will Tell the People*, p. 360.

36 Owen, B., *The Pure Cure*, p. 73.

37 McWilliams, P., *Ain't Nobody's Business*, p. 551.

38 *Nobody's Business*, p. 190.

39 *Nobody's Business*, p. 551.

40 *Nobody's Business*, p. 735.

41 *Nobody's Business*, p. 735-6.

42 *Nobody's Business*, p. 1.

43 *Nobody's Business*, p. 745.

44 The New England Journal of Medicine, 10/7/93.

45 Milwaukee Sentinel, 10/12/93, 5A.

46 Durant, Vol. 2, p. 268.

47 Milwaukee Journal, 10/13/93, D1.

48 Gaddis, J., *The United States and the End of the Cold War*, p. 10.

49 Greider, W., Who *Will Tell the People*, p. 102.
50 *Who Will Tell*, p. 103.
51 Euripides, *Oedipus at Colonus*.
52 *Who Will Tell*, p. 155.
53 Aristotle, *Politics*, 1296a.
54 *Who Will Tell*, p. 155.
55 *Who Will Tell*, p. 264.
56 *Who Will Tell*, p. 268.
57 *Who Will Tell*, p. 269.

Conclusion

1 *The Sixth Continent*, p. 257.
2 *The Second Sex*, p. 728.
3 Nietzsche, *Portable*, p. 72.
4 Gray, J., *The Warriors*, p. 226.
5 *The Warriors*, p. 227.

Index

Bibliography

Adams, Henry, *The Degradation of the Democratic Dogma*, New York: Torchbooks, 1969.

Adney, Tappan, *The Klondike Stampede*, Vancouver: UBC Press, 1994.

Aeschylus, *The Oresteia*, translated by Robert Fagles, New York; Penguin, 1966.

Aeschylus, *Prometheus Bound, The Supplicants, Seven Against Thebes, The Persians*, translated by Philip Vellacott, New York: Penguin, 1961.

Alcoholics Anonymous, Third Edition, New York: AA World Services, Inc., 1976.

Alexander, Paul, *The Ancient World to A.D. 300*, 2nd edition, New York: Macmillan, 1968.

Ambrose, Stephen E., *Undaunted Courage: Meriwether Lewis, Thomas Jefferson, and the Opening of the American West*, New York: Simon and Schuster, 1996.

American Puritans: Their Prose and Poetry, edited by Perry Miller, Garden City: Anchor, 1956.

Aquinas, St. Thomas, *Basic Writings of St. Thomas Aquinas*, volume one, translated by Anton Pegis, New York: Random House, 1945.

Ardrey, Robert, *The Territorial Imperative*, New York: Delta, 1966.

Arendt, Hannah, *Between Past and Future: Eight Exercises in Political Thought*, New York: Penguin, 1956.

Arendt, Hannah, *The Human Condition*, Chicago: University of Chicago Press, 1958.

Aristotle, *The Basic Works of Aristotle*, edited by Richard McKeon, New York: Random House, 1941.

Augustine, *Against the Academicians*, translated by Mary Garvey, Milwaukee: Marquette University Press, 1957.

Augustine, *The Confessions*, translated by John Ryan, Garden City: Image, 1960.

Augustine, *On Free Choice of the Will*, translated by Anna Benjamin and L.H. Hackstaff, Indianapolis: Bobbs-Merrill, 1964.

Aurelius, Marcus, *Meditations*, translated by M. Staniforth, New York: Dorset Press, 1964.

Bailyn, Bernard, *The Ideological Origins of the American Revolution*, Cambridge: Belknap, 1967.

Bainton, Roland, *Christianity*, Boston: Houghton Mifflin, 1985.

Bair, Deirdre, *Simon de Beauvoir; A Biography*, New York: Simon and Schuster, 1990.

Barnet, Richard, *The Giants: Russia and America*, New York: Simon and Schuster, 1977.

Barthel, Manfred, *The Jesuits: History and Legend of the Society of Jesus*, translated by Mark Howson, New York: Morrow, 1984.

Beauvoir, Simone de, *The Ethics of Ambiguity*, translated by Bernard Frechtman, Secaucus: Citadel, 1948.

Beauvoir, Simone de, *The Second Sex*, translated by H.M. Parshley, New York: Vintage, 1989.

Bergson, Henri, *Creative Evolution*, translated by Arthur Mitchell, Westport: Greenwood, 1975.

Berkeley, George, *Principles, Dialogues, and Philosophical Correspondence*, Indianapolis: Bobbs-Merrill, 1965.

Berlin, Isaiah, *Karl Marx: His Life and Environment*, New York: Oxford, 1963.

Bernstein, Peter, *Against the Gods: The Remarkable Story of Risk*, New York, John Wiley and Sons, 1996.

Berton, Pierre, *The Klondike Fever: The Life and Death of the Last Great Gold Rush*, New York: Carroll and Graf Publishers, 1985.

Bhavagad-gita: AsIt Is, A.C. Bhaktivendanta Swami Prabhupada, The Bhaktivendanta Book Trust, 1968.

Bible, The New Oxford Annotated with the Apocrypha, Revised Standard Version, New York: Oxford, 1973.

Bishop, Morris, *The Middle Ages*, Boston: Houghton Mifflin, 1968.

Bloom, Allan, *The Closing of the American* Mind, New York: Simon and Schuster, 1987.

Blythe, Ronald, *The View in Winter,* New York: Harcourt, Brace, and Jovanovich, 1979.

Boethius, *The Consolation of Philosophy*, translated by Richard

Green, Indianapolis: Bobbs-Merrill, 1962.

Boorstin, Daniel, *The Americans: The Colonial Experience*, New York: Random House.

Boorstin, Daniel, *The Creators: A History of Heros of the Imagination*, New York: Random House, 1992.

Boorstin, Daniel, *The Discoverers: A History of Man's Search to Know his World and Himself*, New York: Vintage, 1985.

Bradley, J., *The International Dictionary of Thoughts*, Chicago: J.G. Ferguson Publishing, 1969.

Brady, Cyrus, *The Sioux Indian Wars: From the Powder River to the Little Big Horn*, New York: Indian Head Books, 1992.

Braudel, Fernard, *Civilization and Capitalism, 15th-18th Century: The Structure of Everyday Life*, volume one, translated by S. Reynolds, New York: Harper and Row, 1981.

Braudel, Fernard, *Civilization and Capitalism, 15th-18th Century: The Wheels of Commerce*, volume two, translated by S. Reynolds, New York: Harper and Row, 1982.

Braudy, Leo, *The Frenzy of Renown: Fame and its History*, New York: Oxford, 1986.

Brentano, Franz, *On the Several Senses of Being in Aristotle*, translated by Rolf George, Berkeley: University of California Press, 1975.

Brown, Norman, *Life Against Death: The Psychological Meaning of History*, Middletown: Wesleyan University Press, 1959.

Buddhism: The Dhammapada, translated by John Carter and Mahinda Palihawadana, New: QPBC, 1992.

Carr, David, *Phenomenology and the Problem of History*, Evanston: Northwestern University Press, 1974.

Cassirer, Ernst, *An Essay on Man: An Introduction to a Philosophy of Human Culture*, New Haven: Yale University Press, 1944.

Cassirer, Ernst, *The Philosophy of Symbolic Forms: Language*, volume one, translated by RalphManheim, New Haven: Yale University Press, 1953.

Caton, Hiram, *The Origin of Subjectivity: An Essay on Descartes*, New Haven: Yale University Press, 1973.

Catton, Bruce, *The Army of the Potomac*, 3 volumes, New York:

Doubleday, 1951.

Catton, Bruce, *The Civil War*, Boston: Houghton Mifflin Co., 1960.

Catton, Bruce, *Grant Moves South*, Boston: Little, Brown, and Co., 1960.

Catton, Bruce, *Grant Takes Command*, Boston: Little, Brown, and Co., 1968.

Charlesworth, M.P., *The Roman Empire*, New York: Oxford, 1968.

Christianity: The Apocrypha and the New Testament, from the Revised English Bible, New York: QPBC, 1992.

Civil War Courtship: The Letters of Edwin Weller from Antietam to Atlanta, edited by William Walton, New York: Doubleday, 1980.

Clark, Kenneth, *Civilisation*, New York: Harper and Row, 1969.

Clark, Ronald, *Freud: The Man and the Cause*, New York: Random House, 1980.

Clough, S. and Cole, C., *Economic History of Europe*, Third Edition, Boston: D.C. Heath, 1952.

Confucianism: The Analects of Confucius, translated by Arthur Waley, New York: QPBC, 1992.

Cooper, Chester, *The Lost Crusade: America in Vietnam*, New York: Dodd and Mead, 1970.

Craik, D., *Inspiring Quotations: Contemporary and Classical*, compiled by A. Wells Jr, Nashville: Thomas Nelson Publishers, 1988.

Cronon, William, *Nature's Metropolis: Chicago and the Great West*, New York: W.W. Norton, 1991.

Crosby, Alfred, *The Measure of Reality: Quantification and Western Society, 1250-1600*, Cambridge: Cambridge University Press, 1997.

Cunningham, Noble E., Jr., *In Pursuit of Reason: The Life of Thomas Jefferson*, Baton Rouge; Louisiana State University Press, 1987.

Daniels, Robert, *Russia: The Roots of Confrontation*, Cambridge: Harvard University Press, 1985.

Darwinism and the American Intellectual, edited by R. Wilson, Homewood, Illinois: The Dorsey Press, 1967.

Descartes, The Philosophical Works of, Volume One, translated by Elizabeth Haldane and G.R.T Ross, London: Cambridge, 1911.

DeVoto, Bernard, *The Year of Decision: 1846*, Boston: Houghton Mifflin Co., 1942.

DeVoto, Bernard, *The Course of Empire*, Boston: Houghton Mifflin Co., 1952.

DeVoto, Bernard, *Across the Wide Missouri*, Boston: Houghton Mifflin Co., 1947.

Dickens, Charles, *Hard Times*, edited by G. Ford and S. Monod, An Authoritative Text, New York: Norton and Co., 1966.

Dostoevsky, Fyodor, *The Brothers Karamazov*, translated by Richard Pevear and Larissa Volokhonsky, San Francisco: North Point Press, 1990.

Dostoevsky, Fyodor, *Great Short Works*, translated by Ronald Hingley, New York: Harper and Row, 1968.

Dostoyevsky, Fyodor, *Crime and Punishment*, translated by Constance Garnett, New York: Vintage, 1950.

Dubos, Rene, *Celebrations of Life,* New York: McGraw-Hill, 1981.

Dyer, Gwynne, *War*, New York: Crown, 1985.

Dyson, Freeman, *Weapons and Hope*, New York: Harper and Row,1984.

Dudley, Donald, *The Romans: 850 B.C.-A.D. 337*, New York: Barnes and Noble, 1993.

Durant, Will, *The Story of Civilization*, 11 volumes, New York: Simon and Schuster, 1935.

Durant, Will and Ariel, *A Dual Autobiography*, New York: Simon and Schuster, 1977.

Durant, Will and Ariel, *The Lessons of History*, New York: Simon and Schuster, 1968.

Eco, Umberto, *The Name of the Rose*, New York: Harcourt, Brace, and Jovanovich, 1983.

Egyptian Book of the Dead: The Papyrus of Ani, edited by E.A. Wallis Budge, New York: Dover, 1967

Emerson, Ralph Waldo, *Essays and Journals*, Garden City: International Collectors Library, 1968.

Engelhardt, Tom, *The End of Victory Culture: Cold War America and the Disillusioning of a Generation*, New York: BasicBooks, 1995.

Euripides, *Oedipus at Colonus*, Penguin Books Ltd.

Erdoes, Richard, *A.D. 1000: Living on the Brink of Apocalypse*, New York, Barnes and Noble, 1988.

Farias, Victor, *Heidegger and Nazism*, translated by Paul Burrell and Gabriel Ricci, Philadelphia: Temple University Press, 1989.

Feuerbach, Ludwig, *The Essence of Christianity*, translated by George Eliot, New York: Torchbooks, 1957.

Fitzgerald, Frances, *Fire in the Lake: The Vietnamese and the Americans in Vietnam*, Boston: Atlantic-Little, and Brown, 1972.

Florinsky, Michael, *The End of the Russian Empire*, New York: Collier, 1961.

Ford, Daniel, *The Button: The Pentagon's Command and Control System, Does it Work?*, New York: Simon and Schuster, 1985.

Frankl, V., *Man's Search for Meaning*, New York: Washington Square Press, 1959.

Frankland, Mark, *The Sixth Continent: Mikhail Gorbachov and the Soviet Union*, New York: Harper and Row, 1987.

Franklin, Benjamin, *Autobiography*, Garden City: International Collectors Library, 1923.

Franklin, John Hope, *From Slavery to Freedom: A History of Negro Americans*, 3rd edition, New York: Vintage, 1969.

Franklin, John Hope, *Reconstruction after the Civil War*, Chicago: University of Chicago Press, 1961.

Frazer, James, *The Golden Bough: The Roots of Religion and Folklore*, New York: Avenel Books, 1981.

Freud, Sigmund, *Civilization and its Discontents*, translated by James Strachey, New York: W.W. Norton, 1961.

Freud, Sigmund, *The Ego and the Id*, translated by Joan Riviere, New York: W.W. Norton, 1962.

Fromkin, David, *In the Time of the Americans: The Generation that Changed America's Role in the World*, New York: Alfred

A. Knopf, 1995.

Fromm, Erich, *The Anatomy of Human Destructiveness*, New York: Fawcett, 1973.

Fukuyama, Francis, *The End of History and the Last Man*, New York: Free Press, 1992.

Fuller, R. Buckminster, *Critical Path*, New York: St. Martin's, 1981.

Gaarder, Jostein, *Sophie's World: A Novel About the History of Philosophy*, New York: Berkley, 1994.

Gabrieli, Francesco, *Arab Historians of the Crusades*, New York; Dorset Press, 1989.

Gaddis, J., *The United States and the End of the Cold War: Implications, Reconsiderations, Provocations*, New York: Oxford University Press, 1992.

Galbraith, John Kenneth, *The Culture of Contentment*, Boston: Houghton Mifflin, 1992.

Galilei, Galileo, *Dialogue Concerning the Two Chief World Systems--Ptolemaic and Copernican*, translated by Stillman Drake, Berkeley: University of California Press, 1967.

Gandhi, Mohandas, *Autobiography: The Story of My Experiments with Truth,* translated by Mahadev Desai, New York: Dover, 1983.

Gaukroger, Stephen, *Descartes: An Intellectual Biography*, New York: Oxford, 1995.

Geisst, Charles, *Wall Street: A History*, New York: Oxford, 1997.

Gibbon, Edward, *The History of the Decline and Fall of the Roman Empire,* 7 volumes, London: Methuen, 1909.

Gies, Frances and Joseph, *Cathedral, Forge, and Waterwheel: Technology and Invention in theMiddle Ages*, New York: HarperCollins, 1994.

Gies, Frances and Joseph, *Life in a Medieval Village*, New York: HarperCollins, 1990.

Gilgamesh, translated by John Gardner and John Maier, New York: Alfred A. Knopf, 1984.

Goldstein, Kurt, *Human Nature in the Light of Psychopathology*, New York: Schocken, 1963.

Gorbachev, Mikhail, *Perestroika: New Thinking for Our Country and the World,* New York: Harper and Row, 1987.

Gouldner, Alvin, *The Hellenic World: A Sociological Analysis*, New York: Torchbooks, 1965.

Grant, Michael, *The Ancient Historians*, New York: Barnes and Noble, 1970.

Grant, Michael, *The Antonines: The Roman Empire in Transition*, New York: Routledge, 1994.

Grant, Michael, *Jesus: An Historian's Review of the Gospels*, New York: Scribners, 1977.

Grant, Michael, *The Rise of the Greeks*, New York: Scribner's, 1987.

Grant, Ulysses S., *Memoirs and Selected Letters*, New York: Library of America, 1990.

Gray, J. Glenn, *The Warriors: Reflections on Men in Battle*, New York: Harper Torchbooks, 1967.

Green Julien, *God's Fool: The Life and Times of Francis of Assisi*, translated by Peter Heinegg, New York: Harper and Row, 1985.

Green, Peter, *Alexander of Macedon, 356-323 B.C.: A Historical Biography*, Berkeley: University of California Press, 1991.

Greider, William, *Secrets of the Temple: How the Federal Reserve Runs the Country*, New York: Simon and Schuster, 1987.

Greider, William, *Who Will Tell the People: The Betrayal of American Democracy*, New York: Simon and Schuster, 1992.

Grillmeier, A., *Christ in Christian Tradition: From the Apostolic Age to Chalcedon,* Vol. 1, 2nd Edition, translated by J. Bowden, Atlanta: John Knox Press, 1975.

Grossman, Leonid, *Dostoevsky: His Life and Work*, translated by Mary Mackler, Indianapolis: Bobbs-Merrill, 1975.

Gurdjieff, G. I., *Meetings with Remarkable Men*, New York: Dutton, 1974.

Gurwitsch, Aron, *The Field of Consciousness*, Pittsburgh: Duquesne University Press, 1964.

Gurwitsch, Aron, *Human Encounters in the Social World*, translated by Fred Kersten, Pittsburgh: Duquesne University Press, 1979.

Gurwitsch, Aron, *Phenomenology and the Theory of Science*, Evanston: Northwestern University Press, 1974.

Haasse, Hella, *In a Dark Wood Wandering*, Chicago: Academy Chicago Publishers, 1989.

Hale, John, *The Civilization of Europe in the Renaissance*, New York: Atheneum, 1994.

Hamilton, Edith, *The Greek Way*, New York: W.W. Norton, 1964.

Hammarskjold, Dag, *Markings*, translated by Leif Sjoberg and W.H. Auden, New York: Alfred A. Knopf, 1964.

Handlin, Oscar, *The Uprooted: The Epic Story of the Great Migration that Made the American People*, 2nd edition, Boston: Little, Brown and Co., 1973.

Hayman, Ronald, *Sartre: A Biography*, New York: Simon and Schuster, 1987.

Hayslip, Le Ly, *When Heaven and Earth Changed Places: A Vietnamese Woman's Journey from War to Peace*, New York: Doubleday, 1989.

Hegel, George, *Phenomenology of Spirit*, translated by A. Miller, Oxford: Clarendon, 1977.

Hegel, George, *The Philosophy of History*, translated by J. Sibree, New York: Dover, 1956.

Hegel, George, *Philosophy of Right*, translated by T. Knox, New York: Oxford, 1967.

Heidegger, Martin, *Being and Time*, translated by John Macquarrie and Edward Robinson, New York: Harper and Row, 1962.

Herington, John, *Aeschylus*, Yale University Press, 1986.

Herkens, Gregg, *Counsels of War*, New York: Alfred A. Knopf, 1985.

Herodotus, *The Histories*, translated by Aubrey de Selincourt, New York: Penguin, 1954.

Herold, J. Christopher, *The Age of Napoleon*, Boston: Houghton Mifflin and Co., 1963.

Hinduism: The Rig Veda, translated by Ralph Griffith, New York: QPBC, 1992.

Historical Statistics of the United States: Colonial Times to 1970, Bicentenial edition, Part 2, Department of Commerce, Bureau of the Census, 1975.

Homer, *The Illiad*, translated by Robert Fitzgerald, New York: Doubleday, 1974.

Homer, *The Odyssey*, translated by Robert Fitzgerald, New York: Doubleday, 1961.

Hoopes, Townsend, *The Limits of Intervention*, New York: David McKay, 1969.

Hourani, Albert, *A History of the Arab Peoples*, Cambridge: Belknap, 1991.

Hoyt, Robert, *Europe in the Middle Ages*, 2nd edition, New York: Harcourt, Brace, and World, 1966.

Hughes, Robert, *Culture of Complaint: The Fraying of America*, New York: Oxford, 1993.

Hughes, Robert, *The Fatal Shore: The Epic of Australia's Founding*, New York: Alfred A. Knopf, 1987.

Huizinga, Johan, *The Autumn of the Middle Ages*, translated by Rodney Payton and Ulrich Mammitzsch, Chicago: University of Chicago Press, 1996.

Hume, David, *Enquiries Concerning Human Understanding and Concerning Principles of Morals*, London: Oxford, 1975.

Hume, David, *A Treatise of Human Nature*, London: Oxford, 1888.

Husserl, Edmund, *Cartesian Meditations: An Introduction to Phenomenology*, translated by Dorion Cairns, The Hague: Martinus Nijhoff, 1973.

Husserl, Edmund, *The Crisis of European Sciences and Trans-cendental Phenomenology: An Introduction to Phenomen-ological Philosophy*, translated by David Carr, Evanston: Northwestern University Press, 1973.

Husserl, Edmund, *Ideas Pertaining to a Pure Phenomenology and a Phenomenological Philosophy*, First Book, translated by Fred Kersten, The Hague: Martinus Nijhoff, 1983.

Husserl, Edmund, *Phenomenology and the Crisis of Philosophy*, translated by Quentin Lauer, New York: Harper and Row, 1965.

Islam: The Qur'an, translated by Ahmed Ali, New York: QPBC, 1992.

Jacobs, Jane, *Cities and the Wealth of Nations: Principles of*

Economic Life, New York: Random House, 1984.

Jacobs, Jane, *Systems of Survival: A Dialogue on the Moral Foundations of Commerce and Politics*, New York: Random House, 1992.

James, William, *The Principles of Psychology*, two volumes, New York: Dover, 1950.

James, William, *The Varieties of Religious Experience*, New York: Random House, 1936.

James, William, *The Will to Believe, Human Immortality*, New York: Dover, 1956.

Jefferson, Papers of Thomas, Volume one, 1760-1776, edited by J. Boyd, Princeton University Press, 1950.

Jefferson, Thomas, *Notes of the State of Virginia*, edited by W. Peden, Chapel Hill: University of North Carolina press, 1955.

Jefferson, Thomas, *Writings*, New York: Library of America, 1984.

Jefferson at Monticello, edited by James A. Bear, Jr., Charlottesville: University Press of Virginia, 1967.

Job, Book of, translated by Stephen Mitchell, San Francisco: North Point Press, 1987.

John Paul II, *Crossing the Threshold of Hope*, translated by Jenny and Martha MePhee, New York: Alfred A. Knopf, 1995.

Johnson, Paul, *A History of Christianity*, New York: Atheneum, 1979.

Johnson, Paul, *A History of the Jews*, New York: Harper and Row, 1987.

Johnson, Paul, *Intellectuals*, New York: Harper and Row, 1988.

Johnson, Paul, *Modern Times: The World from the Twenties to the Eighties*, New York: Colophon Books, 1983.

Jones, Tom, *From the Tigris to the Tiber*, Homewood: Dorsey, 1969.

Journals of Lewis and Clark, edited by Bernard DeVoto, Boston: Houghton Mifflin Co., 1953.

Judaism: The Tanakh, the New JPS Translation, New York: QPBC, 1992.

Justinian, *The Digest of Roman Law: Theft, Rapine, Damage, and Insult*, translated by C.F. Kolbert, New York: Penguin, 1979.

Kaminer, Wendy, *I'm Dysfunctional, You're Dysfunctional: The*

Recovery Movement and the Other Self-Help Fashions, New York, Vintage Books, 1993.

Kamm, Anthony, *The Romans: An Introduction*, New York: Routledge, 1995.

Kant, Immanuel, *Critique of Judgment*, translated by J.H. Bernard, New York: Hafner, 1951.

Kant, Immanuel, *Critique of Practical Reason*, translated by Lewis Beck, Indianapolis: Bobbs-Merrill, 1956.

Kant, Immanuel, *Critique of Pure Reason*, translated by Norman Kemp Smith, London: Macmillan, 1929.

Karnow, Stanley, *Vietnam: A History*, New York: Penguin, 1983.

Kaufman, Walter, *Nietzsche: Philosopher, Psychologist, Antichrist*, 4th ed., Princeton: Princeton University Press, 1974.

Kaufmann, Walter, *Without Guilt and Justice: From Decidophobia to Autonomy*, New York: Wyden, 1973.

Kazantzakis, Nikos, *The Odyssey: A Modern Sequel*, translated by Kimon Friar, New York: Simon and Schuster, 1958.

Keller, Werner, *The Bible as History*, 2nd revised edition, translated by William Neil, New York: William Morrow, 1981.

Kelly, A., and Harbison, W., *The American Constitution: Its Origin and Development*, 4th edition, New York: W.W. Norton, 1948.

Kennan, George, *Around the Cragged Hill: A Personal and Political Philosophy*, New York: W.W. Norton, 1993.

Kerblay, Basile, *Modern Soviet Society*, translated by Rupert Swyer, New York: Pantheon, 1983.

Keyes, Daniel, *The Minds of Billy Milligan*, New York: Random House, 1981.

Kierkegaard, Soren, *Concluding Unscientific Postscript*, translated by David Swenson and Walter Lowrie, Princeton: Princeton University Press, 1968.

Kierkegaard, Soren, *Fear and Trembling and The Sickness unto Death*, translated by Walter Lowrie, Princeton: Princeton University Press, 1968.

Klein, Jacob, *A Commentary of Plato's Meno*, Chapel Hill: University of North Carolina Press, 1965.

Koran, translated by N.J. Dawood, New York: Penguin, 1956.

Kosinski, Jerzy, *Pinball*, New York: Bantam, 1982.

Koyre, Alexandre, *From the Closed World to the Infinite Universe*, Baltimore: The Johns Hopkins Press, 1968.

Krafft-Ebing, Richard von, *Psychopathia Sexualis*, translated by Franklin Klaf, New York: Scarborough, 1965.

Kuhn, Thomas, *The Structure of Scientific Revolutions*, 2nd edition, Chicago: University of Chicago Press, 1970.

Kuttner, Robert, *The End of Laissez-Faire: National Purpose and the Global Economy after the Cold War*, New York: Alfred A. Knopf, 1991.

Lachouque, Henry, *The Anatomy of Glory: Napoleon and His Guard*, translated by Anne S. Brown, London: Greenhill Books, 1997.

Laing, R.D., *The Divided Self*, translated by William Weist and Robert Batson, New York: Pelican, 1965.

Laird, John, *Hume's Philosophy of Human Nature*, Archon, 1967.

Lavender, David, *The Great West*, Boston: Houghton Mifflin Co., 1965.

Lawrence, D.H., *Studies in Classic American Literature*, New York: Viking, 1961.

Lea, Charles, *The Inquisition of the Middle Ages*, New York: Barnes and Noble, 1993.

Leibniz, *Discourse on Metaphysics*, translated by George Montgomery, La Salle: Open Court, 1973.

Leopold, Aldo, *A Sand County Almanac*, New York: Oxford, 1987.

Lesky, Albin, *Greek Tragedy*, translated by H.A. Frankfort, New York: Barnes and Noble, 1979.

Levinas, Emmanuel, *The Theory of Intuition in Husserl's Phenomenlogy*, translated by Andre Orianne, Evanston: Northwestern University Press, 1973.

Lincoln, Abraham, *Speeches and Writings: 1832-1858*, New York: Library of America, 1989.

Lincoln's Generals, edited by Gabor Boritt, New York: Oxford, 1994.

Locke, John, *An Essay Concerning Human Understanding*, two volumes, New York: Dover, 1959.

Luther, Martin, *Three Treatises*, Philadelphia: The Muhlenberg Press,

1943.

Machiavelli, *The Prince*, translated by Mark Musa, New York: St. Martin's, 1964.

Makin, John, and Ornstein, Norman, *Debt and Taxes*, New York: Random House, 1994.

Malone, Dumas, *Jefferson and His Time*, 6 volumes, Boston: Little, Brown, and Co., 1948.

Martin, Malachi, *The Jesuits: The Society of Jesus and the Betrayal of the Roman Catholic Church*, New York: Touchstone, 1987.

Marx, Karl, *Capital,* volume one, translated by Samuel Moore and Edward Aveling, Moscow: Progress, 1954.

Marx-Engels Reader, 2nd edition, edited by Robert Tucker, New York: W.W. Norton, 1978.

Maslowe, Abraham, *Towards a Psychology of Being*, 2nd edition, New York: VanNostand, 1968.

Massie, Robert, *Peter the Great: His Life and World*, New York: Alfred A. Knopf, 1980.

May, Rollo, *The Discovery of Being: Writings in Existential Psychology*, New York: W.W. Norton, 1983.

May, Rollo, *Freedom and Destiny*, New York: W.W. Norton, 1981.

May, Rollo, *The Meaning of Anxiety*, revised edition, New York: W.W. Norton, 1977.

McCullough, David, *Mornings on Horseback*, New York: Simon and Schuster, 1981.

McElvaine, Robert, *The Great Depression: America, 1929-1941*, New York: Times Books, 1984.

McGlashan, C.F., *History of the Donner Party: A Tragedy of the Sierra*, Stanford: Stanford University Press, 1940.

McNamara, Robert S., *In Retrospect: The Tragedy and Lessons of Vietnam*, New York: Times Books, 1995.

McPherson, James M., *Battle Cry of Freedom: The Civil War Era*, New York: Oxford, 1988.

McWilliams, Peter, *Ain't Nobody's Business If You Do: The Absurdity of Consensual Crime in a Free Society*, Los Angeles: Prelude Press, 1993.

Medieval Reader, edited by Norman Cantor, New York: Harper

Collins, 1994.

Medvedev, Roy, *Khrushchev*, translated by Brain Pearce, Garden City: Anchor, 1983.

Mee, Charles, Jr., *The End of Order: Versailles 1919*, New York: Dutton, 1980.

Meeks, Wayne, *The First Urban Christians: The Social World of the Apostle Paul*, New Have: Yale University Press, 1983.

Merleau-Ponty, Maurice, *Phenomenology of Perception*, translated by Colin Smith, London: Routledge and Kegan Paul, 1962.

Meyer, Jack, *Washington, D.C. Monuments in Architectural and Historical Review*, Green Bay: CSU Publications, 1993.

Miller, Walter, Jr., *A Canticle for Leibowitz*, New York: Harper and Row, 1956.

Mosley, Leonard, *On Borrowed Time: How World War II Began*, New York: Random House, 1969.

Muir, John, *Travels in Alaska*, Boston: Houghton Mifflin Co., 1979.

Musil, Robert, *The Man Without Qualities*, two volumes, translated by Sophie Wilkins and Burton Pike, New York: Alfred A. Knopf, 1995.

Naisbitt, John, *Megatrends: Ten New Directions Transforming Our Lives,* New York: Warner Books, 1982.

Natanson, Maurice, *Edmund Husserl: Philosopher of Infinite Tasks*, Evanston: Northwestern University Press, 1973.

Natanson, Maurice, *The Journeying Self: A Study in Philosophy and Social Role,* Addison-Wesley Publishing Co., 1970.

Neely, Mark, Jr., *The Last Best Hope of Earth: Abraham Lincoln and the Promise of America*, Cambridge: Harvard, 1993.

Neihardt, John, *Black Elk Speaks: Being the Life Story of a Holy Man of the Oglala Sioux*, Lincoln: University of Nebraska Press, 1961.

Nevins, Allan, *Ordeal of the Union*, 8 volumes, New York: Charles Scribner's Sons, 1947.

Nietzsche, Basic Writings of, translated by Walter Kaufmann, New York: Modern Library, 1968.

Nietzsche, Portable, translated by Walter Kaufmann, New York: Viking, 1954.

352

Nietzsche, Friedrich, *The Will to Power*, translated by Walter Kaufmann, New York: Vintage, 1968.

1996 Life Insurance Fact Book, American Council of Life Insurance, Washington, D.C.

Ott, Hugo, *Martin Heidegger: A Political Life*, translated by Allen Burden, New York: Basic Books, 1993.

Owen, Bob, *The Pure Cure for Arthritis and other auto-immune and inflammatory diseases,* Health Digest Books, P.O. Box 1100, Cannon Beach, Oregon, 1997.

Pagels, Elaine, *The Gnostic Gospels*, New York: Random House, 1979.

Paine, Thomas, *The Age of Reason*, Secaucus: Citadel, 1974.

Paine, Thomas, *Rights of Man*, Secaucus: Citadel, 1974.

Paludan, Phillip, *The Presidency of Abraham Lincoln*, Lawrence: University of Kansas Press, 1994.

Parkman, Francis, Jr., *The Oregon Trail*, New York: Penguin Books, 1982.

Parrinder, Geoffrey, *Mysticism and the World's Religions*, New York: Oxford, 1976.

Perowne, Stewart, *Hadrian*, New York: Dorset Press, 1960.

Philosophy in the Middle Ages, edited by Arthur Hyman and James Walsh, Indianapolis: Hackett, 1973.

Plato, Collected Dialogues, edited by Edith Hamilton and Huntington Cairns, Princeton: Princeton University Press, 1961.

Plato, *The Republic*, translated by Allan Bloom, New York: Basic Books, 1968.

Plessner, Helmuth, *Laughing and Crying: A Study of the Limits of Human Behavior*, translated by James Churchill and Marjorie Grene, Evanston: Northwestern University Press, 1970.

Plutarch, *Fall of the Roman Empire*, translated by Rex Warner, New York: Penguin, 1958.

Plutarch, *Makers of Rome*, translated by Ian Scott-Kilvert, New York: Penguin, 1965.

Pomper, Philip, *The Russian Revolutionary Intelligentsia*, New York: Crowell, 1970.

Porter, Roy, *Gibbon: Making History*, New York: St. Martin's, 1988.

353

Powers, William, *Oglala Religion*, Lincoln: University of Nebraska Press, 1982.

Rakove, Jack, *Original Meanings: Politics and Ideas in the Making of the Constitution*, New York: Alfred A. Knopf, 1996.

Rauch, Georg von, *A History of Soviet Russia*, 6th edition, translated by Peter and Annette Jacobson, New York: Praeger, 1972.

Readings in Vedic Literature: The Tradition Speaks for Itself, by Satsvarupa dasa Gosvami, The Bhaktivendanta Book Trust, 1977.

Reich, Robert, *The Next American Frontier*, New York: Times Books, 1983.

Reynolds, David S., *Walt Whitman's America*: A Cultural Biography, New York: Alfred A. Knopf, 1995.

Reynolds, G.S., *The Mortality Merchants*, New York: David McKay, 1968.

Rhodes, Richard, *The Making of the Atomic Bomb*, New York: Simon and Schuster, 1986.

Ricoeur, Paul, *Husserl: An Analysis of his Phenomenology*, translated by Edward Ballard and Lester Embree, Evanston: Northwestern University Press, 1967.

Ricoeur, Paul, *The Symbolism of Evil*, translated by Emerson Buchanan, Boston: Beacon Press, 1969.

Rinpoche, Sogyal, *The Tibetan Book of Living and Dying*, New York: HarperCollins, 1992.

Rodis-Lewis, Genevieve, *Descartes: His Life and Thought,* translated by Jane Todd, Ithaca: Cornell University Press, 1998.

Rose, H.J., *Ancient Greek and Roman Religion*, New York: Barnes and Noble, 1995.

Rossi, Paolo, *Philosophy, Technology and the Arts in the Early Modern Era*, translated by Salvator Attanasio, New York: Torchbooks, 1970.

Rossiaud, Jacques, *Medieval Prostitution*, translated by Lydia Cochrane, New York: Barnes and Noble, 1988.

Russian Philosophy, volume one, edited by James Edie, James Scanlan, and Mary-Barbara Zeldin, Chicago, 1965.

Sachar, Howard, *A History of Israel: From the Rise of Zionism to*

Our Time, New York: Alfred A. Knopf, 1979.

Sagan, Eli, *At the Dawn of Tyranny: The Origins of Individualism, Political Oppression,* and the State, New York: Alfred A. Knopf, 1985.

St. John of the Cross, Collected Works, translated by Kieran Kavanaugh, Washington, D.C., ICS, 1973.

Sale, Kirkpatrick, *The Conquest of Paradise: Christopher Columbus and the Columbian Legacy,* New York: Plume, 1990.

Sandoz, Mari, *The Battle of the Little Bighorn,* Lincoln: University of Nebraska Press, 1966.

Sandoz, Mari, *Crazy Horse: The Strange Man of the Oglalas,* Lincoln: University of Nebraska Press, 1992.

Sandoz, Mari, *These Were the Sioux,* Lincoln: University of Nebraska Press, 1985.

Santayana, George, *Scepticism and Animal Faith: Introduction to a System of Philosophy,* New York: Dover, 1955.

Sartre, Jean-Paul, *Being and Nothingness: An Essay on Phenomenological Ontology,* translated by Hazel Barnes, N e w York: Philosophical Library, 1956.

Sartre, Jean-Paul, *Nausea,* translated by Lloyd Alexander, New York: New Directions, 1964.

Saul, John Ralston, *Voltaire's Bastards: The Dictatorship of Reason in the West,* New York: Free Press, 1992.

Savill, Agnes, *Alexander the Great and His Time,* New York: Dorset, 1990.

Scheler, Max, *Formalism in Ethics and Non-Formal Ethics of Values: A New Attempt toward the Foundation of an Ethical Personalism,* translated by Manfred Frings and Roger Funk, Evanston: Northwestern University Press, 1973.

Scheler, Max, *The Nature of Sympathy,* translated by Peter Heath, Hamden: Archon, 1970.

Schopenhauer, Arthur, *The World as Will and Representation,* two volumes, translated by E. Payne, New York: Dover, 1969.

Schutz, Alfred, *Collected Papers, I,* The Hague: Martinus Nijhoff, 1973.

Screech, M.A., *Erasmus: Ecstasy and the Praise of Folly,* New York:

Penguin, 1980.

Sealey, Raphael, *A History of the Greek City States, 700-338 B.C.*, Berkeley: University of California Press, 1976.

Shipler, David, *Russia: Broken Idols, Solemn Dreams*, New York: Penguin, 1983.

Shirer, William, *The Rise and Fall of the Third Reich: A History of Nazi Germany*, Greenwich, 1959.

Smith, Hedrick, *The Russians,* New York: Ballantine, 1976.

Smith, Henry, *Virgin Land: The American West as Symbol and Myth,* New York: Vintage, 1950.

Snell, Bruno, *The Discovery of the Mind: In Greek Philosophy and Literature,* New York: Dover, 1982.

Snow, C.P., *The Two Cultures*, Cambridge: Cambridge University Press, 1969.

Snyder, Louis, *Snyder's Historical Guide to World War II,* Westport: Greenwood Press, 1982.

Sobel, Dava, *Longitude: The True Story of a Lone Genius Who Solved the Greatest Scientific Problem of His Time*, New York: Walker and Co., 1995.

Sokolowski, Robert, *The Formation of Husserl's Concept of Constitution*, The Hague: Martinus Nijhoff, 1970.

Sophocles, *The Oedipus Cycle*, translated by Dudley Fitts and Robert Fitzgerald, New York: Harvest Books, 1949.

Sorel, N., *Ever Since Eve: Personal Reflections on Childbirth*, New York: Oxford University Press, 1984.

Source Book in Chinese Philosophy, edited and translated by Wing-Tsit Chan, Princeton: Princeton University Press, 1969.

Sowerby, Robin, *The Greeks: An Introduction to their Culture*, London: Routledge, 1995.

Soyka, Fred, *The Ion Effect*, Bantam, 1991.

Spinoza, Benedict, *On the Improvement of the Understanding, The Ethics, and Correspondence*, tranlated by R.H.M. Elwes, New York: Dover, 1955.

Spinoza, Benedict, *A Theologico-Political Treatise and A Political Treatise*, translated by R.H.M. Elwes, New York: Dover, 1951.

Statistical Abstract of the United States, 108th edition, Department of Commerce, 1988.

Stewart, George R., *Ordeal by Hunger: The Story of the Donner Party,* Boston: Houghton Mifflin Co., 1988.

Strayer, Joseph, *The Albigensian Crusades*, Ann Arbor: University of Michigan Press, 1992.

Stuckenberg, J.H.W., *The Life of Immanuel Kant*, Lanham: University Press of America, 1986.

Sykes, Charles, *A Nation of Victims: The Decay of the American Character*, New York: St. Martin's Press, 1992.

Tarnas, Richard, *The Passion of the Western Mind: Understanding the Ideas that have Shaped Our World View*, New York: Harmony, 1991.

Taylor, William, *Cavalier and Yankee: The Old South and American National Charcater*, New York: Torchbooks, 1969.

Thomas, Emory M., *The Confederate Nation: 1861-1865*, New York: Harper and Row, 1979.

Thomas, Hugh, *Conquest: Montezuma, Cortes, and the Fall of Old Mexico,* New York: Simon and Schuster, 1993.

Thompson, J.M., *Napoleon Bonaparte*, New York: Barnes and Noble Books, 1996.

Thompson, William, *Wisconsin: A History*, 2nd edition, Madison: University of Wisconsin Press, 1973.

Thoreau, Henry David, *A Week on the Concord and Merrimack Rivers; Walden, or Life in the Woods; The Maine Woods; Cape Cod*, New York: Library of America, 1985.

Thurow, Lester, *Head to Head: The Coming Economic Battle among Japan, Europe, and America*, New York: Morrow, 1992.

Tierney, Brian, *The Middle Ages: Sources of Medieval History*, volume one, New York: Alfred A. Knopf, 1970.

Tocqueville, Alexis de, *Democracy in America*, two volumes, New York: Vintage, 1945.

Troyant, Henri, *Catherine the Great*, translated by Joan Pinkham, New York: Dutton, 1980.

Tuchman, Barbara, *The March Of Folly: From Troy to Vietnam*, New York: Ballantine Books, 1984.

Tusa, Ann and John, *The Nuremberg Trial*, New York: Atheneum, 1986.

Unamuno, Miguel de, *Tragic Sense of Life*, translated by J.E. Crawford Flitch, New York: Dover, 1954.

Unruh, John, Jr., *The Plains Across: The Overland Emigrants and the Trans-Mississippi West, 1840-60*, Urbana and Chicago: University of Illinois Press, 1979.

Utley, Robert, *The Lance and the Shield: The Life and Times of Sitting Bull*, New York: Ballantine, 1993.

Vasari, Giorgio, *The Great Masters*, translated by Gaston Du C. de Vere, Beaux Arts Editions, 1986.

Veblen, Thorstein, *The Theory of the Leisure Class*, New York: Penguin, 1967.

Viorst, Milton, *The Great Documents of Western Civilization*, New York: Barnes and Noble Books, 1994.

Virgil, *The Aeneid*, translated by Robert Fitzgerald, New York: Random House, 1981.

Voltaire, *Candide*, London: Penguin Books, 1947.

Wall, The: Images and Offerings from the Vietnam Veterans Memorial, Sal Lopes, Collins Publishers, 1987.

Weber, Max, *The Protestant Ethic and the Spirit of Capitalism*, translated by Talcott Parsons, New York: Scribners, 1976.

Wells, H.G., *The Outline of History: Being a Plain History of Life and Mankind*, Garden City: International Collectors Library, 1971.

Wheeler, Richard, *Witness to Gettysburg*, New York: Meridian, 1987.

Whitman, Walt, *Complete Poetry and Collected Prose*, New York: The Library of America, 1982.

Wilderness World of John Muir, edited by E. Teale, Boston: Houghton Mifflin, 1954.

Wilkens, Robert, *The Land Called Holy: Palestine in Christian History and Thought*, New Haven: Yale University Press, 1992.

Wills, Garry, *Inventing America: Jefferson's Declaration of Independence*, New York: Doubleday, 1978.

Wills, Garry, *The Kennedy Imprisonment: A Meditation on Power*, Boston: Atlantic-Little, Brown, 1981.

Wills, Garry, *Lincoln at Gettysburg: The Words that Remade America*, New York: Simon and Schuster, 1992.

Wittfogel, Karl, *Oriental Despotism: A Comparative Study of Total Power,* New York: Vintage, 1981.

Wolin, Richard, *The Heidegger Controversy: A Critical Reader*, Cambridge: MIT Press, 1993.

World Religions: From Ancient History to the Present, edited by Geoffrey Parrinder, New York: Facts On File, 1983.

Wren, Melvin, *The Western Impact upon Tsarist Russia*, Chicago: Holt, Rinehart, and Winston, 1971.

X, "The Sources of Soviet Conduct," Foreign Affairs, Summer, 1947.

Yourcenar, Marguerite, *Memoirs of Hadrian*, translated by Grace Frick, New York: Farrar, Straus, and Giroux, 1954.